BERNARD LEVIN

The author was born in 1928 and educated at Christ's Hospital and the London School of Economics. He has written regularly since 1953 for almost all of the leading newspapers, and is widely regarded as the greatest journalist of his generation. He has been a book, television and theatre critic, and for many years now he has been the chief columnist of *The Times*. In 1990, he was awarded the CBE.

Bernard Levin's first book, THE PENDULUM YEARS, was published in 1970. He has since then written ENTHUSIASMS, CONDUCTED TOUR, TAKING SIDES, SPEAKING UP, THE WAY WE LIVE NOW, IN THESE TIMES, ALL THINGS CONSIDERED and NOW READ ON. He is also the author of three travel books which were linked with Channel 4 television series – HANNIBAL'S FOOT-STEPS, TO THE END OF THE RHINE and A WALK UP FIFTH AVENUE.

Bernard Levin

IF YOU WANT MY OPINION

First published in Great Britain in 1992 by Jonathan Cape Ltd

Sceptre edition 1993

Sceptre is an imprint of Hodder and Stoughton Paperbacks, a division of Hodder and Stoughton Ltd

Printed and bound in Great Britain for Hodder and Stoughton Paperbacks, a division of Hodder and Stoughton Ltd, Mill Road, Dunton Green, Sevenoaks, Kent TN13 2YA. (Editorial Office: 47 Bedford Square, London WC1B 3DP) by Cox and Wyman Ltd, Reading, Berks. Photoset by Rowland Phototypesetting Ltd, Bury St Edmunds, Suffolk.

British Library C.I.P.

A CIP catalogue record for this title is available from the British Library

ISBN 0-340-58923-X

10 9 8 7 6 5 4 3 2 1

Contents

Acknowledgments   vii
Introduction   ix
The forty horses of the Apocalypse   1
Bang, bang . . .   5
. . . you're dead   9
They also serve   13
The good book   17
Ah, sweet mystery of life   22
Out, damned spot   26
Of mice and men   30
The Big worm-eaten Apple   34
Evening dress strongly recommended   38
More out than in   44
Waiting for Godot   48
Going Nap   52
Black tragedy   56
Ten years hard   60
Mr Wilson forgives God   65
A man's a man for a' that   69
Silent night   73
Oriental Express   77
Dead men talk no sense   82
A bite and a sup   86
Here and there   91
This little piggy stayed at home   95
The reason why   99
And half a pound of liver   104
The keys and the Kingdom   108

Patience on a monument 112
How long is a piece of rope? 116
Eating people is wrong 120
Caliban's mirror 124
It's a jingle out there 128
One man in his time plays many parts 132
Picking up the pieces 138
Sororicides of the world, unite 142
Dons delight to bark and bite 146
Supplementary benefit 151
Des. res. 155
Arcadia on Thames 159
Civilising mission 163
And kiss his dirty shoe 168
Decline and fall 172
Neither a borrower, nor a lender be 177
Sub specie aeternitatis 181
Woodman, woodman, spare that tree 185
Arabian, and other, nights 189
And all who sail in her 193
Putting it in words 197
From little acorns . . . 203
Three days that shook the world 207
Of making many books 211
When scorpions ruled the earth 216
The heart has its reasons 220
Merrily on high 224
A little local difficulty 228
Countercheck quarrelsome 232
You say tomato 236
Time, gentlemen, please 240
Index 246

Acknowledgments

Happy the author who, book after book, has the same band of helpers, colleagues and friends to acknowledge.

I am such an author, and I thank most warmly my dear friend and assistant Catherine Tye, who spotted many an error (including even the length of time I have been writing for *The Times*); Brian Inglis, who read the proofs of this, my thirteenth, book as he has done with the previous twelve; C.H. Rolph, who actually invited himself to proof-read the previous book, and happily embarked on the same course with this one; my beloved sparring partner and (much more to the point) indexer, Oula Jones of the Society of Indexers, who brought unfailing skill and enthusiasm to her task; and many of my colleagues and friends at *The Times*.

Introduction

THIS IS THE seventh volume of my selected journalism to appear; the first was *Taking Sides*, published in 1979, and there followed *Speaking Up* (1982), *The Way We Live Now* (1984), *In These Times* (1986), *All Things Considered* and *Now Read On* (1988). I have chronicled these 13 years for those of my twice-weekly readers of *The Times* who want such a chronicle; it has been a very personal view, of course, even an eccentric one, but it may have a brief extra shelf-life (a word, incidentally, wholly unknown when the series began), in the fact that at the least the world has throughout been seen by the same pair of eyes, and recorded by the same pen. (Come to think of it, the Atex magic word-machine on which I am typing these words did not exist when I launched myself on my first stint.)

Naturally, each slice of time, thus buttered, had its special events and even special tone to put the jam on, but half a baker's dozen over 13 years seems to me an opportunity to look right through an arc of time to see if there are any permanent conclusions to come to. There are, of course, no permanent conclusions to anything, but I have never let that stop me; journalism is an eternally ephemeral trade, and although yesterday's sensation was always forgotten by tomorrow, it has always looked, or was always made to look, carved in the stone of the years. That probably did not fool the readers, but for some reason they never seemed unhappy with this state of affairs.

To that end, I have browsed through the six previous Introductions in compiling this one, to see whether there is even an illusory feeling of a series, of continuity, of torches being handed. Think of the possibilities of revolution in attitudes, politics, entertainment, speech, international affairs, crime (and laws), health, travel, food and drink – the list could go on for some time. Does *b* follow *a* in our ordered alphabetic world?

Oh, my word, *no*.

The first shock in going back to 1979 was felt four pages in; it was a reference to Harold Wilson. Men who have lived long in the limelight naturally cast a considerable shadow on it, or so most of us would think, nor does it seem to matter that they rarely or never visit the same limelight. As I write, Harold Wilson has been very ill for a long time, and not seen in public; though I was one of his most tormenting critics, I can only wish him serenity and years to enjoy it. But his seclusion is not the point; he was certainly not ailing in 1979, yet as I read the name I was instantly gripped by the most powerful attack of nostalgia I have ever felt, so far away were the years when Wilson was on every lip, or at least on every newspaper's front page. After all, he was Prime Minister more than once; very few men in our history (and only one woman) can say that, and whatever view was taken of him and of his governing, no one during the Wilson years (there's a clue – they were indeed referred to as 'the Wilson years') could have thought, even jocularly, that a day would come when the very sight of the name in the introduction of a book would bring out the scent of the dust of history.

Now I, during those years, was close to the world of politics. For some time, indeed, I was a full-time political commentator, yet I, too, felt astonishment at my astonishment; what would the average reader, with the average interest in politicians, feel? And, let me tell you, it immediately got worse; a very few lines away there was a reference to someone called Sir Reginald Manningham-Buller, and another to Anthony Barber. I must have heard speeches in the House of Commons by them on innumerable occasions, yet I had to shake myself to bring them to recognition.

There are ephemera other than political ones to come in this 13-year survey I have embarked upon, of course, but I want to continue with politics for a moment longer. In the Introduction to the second of my anthologies, *Speaking Up*, I see that in what must have been a very desperate moment, I wondered how the politicians' *words* would stand the test, rather than their actions and or careers. Please allow me to quote a few lines from the text:

> Take a sheet of paper; think of the seven Prime Ministers from Eden to Thatcher; write down anything you remember them having said. I do not believe that the following list can be far extended. Eden: 'A property-owning democracy' (whatever, incidentally, he meant by that). Macmillan: 'Most of our people have never had it so good', and 'The wind of change' (though the latter was not his own). Home: nothing. Wilson: 'The pound in your pocket.' Heath: 'The unpleasant and unacceptable face of capitalism.' Callaghan: nothing. Thatcher: 'There is no alternative.'

I forbear to guess at the result of the test applied to Mr John Major.

Well, then, here are two Introductions lavishly sprinkled with politics, and nothing but moths rise from the pages. Or rather, the politics instantly vanishes when breathed on, and a very different theme is now heard. In the second of the prefaces I noted a series of hideous brutalities – mostly physical, but some verbal – recorded from here and abroad, and I began to wonder how long it would be until the citizens of my native country, Britain, and particularly my native city, London, would be obliged, like the cities of what we like to think of as lesser breeds without the law, to shun certain well-known thoroughfares or even entire areas, because of the danger of violence. Unfortunately, I broached that very question one evening in a company of friends including one or two who would now be called 'streetwise'. They gaped at my innocence, and told me that I was a good few years behind the times; such danger had long taken root throughout the country.

Things got worse. A book or two later, I was filling many pages with the abominations of tyranny; and the world then (as now – though the cast has changed the play has not) had no shortage of tyrants who killed or imprisoned or exiled thousands and tens of thousands, while in any case turning their countries into yet vaster prisons. Beastliness here, beastliness there; such beastlinesses as no beast would carry out were carried out a thousand times a day somewhere in our world. We – I, anyway – had long preached the doctrine of the decline of wickedness; I argued that the crimes of Hitler and Stalin were so monstrous, so limitless, so unparalleled in all history, that the world would instinctively know that at the end of any tunnel of evil there were things that the universe would not, could not, tolerate. Oddly enough, I think I was right *at the time*; for a generation or two, I did feel that evil – the real thing – had hid its head in shame, and that crimes and horrors, whether from the underclass or the rulers, had significantly diminished.

Whether or not I was right then, I was certainly wrong another book or two later. Not only had 'ordinary' violence increased (as I write these words I am conscious that in the previous month I have read of at least a half-dozen rapes of women over 70 years of age, and two well over 80). We all know that 'mere anarchy is loosed upon the world'; what we could never have imagined is the variety of dreadfulness such anarchy can embrace.

At the same time, or a little later, I began to sense two more kinds of pressure on us, on our safety and our liberties. Once again, in the teeth of incredulity, I must repeat that it is true that in Britain, if you find a bat, flittering about or hanging apparently senseless, in your barn or indeed your attic – or for that matter your dining-room, your bathroom or even your kitchen – and you take it, however gently, and put it carefully out of the window, you can be arrested, charged, and fined £1,000 for a first offence. No, this is not some macabre jest on my part; it is the law of the land.

Let that stand for many dozens of such encroachments on what we once thought of as freedom, and come along a little later; there we shall find that some malodorous wind has blown across the Atlantic and brought with it the pestilence that goes by the name of 'Political Correctness', which began as an American joke, then became an American danger, then reached Britain as a British joke, and is now, as I write, reaching out to make a British danger worse than the American one. (Have you ever noticed what I have just this minute named the Law of Atlantic Extension? It says that the good things America sends us get even better on the way over – time-saving devices, excellent design, new games – but that the bad things get worse in passage – their television, their insularity, and now their intolerance.) Thus Political Correctness, recently arrived, will be carried out as dishonestly and as unpleasantly as in the United States, but also with incompetence and with the kind of vile self-righteousness which has led to the smashing of the windows of butchers' shops in the name of vegetarianism.

The sixth and most recent volume brought an irony so painful that it hurts even to think of it, much less repeat it here. But I must do both.

1989 was truly *annus mirabilis*, a year (to be precise it was seventy-two days near the end of the year) which saw the collapse of one of the mightiest empires the world has ever known ... Even in the darkest times of the post-Stalin Soviet Empire, I never wavered in my certainty that it would fall one day, and that I should live to see that day ...

It fell, and great was the fall of it; I saw it fall, and having rejoiced exceedingly in my book of the year of its end, I went on to what really troubled me, once Eastern Europe was free. It was 'the Nanny State', and it was occupying my thoughts a great deal, for hardly a day went by without an example of it. But my fears of it went further than any examples; it seemed that the people of Britain did not mind being nannied, indeed wanted to be nanny's charges. I savaged such attitudes, and for an example of those who had thrown off the swaddling-clothes I gave, obviously, the long-imprisoned nations of the Eastern Empire. I did not think – who could have done? – that many of the eastern lands – including the mightiest of them – would find themselves in such difficulties, difficulties of hunger, poverty, upheaval, banditry and national collapse.

That story has not yet been finished, and will not be finished for a considerable time; I wrote little on the subject while it was happening, because it was impossible to guess next week's future, let alone next year's. I am sure that my next anthology – *absit omen* – will contain more than one review of these grim days for the liberated lands, but there is no shortage of other subjects pressing closely for examination. These are the ones that have been filling my thoughts as I arranged my most recent *Times* articles for this Introduction, the seventh of the line, and to which I must now turn.

I have to begin at the end of the period, because the story which ended 1991 was so astounding, so enormous, so enigmatical and so persistent that not to start with it would seem perverse. When, on November 5th (an almost preposterously fitting date for the fireworks that were to come), Robert Maxwell's substantial corpse was found floating in the Atlantic near his luxurious private ship, it naturally caused a sensation, not least because the variety of possibilities of how he met his end were enough to excite any bookmaker in the land, normally the most placid of men. Little did the bookies know that within a week, they would be swept up like all of us into one of the most fascinating stories any day's newspaper has ever carried; indeed, I can remember nothing remotely like it for sensation since the end of the second world war. From that day, for *months* on end, there was no rest for headline-composers; every day, and frequently several times a day, there was – and as I write still is – a new story of depredation, theft, forgery, swindle, blackguardliness of colossal size and power, and daylight robbery done in the dark. To sort out the details of the mess, to see who else had one or more fingers in the pie, to trace billions of pounds, will take years, and those who did not suffer from his crimes (he stole from the poor as well as from the rich) will be entertained most hilariously until the last tolling of the bell announces that the symbolic body of Robert Maxwell – his real one being buried, in an unbelievably grotesque and improbable gesture by the Israeli Government, in the holiest place of the Promised Land – can now sleep in peace.

Now: In June 1990, *The Times*, which by then had had for a year or two an attractive Saturday magazine, as part of the parent paper, began in it a feature headed 'Enthusiasms'; since I had written a book with that exact title, I had the honour of inaugurating the idea in the magazine. My choice of an Enthusiasm for the page ('Going Nap' p.52) was my response for the second time to Abel Gance's film of Buonaparte, almost the last, surely the longest, and quite certainly the greatest, of all the products of the silent cinema. From then on, I have contributed from time to time to this feature, offering Enthusiasms on a wide variety of subjects, such as François Villon ('Putting it in words' p.197), Glyndebourne ('Evening dress strongly recommended' p.38), Michael Holroyd's three-decker biography of Bernard Shaw ('Ten years hard' p.60), my love of the Mandarin Hotel in Hong Kong ('Oriental Express' p.77) and a good many more.

Now the reason I offer you this bibliographical record is a curious one, not at all easy to deduce, I think, from my catalogue. Here is a clue: of the 57 *Times* articles included in this volume, no fewer than ten came from my submissions to the *Saturday Review*, which is the title of the paper's magazine in which my Enthusiasms and those of many other people are chronicled. When a man with as many opinions as I have turns so frequently to subjects almost devoid of opinions, and does so with relief and gratitude, commending not this or that point of view, but beauty, excitement, fine labour and the fine results of it, there must be a reason.

The reason, of course, is that so many of the other items I have selected for inclusion in this, my seventh biennial anthology, let alone those I left as browning newspaper cuttings, were on subjects to make quail the stoutest heart, to bring tears to the driest eye, and shock the most blasé. I fled to the *Saturday Review* to close my ears and eyes and feelings to the real world by immersing myself in the much more real world of art and its brothers and sisters.

Que l'humanité se débrouille sans moi! How wonderful, I thought again and again, if I could live in the spirit of that wonderfully cynical motto. But I cannot and must not; as it is, I have very little hope of being welcomed into Heaven, and any scrap of evidence that might soften St Peter's doorkeeper heart I must clutch. I *could* spend all my articles on enthusing – there are, thank God, enough possibilities to weave words and pictures from – but I have to steel myself to return to the diurnal round of horrors and pains. Hence, the following.

Regimes and places, for instance; we have enough to serve the most finicky customer. How about ('Black tragedy' p.56) the dreadful and deathly mess Africa made with most of the freedom the colonisers left them? No novelist, no playwright, could think up Mobutu of Zaire, who bought 15 luxurious European houses, many of them palatial *châteaux*, and stole from his people for storage in European banks so many billions in European currencies that they must have by now become literally countless, while his people no less literally starved? Then again ('And kiss his dirty shoe' p.168), sample the British Foreign Office's attitude to Saudi Arabia, one of the vilest and most tyrannical lands in the world, where the ruler rules everything and everybody, and which has nothing like a written constitution, let alone independent judges, to deflect injustice, while Britain plays host to the princelings, bastards and favourites of the land when they feel like a few weeks' boozing, gambling and whoring in London. This article particularly discusses an abominable crime in that country – a dreadful murder with the ruler's approval – but that is not the core of the wickedness. For that, you have to go once more to our Foreign Office to find the most slavish and grovelling apologies for the fact that a brave British citizen exposed the crime, and did so on television, thus attracting a campaign of vilification from on high – *British* vilification and *British* high.

Come home now, and gaze upon 'Caliban's mirror' (p.124), the story of a gang which broke into a beautiful and lovingly furnished empty mansion, and who in less than a week smashed everything in the place and befouled what they smashed, for no better reason than that they felt like doing so. Or 'Bang, bang . . .' (p.5) and '. . . you're dead' (p.9) which indicate that our masters think we are all cowards, presumably because our masters actually are. Or 'And half a pound of liver' (p.104) – more madness from the human transplant game, or – abroad again – 'The forty horses of the Apocalypse' (p.1) which touches upon the Kurds, perhaps the most wickedly treated people since Hitler turned upon the Jews and Stalin turned on everybody (including the Kurds, incidentally). Or 'A man's a man for a' that' (p.69) which discusses the delights of boxing *by women* (some of them use plastic breast-protectors, it seems, while others do not); I never heard the word 'denatured' more correctly used.

Of course, it is not all like that; I have a substantial packet of articles which are designed for no other purpose than to make my readers smile, or even laugh, from 'One man in his time plays many parts' (p.132), which is *my* theatrical reminiscences, not upon the stage but in the critic's aisle seat, and 'More out than in' (p.44), the story of a gentleman in

India who applied to have the Prime Minister tested for insanity, under the provisions of the Indian Lunacy Act, to 'Dons delight to bark and bite' (p.146), a title which does indeed indicate that here is an invisible provocation meeting a non-existent complaint between scholars in – why, where else? – the columns of the *The Times Literary Supplement*, and 'When scorpions ruled the earth' (p.216) about a man who is always falling over gigantic fossils when out on a country walk.

There is, of course, another kind of mirth, which can freeze the blood, as witness 'Waiting for Godot' (p.48), a true and faithful account of what a leading politician in this country has to go through (or at least feels he must go through) if he wants to be an even more leading politician, and there is a grim laugh to be extracted, too, by 'Counter-check quarrelsome' (p.232) which details the length some people can go to to find a reason never to speak again to some former friend.

There are even two heroes: Lord Longford's decades-long struggle to point out that even in the wickedest heart there is room for change, so that the blackest villain, having done penance in prison, may yet find true repentance ('The keys and the Kingdom' p.108), has been a struggle indeed; he is too polite to point out to this Kingdom's Christian ecclesiastical leaders (eternally silent on such matters) that redemption does, on the whole, play a rather important part in the Christian religion, and that the Founder of it was particularly taken with the idea. (I am not at all too polite to point it out, and have often done so, with no more effect than Lord Longford.)

The other hero is Quentin Crewe, author, journalist, thrice-wed and funny with it, whose body was struck in the womb by a terrible wasting disease called muscular dystrophy, so that he has been physically deteriorating since he was born, and can now do very little indeed for himself, not even so much as turning over in bed. ('A little local difficulty' p.228.) Yet his insouciance, his wit and his iron-clad refusal to treat the universe as anything but a tremendous joke has led him to gigantic exertions such as crossing the Empty Quarter of Arabia in a wheelchair, and following that feat crossing the Sahara as well.

I salute them both, but not only for what they do; they are needed to tip the balance back when from time to time we think – I do, anyway – that if a huge meteorite hit the earth and blew it to fine dust it would not be something to get angry about, and if we did cut up rough we would be given short shrift from whoever settles these cosmic plaints, and deserve even shorter shrift.

This world is getting grubbier and grubbier. It is doing so literally, as more mess and filth is strewn about, however many pleas, in however many languages, beg the passers-by to refrain from making things worse. But it is also getting grubbier metaphorically. No society is without quarrels, but it really does seem that quarrels are now noisier than ever before, and based on smaller causes. Selfishness in all its guises can be found in even the most unlikely places: as I write, the level of hate and obstinacy that Christian clerics have reached at Lincoln Cathedral has risen yet higher, and there is no dove of peace in sight. Our leaders, and everybody else's, are more inadequate than ever, and no better replacements are in sight. There is more war, not less, than before in the world, and even that was enough to keep the fiercest armchair general happy. The freed Soviet lands, freed by another kind of heroes, are stumbling about like men in pitch-dark, which they are, and no one in his senses would bet a new kopek on the outcome. Most tragic in that scene is the horrible sight and sound of former Communist serfs beginning to ask how and where they are better off, and, when told that they are at least free now, responding that they cannot eat freedom. (Which, I have to say, is perfectly true.)

Is it any wonder that a man like me will be tempted to wash his hands of the chronicling of the world as it is, and concentrate on writing about the world as it might be, and from that experience to go further, and write about the world as it never was or could be? I go back to the *Times*'s *Saturday Review* and its Enthusiasms, which shows the way. Why cannot I bind myself to write only on subjects that do not bring gloom and despondency, why cannot I mount into an ivory tower?

Well, first, anyone trying to build a tower of ivory will be immediately arrested by the Political Correctness Police for using ivory for anything – *even if the builder could prove that it all came from elephants which had died of old age, with their children and grandchildren round their beds*. (The Political Correctness Police are not very logical, and for that matter not very honest.) But even if no such ukase were in force worldwide, and anyone could have ivory by the lorry-load, and workmen who wanted no fee would do the building, I suppose I would, in the end, settle for the real world, however unreal it actually is.

Why? I hardly know myself. Perhaps however horrible the world gets, it still retains its lodes of beauty and happiness and art and love and unselfishness and honesty and goodness. It is true that those things make no noise and do not strut about to be seen, unlike the rest, so that a newcomer, and plenty of oldcomers, are inevitably under the impression that that is all the world affords. If I have any tiny influence in any tiny corner of any tiny half-forgotten spot, I can at least try to persuade a few, a very few, of those newcomers and oldcomers, that the world is not *entirely* like that. A modest ambition, you would say? Well, I could boast about it.

April 1992   B.L.

The forty horses of the Apocalypse

I DO NOT have the ear of the Almighty, and I shrink from guessing His plans for this world; but there must be a file somewhere in the heavenly archives marked 'Total destruction by Fire/Brimstone/Plague/Flood/Great Beast/Other', and I have an uneasy feeling He may be about to blow the dust off it.

If so, it will be not only the wickedness that invokes the ultimate wrath; after all, evil was allowed for in the original design, when we were given choice. But the madness – has there ever been a time when so much of it has stalked the world? – may be enough to put Operation Last Days into motion.

If you were God, what else would you do when you came upon the picture from Australia, published in the *Telegraph*, of a vast throng of sheep – many thousands of them – lined up to be shot and their carcasses abandoned? It seems that fattening the beasts and taking them to market would fetch so little that the farmers would be out of pocket, so it is better to kill them and let them rot. The previous day the same newspaper had been estimating the number of millions of human beings who will shortly die of starvation in the Horn of Africa, but it is not essential to combine the two stories; the madness of the Australian cull can stand alone as a symbol of what the human race has done with God's promise. I am sorry that Graham Greene did not live another day to see the picture; my admiration for him was greatly restrained, not least because of his flabby Soviet fellow-travelling, but he was a dab hand at moral dilemmas in his novels, and somebody ought to be endowing a chair of them (the dilemmas, not the novels) in his memory.

There are enough to choose from, these days. Did we not cheer – I more loudly than anybody – when the Soviet Union began to crumble? The crumbling goes on apace, but there is no food in the shops and no money to buy it if there were: go tell the people to eat freedom. For that matter, I was well to the fore when it came to cheering the collapse of Yugoslavia, but I do not think that civil war will greatly improve things there. As for South Africa, where one-man one-vote is on the way, blacks now slaughter blacks in such numbers that there may be no adults left to do the voting when the great day dawns. And here is a story, every month the number of people with AIDS increases by 10,000, while experts claim that the world total of those suffering the condition is well over a million, and those who register HIV positive are numbered between 9 and 11 million; how splendid, brave and right, only a few years ago, was the sweeping away of all sexual and other restraints that hampered people's pleasure!

But if the Graham Greene Chair of Moral Dilemmas comes about, the very first course in the subject must be the consequences of the Gulf war, and in particular the plight of the Kurds. There will be three papers in the degree exam, viz., the plight itself; what should or could be done about it; and what we feel. Today's lecture will concentrate on the third.

Many of the despatches and photographs that journalists have been sending back from Iraq are among the most terrible of our times; to see the like of Saddam's genocidal killing you have to go back to the indiscriminate and relentless slaughter by Pol Pot and his Khmer Rouge.

That, however, only lays down the things about which we are to have feelings. I assume that we are not, as individuals, in a position to save any Kurd; at least very few of us are. (I think that anyone safely in a position to kill Saddam, and who does not embrace the philosophy of complete non-violence, ought to think seriously about doing so; come to think of it, what do the operatives of Mossad do for their wages?)

If we can do nothing to alleviate the plight of these hideously persecuted people, are we not hypocritical in weeping over them? After all, throughout all history abominable deeds have been done to the innocent and helpless; Saddam's revenge for his defeat is worse than most, but there are many such people hardly better off. Can we spend our entire time weeping? Or rather: how much time have we spent weeping for other victims? If the answer is little or none, what provokes the tears now, and whatever it is, are we not, as we weep for the Kurds, really expiating *our* guilt for *not* weeping at the slaughtered Cambodians?

That may be too crude; let us refine it a little. No sorrow excludes any other. If we shrugged off the dead Cambodians, not from indifference but from inability to do anything about them, we are not precluded from feeling pain at the plight of the Kurds. Indeed, we may each have a threshold of weeping; the tears refused before are now ready to fall.

Here, though, is a trap. Newspaper people say one picture is worth a dozen stories, and it is true. No one who has seen the photograph of the little boy from the Warsaw ghetto, his hands up, his overcoat neatly buttoned and his flat cap on his head, being driven along with the crowd to a terrible death, will ever forget it.* The same is true of the picture of the member of the Vietcong being shot in cold blood. When the close-ups of mounds of slaughtered Kurds arrive, what shall we do, other than remember them always? But why did we wait to *see* the horror before we could respond emotionally?

Am I, or am I not, my brother's keeper? If I am, there will be many times when he is in trouble and I am unable to help him, though I would wish to. What can I do then? I can grieve; but it is his grief that is central to the argument,

*When this appeared I got a letter from New York, revealing that the boy survived and is now an American citizen and by profession a dentist.

not mine. If the Kurds are our brothers, and we cannot help them, what price fraternity? Suppose someone who felt very deeply the plight of the Kurds and to demonstrate his fellow-feeling, shaved his head, shut himself up in a cage and fasted for a fortnight: if the Kurds heard about it, would it comfort them? I imagine not. But what if they never knew the gesture had been made; is it wasted?

That, surely, is the crux. The materialist view is that to exude sympathy into the world, without a name and address on it, is useless, indeed meaningless. But the rest of us know that the world can feel goodness even as it can feel evil. Almost all of the time, almost all of us are impotent to affect the course of history. But unless we practise an unwavering solipsism (it is possible), we are, for good or ill, members one of another. Why do we mourn beside the graves of our loved ones, though we know they cannot hear us? Why do we concern ourselves with events in Borrioboola-Gha? Well, why did the Creator give us pain? Because all flesh *is* grass; and the only way to cheat death (unless you can write the Ninth Symphony) is to touch, metaphorically or literally, another hand, before passing on into the night. I can do nothing for the Kurds, but if it comes to that I can do nothing for the five sparrows which were sold for two farthings. Yet they have had the last word.

The Times April 4th, 1991

Bang, bang . . .

AMONG ALL THE millions of words of comment so far spent on the Gulf war, and the thousands on the Victoria station bomb, I have read none which suggests to me that the authors are my age, let alone older. Some of them must be, of course, but their silence seems to me significant. Let me break this silence today.

I lived through the second world war, beginning as a child and ending as a youth. Most of the time I was at my school in Sussex, where the greatest danger was that the tuck-shop might run out of produce. On one occasion a very small jettisoned bomb fell just within the school's boundaries, damaging nothing but the grass, and on another a Spitfire with engine-trouble made an emergency landing on the cricket-field; the two events were cheered with equal fervour.

My family lived in Bedford, where I spent the holidays. The air-raid sirens sounded a dozen times a night; there were frequent bombing raids, but the city was plainly not on the enemy agenda for destruction. Mere gig-lamped schoolboy though I was, I followed the war news closely; we all had maps with coloured pins to record the ebb and flow of battle. The newspapers and broadcasters naturally rejoiced in allied successes, and put the best face possible on allied reverses; but the greatest rejoicing, at least before the tide of war began to turn and victory was seen as certain, was in the bombing of Germany.

I offer no opinion on the still-vexed argument over the value of the second world war bombing offensive, or the role of 'Bomber' Harris. This, however, I can say: on neither side in the second world war was there any question of the *rightness* (as opposed to the *usefulness*) of the bombing of civilian targets. Neither the Luftwaffe nor the Royal Air Force gave any thought at all to such a question; neither made any distinction (other than strategic ones) between a raid on a munitions factory and a raid on a block of flats. To speak bluntly, the policy – on both sides, I repeat – was to destroy as many dwellings in as many cities as possible, together with, most emphatically, the human beings in them.

My purpose, however, is not to make my younger readers' flesh creep. It is twofold: to make clear that practically nobody thought the policy was in any way wrong, and to emphasise that even while the night's death and debris were smoking in the ruined streets, the people were going about their normal purposes. When the employees of a bombed shop arrived for work, they first hung out a banner reading 'Business as Usual', even before they swept up the broken glass. I am not exaggerating when I say that if people had then found all the main-line railway stations shut because a bomb had hit one of them, their unanimous conclusion would have been that some official had gone mad.

The truth is that there was *no* distinction between civilians and soldiers; on both sides such a separation would have been quite incomprehensible. 'Total war', as it was called, was truly total, and killing hundreds of thousands of civilians could be, and was, easily accommodated under that heading. I am not sure, but I think that even that great man, George Bell, Bishop of Chichester, who consistently pleaded for a mitigation of the wartime horrors and, later, a negotiated peace, did not denounce the policy.

It must be understood, though, that the indiscriminate killing of civilians, again on both sides, was not done for the pleasure of it, nor even for revenge. It had a purpose, and the purpose was the destruction of morale.

Whether it worked, on either side or both, I shall not

discuss. But that there is something called morale, which can be damaged or destroyed, is undoubtedly true; what everybody has now forgotten is that in the second world war, as in most wars in history, the attack on morale had a very high priority. The reason it has been forgotten can be seen from the date; no war has threatened the British Isles for almost half a century, and in that time the very idea of war has faded from British minds.

Certainly, the world has not wearied of fighting; the Vietnam war is embedded for ever in American hearts. We did not participate directly in that, but British troops fought in the Korean War, at Suez and the Falklands. In none of those conflicts, however, did the war impinge closely on the general population here; not even in the Korean War, in which, after all, there were many families waiting in fear for the official telegram.

It is surely this which explains the reaction to the attacks (even though these were neither knowing nor deliberate) on 'civilian' areas in the Gulf war, as well as the astonishing willingness of BR to discommode millions of travellers. Only we who lived through the second world war have remembered the terrible truth that in war we are all, down to the youngest baby, soldiers; those too young to remember the war at all can hardly be criticised for not understanding the terrible truth. But that does not mean it is untrue. (It can be argued that the people of Iraq are not responsible for Saddam Hussein, and some would say that they are as much his victims as the Kuwaitis and for that matter the dead on the allied side. Something of the sort could have been said about Hitler with almost as much truth, but the point of any offensive on morale is that it cannot, and does not, distinguish between one kind of civilian soldier and another.)

All wars turn into history, while those who live through them are indelibly marked on their souls or bodies or both. Those who have first-hand memories of the second world war must be the most amazed at the remarkable storm over the bombs which went astray, and at the decision to stop

London altogether in the rush-hour. More amazing yet is that in the Gulf war an attack on morale has apparently not even been contemplated, let alone launched, while the Victoria terrorists have been presented with a colossal success by doing no more than murdering one person and seriously injuring half a dozen others.

Like anyone with feelings, I deplore the loss of life in this war; I deplore also, and more strongly, the carnage wrought by the few bombs that went (if they did) to the wrong targets. And no one can fail to be moved by the thought of Adam Corner, fatherless after the Victoria station murderers had done their work. But I lived through years in which, *every night*, the toll of death from bombs ran into hundreds, yet when morning came the living went on with their lives.

I am not advocating a rain of nuclear missiles on Baghdad, or urging my readers not to report unattended and sinister parcels in public places. I am pleading only for a sense of proportion, basing the proportion in question on the measurements of the second world war. By those, the allies are pursuing the Gulf war with a restraint that is as squeamish as it is commendable, and the interjections of the IRA gangsters should be treated, in the words of the late George Brown, with total ignoral.

The Times February 26th, 1991

. . . *you're dead*

SOMEWHAT TO MY surprise, I feel obliged to return to the subject of my column published on February 26th, in which I combined two themes. The first of them concerned the striking difference between the civilian attitudes to what was happening in the Gulf in these recent days and those, which I remembered from my childhood, which were felt and expressed during the second world war. The other was a discussion, obviously linked to the first, of the measures, as unnecessary as they were hysterical, which were taken (with, as far as I could see, general approval) in the wake of the Victoria station bomb.

I cannot remember any previous occasion on which my readers have written to me with unanimous agreement. Significantly, they did not just commend my thoughts on the subject as similar to their own; in very many of the letters there was an expression of gratitude. Now for a columnist to be thanked is an event sufficiently unusual to warrant examination. In this case the letters themselves provided the clue. The writers were thanking me for strengthening them amid what they saw as a tragic and shocking decline in that indefinable, but essential, quality required in any conflict: morale. Again and again the word 'wimps' occurred in their letters, equally distributed between British Rail and those who deplored (except for religious or pacifist reasons) the allies' intention of pressing the war home by all legitimate means.

The reason for my correspondents' feelings stemmed from the same source as my original article: they had lived through the second world war, and could remember at first hand the all-encompassing danger from bombs and the general insouciance with which they were regarded, as well as the resolve on both sides to use any degree of force or fire power on any enemy target – an enemy target being any place, whether a barracks or an orphanage, in which members of the enemy nation, soldier or civilian, might be found. (I was somewhat too sweeping in my claim that there were practically no voices raised against the policy of saturation bombing; Max Hastings sent me a copy of his book *Bomber Command*, which shifted the perspective, not least because it reminded me of that remarkable man Richard Stokes, MP, a kind of saner Tam Dalyell.)

Let us look at the Victoria station bomb first. The gangsters who planted it naturally wanted to kill as many people as possible, and must have been dismayed at the small number of casualties it caused (while the Paddington one hurt nobody). But murder, however gratifyingly numerous its victims, was not their principal aim. What they wanted was chaos, and they not only achieved their goal with a satisfying completeness, they are still getting it almost daily with telephone calls.

For readers who have no first-hand recollections of the second world war, let me describe another practice from those times. When the air-raid sirens sounded, an illuminated sign would be switched on in places of entertainment; it announced that a bombing raid was expected, and calmly added that those patrons who wished to leave were requested to do so without disturbing those who did not. The point I am making is not that the people were brave then and are cowardly now, but that the long years of peace have contributed to a lamentable loss of balance; we cannot see the haystack of normality and safety because we are so wedded to finding the needle of a chance injury. After all, in the second world war many places where many people came together, including churches, were hit by bombs, sometimes killing large numbers. But I have no recollection of any catastrophe in the form of a panic stampede. Indeed, so unpopular was a government decree ordering the closure of theatres that it did not last long; the Windmill theatre (alas for history, it is now a porn shop) actually refused to comply, and for many years after the war its proudest boast, blazoned on its frontage, was 'We never closed!'

Why, then, do we close instantly now? Another memory springs relevantly to mind. The civilians on whom the bombs were falling constituted, and in no mere token formed, another theatre of war; the British Isles were designated the 'Home Front', to emphasise the truth that there were not two species – soldiers and civilians – but only one, with different duties and for that matter different uniforms, but equally essential. Now, however, though assuredly British troops in the Gulf were admired, I think there was something of a division between the two; the sense of one nation under arms was missing, and I do not believe that that was because the enemy was unable to attack the Home Front directly.

Another subject discussed in the unsolicited letters I received was the modern invention of 'counselling'; my correspondents were contemptuous of the enormous quantities of cotton wool now offered free to those who, say, have been in a terrorist attack, though not themselves even injured.

Closely parallel are the recent claims by 'experts' that those civilians trapped in Iraq when the war broke out, and who for a week or two were sent as hostages to military installations, would need long and careful psychiatric treatment for this traumatic experience. So they will if the experts get to them first, though the truth is that any sensible man or woman in a war – or in the London traffic, for that matter – is in danger of death a hundred times a day.

Is there no one in the generation younger than mine who shares my outrage that it is now possible to get public money from the courts for suffering 'stress' at the scene of a disaster – not for receiving injury but simply observing it? And will he or she go the next mile with me, and back me in arguing that even damages for real injury should be compensated commensurately with the wound, so that someone confined to a wheelchair would be reimbursed for the lost years of activity but a victim with a broken leg which heals completely should get only the cost of missed wages and medical expenses?

We have fallen asleep on our laurels. I do not, of course, believe that the British Isles will ever again suffer direct attack, and I think it very unlikely that we shall even need to participate in a coalition war such as the one that has just finished. Good; entirely good. But the crucial lesson for time of peace, so grimly learned in the second world war, has apparently been jettisoned; if it had not been, we would count ourselves lucky that we were not involved in a war which knew no mercy, and marvel at those who thought that the Gulf war was one such. And we would rise in revolt when the entire railway network is stopped because of a couple of loud bangs.

The Times March 2nd, 1991

They also serve

LIFE, YOU MUST agree, holds many surprises. The most recent one, as far as my observation goes, is to be found in any telephone-box in central London. (Perhaps elsewhere, too, but I have not made a detailed investigation.)

A year or two ago, a curious phenomenon appeared; anyone going into a public phone-box was likely to find its walls decorated, in thick crayon, with many telephone numbers. These, except in the literal sense, were not graffiti; no wicked words or rude pictures, indeed no words or pictures at all, accompanied the numbers. What, then, was their purpose?

Unable to solve the riddle, I asked about until I found, among my acquaintances, someone sufficiently streetwise to know. He told me that this was the latest form of advertising for prostitution; those seeking such sexual services could find them at the other end of the number. Only a day or two after I got my explanation, I read of a court case in which the defendant was asked what he did for a living, and it transpired that his work consisted – entirely, as I recall – of adorning the interior of telephone-boxes with prostitutes' numbers, a vocation sufficiently uncommon, I imagine, to cause puzzlement at dinner-parties: 'And what do you do?' 'I write prostitutes' telephone numbers in phone-boxes.' 'Er, how frightfully interesting.'

We must, however, move with the times. As it happens, we *have* moved with the times, because the gentleman at the dinner-party has gone up-market. The telephone-boxes are no longer defaced by crayon; instead, the information is now provided on tastefully printed visiting cards, which are tucked into any niche that will fit.

Moreover, another great stride for civilisation has been taken, because, in addition to the phone-number, the cards also advertise the services provided by each establishment. Here, for instance, 'Kim invites you to her "office" for a relaxing massage', 'Lindy, 18-year-old Blonde, offers afternoon love games', and 'Tall, Talented, Young and Lovely Charlie Girl is a tantalising madam'.

Others are even more specific: one of the ladies, doubtless too shy to give her name, says 'Full of Eastern Promise – 42in bust' (though a rival offers '44ins of pure Heaven'), and another, similarly discreet, declares that 'Sticks and Stones May Break Your Bones But Whips and Chains Excite ME!'

Then there is 'Sexy Sarah, Silky Long Hair – from 12 to 8pm', 'Busty Brunette has been a naughty girl', 'The lovely young Charlotte in RUBBER', and – from '18-year-old blonde' – 'Ooh! I'd love some Hanky-Spanky!'

You get the idea. But I have to say that I'm damned if I do. To the end of my days, I shall never understand prostitution, oldest profession though it may be. (And don't forget that mine is the second oldest.) I know that there is no society without it, and probably that there has never been such a society at any time in history. I can, with difficulty, understand a man so exceptionally ill-favoured that he can find no sexual partner at all without payment; I can just understand the Baron de Charlus and others who can get no satisfaction except in flagellation (though surely even they could find a consenting adult whose tastes fitted); beyond that, my imagination stops dead and will go not a step further.

Mind: I am not censorious, nor do I wish the trade to be further harried by the law, but one of the nastiest aspects of the present legislation is that it feeds the apparent need among some of the public for regular whorehunts. The judges are much worse: whenever matters prostitutional get into courts higher than those of the magistrates (who mostly still remember what human beings are, information long forgotten in the High Court and upwards), a fit of righteousness seizes the bench.

I still feel rage whenever I recall a case, many years ago, in which the court decided that certain prostitutes were breaking the law against plying their trade in the streets, though they were sitting inside their houses with the windows shut: the judges diddled them out of justice by claiming that since they could be seen through the glass by passers-by, the prostitutes were, presumably in some metaphysical sense, 'in' the streets.

That leads me to another paradox in our attitudes to prostitution. There can hardly be an adult anywhere in the land who does not know what prostitution is, and how ubiquitous are its roots. They may understand the necessity of it, or – like me – remain baffled, but none can argue, surely, that it does not supply a need, satisfied by a voluntary seller and a voluntary buyer. Yet the ancient stigma is as powerful as ever, and millions of respectable folk shudder at the thought of the entire trade; all jokes about prostitutes cast them as the essence of sin.

I confess that although not censorious, I have twice been shocked. The first time was in Israel: I can still recall my absurd indignation, in Tel Aviv, at the sight of Jewish prostitutes. On the second occasion, a long time ago, I was walking through an alley in Soho and saw in front of me a man I knew, indeed a man who worked for the same organisation as I did. I was about to hail him, when he stopped before a door, which opened almost immediately; as he entered, I got a glimpse of the interior, which left me in no doubt as to what he would shortly be buying.

Prostitution must have generated more hypocrisy than money, or even religion; in a contest, homosexuality would hardly get a look in. The starkest version is, of course, in Shakespeare: *Measure for Measure* is not one of his greatest achievements, but he has got Angelo spot on. (It is the only one of Shakespeare's plays with a title from scripture; that must be a coincidence, but it is a tantalising one.)

If there is a special taint to prostitution, I have to say that it has an ancient lineage, also Shakespearian. Think of Polonius, briefing Reynaldo to keep an eye on Laertes in France; he is to invent a few mild slanders and drop them in company, whereupon someone of the party will recall a real naughtiness on the part of the boy ('. . . your bait of falsehood takes this carp of truth . . .'). Between them, they list such sins as Laertes might have been thought guilty of ('. . . none so rank As may dishonour him . . .'): these include gaming, drinking, fencing, swearing, quarrelling, drabbing. And only at drabbing does Reynaldo jib: 'My lord, that *would* dishonour him.'

And now the ladies of the night offer their services on visiting-cards, some of which are laminated. I did wonder, after spending an hour or so collecting them from phone-boxes, what would happen if I absent-mindedly put them in the wrong pocket and pulled the lot out with my handkerchief in company. I suppose I should have to put up with a widespread belief that I was seeking 'Intimate Pleasure in Discreet and Luxurious Surroundings', 'Imaginative mistress, fully equipped', and even 'Deep Throat'.

Incidentally, can it be true that 'Blondes Prefer Gentlemen'? Marie says they do.

The Times September 10th, 1990

The good book

IN THE BEGINNING was the word. Yes, but many centuries had to pass before it could be printed. It is very unlikely indeed that when Johann Gutenberg woke up one morning somewhere about 1450 and said to his wife 'I have an idea,' he had even the slightest premonition of what he was about to start. If he had, he would certainly have abandoned it at once – not because of what has been done with his invention over the centuries, but because it drove him into bankruptcy; a wealthy merchant staked him for the cost of his printing machinery, but when he could not repay the loan his sponsor repossessed the lot.

History does not record what Gutenberg's wife had to say in the matter, but if he had asked me to advance the money to satisfy his creditor, I should willingly have done so, for the debt I owe him by now must easily outweigh his. For I am Gutenberg Man not only in the sense that I live by the printed word. I have been fascinated all my life by the art and craft of printing, and above all, the letters of the alphabet – of many alphabets. One of my very earliest memories is the wonder I experienced when I acquired my first set of wooden bricks, each with a letter on it, and whenever I visit one of my small friends with such a set, I squat on the floor, the better to shuffle the pieces about; I would not exchange for all the gold of the Indies the look on the face of a child who has just made the connection between C A T and his furry friend.

One of my most loved books – I return to it again and again – is that classic of bibliographical detection, a thousandfold more exciting than anything Agatha Christie and her kind ever penned, the majestically titled *An Enquiry into the Nature of Certain Nineteenth Century Pamphlets* by John Carter and Graham Pollard, which nailed one of the greatest bookmen in British history, Thomas J. Wise, as a forger, a swindler and a thief. The detection, however, was made possible only because the detectives were versed in every detail of bibliography, printing and the book trade; a lover of books and of books' integrity can find tears in his eyes when contemplating the plate between pp.58 and 59 of *An Enquiry*, in which the famous 'broken-backed f', with its missing kern, brought nearer the solution of the mystery.

The route from the hieroglyphic writing of the Egyptians, via the Greeks, to the western alphabet of today, is not difficult to follow, though in the earlier stages the eye of faith may be necessary to cross a bridge or two. What is astonishing about the path is that it petered out entirely around the beginning of the Christian era; the letters of the Roman capital alphabet (minuscule came much later), as used for incising letters into stone, are the letters we use today, and however many variations have been played on that majestic original (I possess an encyclopaedia of typefaces, which contains getting on for a couple of thousand of them), there is no getting away from it; no wonder the largest group of faces are called Romans. More to the point, there is a face, still in widespread use throughout the world, called Times New Roman. It was designed for this newspaper by one of the greatest of typographers, Stanley Morison, who was typographical adviser to this newspaper for more than 30 years. (Alas, *The Times* is no longer printed in the face that it gave to the world.)

The adoption of the invention of printing with movable type must be accounted one of the swiftest revolutions ever made; I think that not even the internal combustion engine established itself so quickly. The scribes must have been devastated, but I know of no commination launched against printing as an invention of the devil, which is strange, seeing that throughout all history new techniques have been condemned as flying in the face of nature. ('Television?' said C.P. Scott; 'Television? No good will come of this device; the word is half Greek and half Latin.') All over the western world, far-seeing men hurried to set up the presses and began to print, and some of them have made for themselves a permanent niche in history. The Venetian Aldus (born at almost the same moment as Gutenberg's invention), for instance; Plantin at Antwerp, Garamond in Paris, Caxton, of course, in London; and Froben in Basle. Froben is my hero, because at his elbow, seeing his own works through the press, and at times employed as a general proof-reader, stood Erasmus, whom I love more than any man in history except The Man himself. (Most of the leading printers of the early days have typefaces named after them, but I know of none called Froben.)

The rot started with Linotype. There, surely, was a fitting object for a crusade against an invention of the devil, and whatever the experts say, I shall go to my grave convinced that nothing beautiful ever came out of a Linotype machine. True, to have watched the Linotypers at work (on, that is, the rare occasions when their union leaders had not called them out on strike in order to blackmail the newspaper owners) was a fascinating experience. Perched on his elevated seat, keeping an eye on the pot of boiling lead bubbling away beside him, the operator thumped his giant keyboard to produce his tiny letters. Oddly enough, the Linotype had a keyboard radically different from that of the standard Qwerty layout which still commands typewriters, and now also the Atex on which I am 'writing' these words. (In recent years Qwerty has been denounced as ergonomically unsound, and other keyboard shapes recommended as more rapid and error-free, but I can no more envisage such a change than I can believe that we shall one day switch over to driving on the right.)

As the uglification of printing gained speed, there arose a body of men and women who were determined to keep alive the beauty of the printed letter, the printed word, the printed line and the printed book. These devoted themselves to the modern versions of the private presses; anyone who knows or cares anything about printing, or for that matter about beauty, will thrill to names such as Golden Cockerel, Hogarth, Ashendene, Gregynog, Kelmscott, Nonesuch and Dropmore. Almost all of these have ceased to function, to our great loss. But I was delighted, the other day, to read that something called the Fine Press Book Fair was to take place at Oxford on a coming Saturday, and off to Oxford I went, to see what has taken the place of those noble houses. (The first thing I learnt was that the proprietors of today's fine presses are in no danger of falling down the stairs while getting dressed in the dark; the fair was officially open from nine in the morning, but at half-past ten fewer than half the stands had been set up.)

O, but my heart sang to know that there are people, here and in other countries (there were entries from America, The Netherlands, Germany, France and Switzerland), who love beautiful print so much that they have made it their lives and their business to ensure that the tradition will continue. The printing and layout of the very catalogue of exhibitors was a thing of beauty, and it led the way to a vast range of beautiful things; nor was the beauty only to the eye – the tactile pleasure of lovely rag paper is an important part of fine printing, and so is its scent, though I was a little disappointed (I am an inveterate sniffer of books and paper) to find that only a minority of the exhibitors had taken the point.

I listed some of the older private presses; let me do the same for some of the newer ones: I strolled among the Alembic Press, the Chimaera Press, the Five Seasons, the Hanborough Parrot, the Hayloft and the Hedgehog and the Hermit, the Libanus, the Newdigate, the Oleander, the Rampant Lions, the Simon King, the Tabard, the Woodcraft, the Worlds End, and everywhere I saw beauty and care and love. The treasures on show were by no means cheap; but when you consider what has to be done with hand-set type and hand-operated presses, they were certainly not dear. But even if a visitor to the fair could only look, not buy, it would have been an uplifting experience. Some of the works on offer had been printed in editions as small as 50, a few in an edition of only ten, and there was an exhibitor who opened for me a handsome slip-case, inside which was a thing of strange and wonderful colours, which was all on its own, an edition of *one*. I am glad, very glad, that Gutenberg, when he had his revelation, did not, on second thoughts, conclude that it would not work, and that even if it did, no one would want to buy it.

The Times (Saturday Review), November 24th, 1990

Ah, sweet mystery of life

PILTDOWN MAN AGAIN; will that tap never stop dripping? What is it that draws to the mystery men and women, experts and passers-by, detective-minded people with time on their hands and serious scientists whose time is precious?

In some ways the mystery fits into a well-known pattern: the Unprovable Solution. This, as its name implies, is the one that is vulnerable to every serious student and every lunatic alike. A perfect example is the mystery of the *Mary Celeste*. All we know for certain about her fate is that she was found abandoned by her entire crew, with evidence of great haste, even panic, in the evacuation, though she was perfectly sound and in no danger of sinking. The answers range through cannibals, sea-monsters, hallucination, mutual massacre, collective insanity and the belief that Bacon wrote Shakespeare, but no seeker after the solution has ever been able to convince anyone with a rival solution, which must surely be the one inescapable test.

There is another form of puzzle which attracts followers over the years, with new recruits always available: the Mystery Cleared Up. This is the kind which baffles everybody for years or even centuries, only to be conclusively settled in a way which leaves no one in any doubt that it has been.

Piltdown Man, although having affinities with the *Mary Celeste* is not quite the same as it. Experts may still bicker over the details, especially the identity of the 'Second Man' (it is appallingly reminiscent of the spy nonsense), but there is now a general consensus among students of the subject that the perpetrator of the hoax was almost certainly Charles Dawson, a perfectly respectable solicitor. Two obstacles prevent the book being finally closed. The first is that although the weight of evidence against Dawson is overwhelming, most of it is negative: that is, no solution other than Dawson's guilt will fit. The second is more intriguing; throughout all the years and arguments, nobody, not even the most fervent Dawson-fingerer, has come up with a solution to the obvious question: why did he do it?

The ground has been bitterly fought over; indeed, when the scientific approach by three real experts made clear that Dawson must be the 'villain' (I put it in quotation marks because no crime was committed, nor was any money gained by the hoax), a friend of Dawson wrote an entire book in a splendidly waspish tone to vindicate his maligned hero. The experts had published their findings in a scholarly form in the *Bulletin of the British Museum (Natural History)*, and you can't get any more scholarly than that. However, so much interest was generated by their study, called *The Solution of the Piltdown Problem*, that a more popular version was called for, and one of the three, Dr J.S. Weiner, took it upon himself to write the book. It was called *The Piltdown Forgery*, and the book that Dawson's friend wrote was entirely devoted to answering Weiner: he even called it *The Piltdown Fantasy*.

A story which can generate such heat must have staying power; that power is such that yet another book is about to burst on the controversy and wake the long-dead participants. Weiner, in his meticulous study, allowed a tiny chink of possible innocence into the formidable argument for Dawson's guilt; apart from that, the only remaining mystery is the identity of the Second Man. The long cast of possibles for the role includes William Sollas, formerly Oxford professor of palaeontology; Father Teilhard de Chardin; Lewis Abbott, an amateur collector of fossils, and Conan Doyle (though this is getting very extravagant). But the theory to be put forward by Professor Frank Spencer of the City University of New York does not purport to have established the name of the Second Man; he argues that Weiner's conclusive identification of the *first* man was wrong: Spencer's candidate is to take the number one spot on the ballot. He is Sir Arthur Keith, one of the most distinguished scientists in the field of anthropology and allied endeavours that this country has had.

As far as I know, nobody has ever suggested that Keith was even the Second Man, let alone the First, and the claim is sure to be hotly contested, even though there can hardly be any friends, let alone relatives, to get indignant: Keith died in 1955, childless, at the age of 88. But that is the best thing about these pointless disputes; they raise passions so intense that you might think that the disputants include brothers, sons and wives of most or all of the persons who caused the original uproar.

Keith's reputation was worldwide; professorships and honours were showered upon him, and he was sent prehistoric relics from everywhere, usually for authentication. It is difficult to believe that he was a kind of palaeontological Berenson, certifying fakes with both hands and taking a rake-off from each. In the first place, there is no evidence that Keith did anything underhand, and in the second, it was all very well for Berenson to take 5 per cent of the value of a bogus Titian he had certified as genuine, but Keith would have had to do about forty thousand authentications to raise the price of a small cake, even without currants in it.

He did have a connection with Piltdown Man. When it was found, it was naturally shown to Keith; his verdict was that it was genuine: part man, part ape. After Weiner's book appeared, he was asked what he thought now, and replied, 'I think you are probably right, but it will take me some time to adjust myself to the new view' – hardly the terms in which a faker would discuss the faked.

Bacon didn't write Shakespeare, you know. On the other hand: 'Who fished the murex up? What porridge had John

Keats?' I once tried to find out the answer to Browning's question. I got hold of every biography of Keats I could find; not one even had 'porridge' in the index. I did not stop there, though; I tried ringing up the manufacturers of packet porridge, and asking them if they would look through their archives to see whether one John Keats had been a customer. I got some pretty peculiar answers, I can tell you, though I suppose I should have known I would get nowhere.

Then there was Swedenborg. I had read somewhere that the first edition of his *Heaven and Hell* had sold only four copies, one of them to Immanuel Kant, who recorded his purchase in his diary. I thought it would be fun to discover who bought the other three copies, but since I had no idea where to start and spoke not a word of Swedish I rapidly abandoned my project.

I would not stake my life on the Piltdown forger being Dawson, but I would stake a tenner; I certainly would not put a penny on poor Sir Arthur Keith, thus hugger-mugger dragged from his grave to answer impertinent questions by Americans. Suffice it that *somebody* with a sense of humour, all those years ago, smote the academic Philistines with the jawbone of an ape.

The Times June 21st, 1990

Out, damned spot

A N ODD CLAIM, but I make it with confidence: of all heterosexual journalists in this country, I think I have written more than any other in defence of homosexuals, particularly in exposing and condemning the injustices so often visited upon them, collectively and singly. Such defence has been needed too often for us to believe that there is no longer any widespread homophobic prejudice in Britain; when Paul Johnson can write, in a respectable paper, about 'screaming perverts', and men can be dismissed from their jobs for no reason other than their sexual orientation, it is clear that a good deal of education in these matters is still needed.

I hope I have, in a small way, contributed to that education; all I got out of it was favourable reviews of my books in *Gay News*, and a fat lot of good that did me. Today, however, I would like to cash a voucher. All I ask is that the homosexual community gives me an attentive, open-minded reading of what I am going to say.

As any homosexual, or understanding heterosexual, will realise, I have deliberately begged the question already, with my use of the phrase 'homosexual community'; there is no such thing, which is the first and most important lesson to learn in this fraught syllabus, and to think of homosexuals as an undifferentiated mass is already to fail the test. There is as wide a homosexual spectrum as a heterosexual, measured by character, attitudes, beliefs, feelings, tastes, interests, intelligence, appearance and talent.

It is true that in a few professions (notably the theatre and the ballet), homosexuals are represented in much greater numbers than their proportion in the community would suggest, but the same could be said of Jews in banking, and with as little significance. What distorts the picture, unfortunately, is the strident tone adopted by the 'leaders', 'spokesmen' and 'strategists' of the homosexual world, and my quotation-marks are necessary; nobody, as far as I know, has been elected to any such position, and I am sure that many homosexuals resent the assumption that they are incapable of speaking for themselves or, perhaps more important, remaining silent for themselves.

For a long time that resentment was the only special attitude recognisable as part of the general discussion of homosexuality. Now, however, a new one has appeared, and may soon have devastating consequences: fear.

In this matter, as in so many others, the United States leads the way. A striking paradox of America is that while it boasts, truly, that it leads the way in freedom, it is at the same time the most intolerant country in the democratic world. The intolerance comes not from authoritarian government but from ludicrously unrepresentative pressure groups which bully, threaten and generally make a pestilent nuisance of themselves. (In what other civilised country could Prohibition have been thought up, or Un-American Activities Committees, at least without being immediately hooted off the stage?)

What has this got to do with homosexuality? Prepare, if you have not already encountered it, to accept into the language the word 'outing' – not as a noun meaning a pleasant day at the seaside, but as the present participle of the active verb 'to out'. A group of homosexual fanatics, claiming, falsely of course, to speak for all American homosexuals, have devised a vicious form of blackmail. Noting that many homosexuals have publicly admitted their sexual nature (in the *argot* of these matters, they have 'come out'), they demand that all should follow that example, and those who refuse will be identified against their will, as homosexuals – they will be 'outed'.

I can think of nothing more likely to set back for years, possibly for ever, the longed-for understanding and acceptance of homosexuality in the mainstream of American culture and life, and *a fortiori* in ours. Here, over the years, there have been absurd claims, substantiated by nothing but a belief that sufficient repetition will (rightly, I fear) in time produce acceptance, as to the number of homosexuals in the population. The original claim was 4 per cent: then it went up to 10 per cent. Since there was no evidence at all for the figure, all were free to extend it; when it reached 25 per cent I declared that the only heterosexuals in the entire country were Willie Whitelaw and myself, and I later added Frank Bruno, because I didn't want a bunch of fives from that impressive fist. But whatever the number of homosexuals, only a very small proportion have been willing to 'come out'.

For those who have not done so, I have sympathy, but this is a matter for a feeling much more important: justice. Most homosexuals lead lives as decent as the rest of us: at any rate I know of no evidence to contradict that claim. From time to time, the less expensive newspapers splash the previously unrevealed fact of, say, some actor's homosexuality; a wicked action. But what faces homosexuals now is the prospect of being 'outed' against their will by their own kind, with ruin, for many, as the consequence.

This moral thuggery is to be deployed, it seems, by a small number of homosexuals with no authority other than their own self-righteous malice, promoted as the route to homosexual acceptance. No doubt some are driven to this wickedness by a suppressed loathing of their own condition, but it is the effect, not the cause, which matters. There is also no doubt that real, not metaphorical, blackmail will be practised behind the 'outing' movement, but that is unlikely to disturb the consciences of the 'outers'. It is unlikely that these could offer a rational explanation of their wish to damage or destroy thousands of their own kind; certainly the American version of 'outism' has been defended in terms as incoherent as they are dishonest.

There is a dreadful irony in this story. Most of those who plan the 'outings' are too young to know about it, but I well remember the first attempts to free homosexuals, when it was a matter of literally freeing them; homosexual actions, however private, discreet and mutual, constituted a criminal offence, punished by savage sentences. The fanatically homophobic Maxwell Fyfe, as Home Secretary, launched a kind of pogrom against homosexuals (when, incidentally, there was a known homosexual in the Cabinet), which led not only to imprisonment for many but also to countless personal tragedies, including suicides. (As far as I know, nobody has ever managed to identify the civil servant hero who dissuaded Maxwell Fyfe from prosecuting Benjamin Britten and Peter Pears.) Now they face another kind of torment, this time from the enemy within.

Serve them right, some would say. Most of us, I trust, would not. Surely, the years of misery, ostracism, concealment and persecution should have instilled, in those who came after, a spirit of tolerance towards those of their brethren who, for a variety of reasons, do not wish the fact of their homosexuality to be known.

Hitler persecuted homosexuals; in the Third Reich they were forced to wear a pink triangle, akin to the Jewish star. Now, if this horrible 'outing' threat is put into practice, they will have to sport a similar brand, no less shaming for being invisible, and pinned upon them not by their persecutors but by their own kind.*

The Times June 4th, 1990

---

*The 'outers' lost their nerve and withdrew, claiming that they had never intended to go through with it.

Of mice and men

THE RECENT DEATH of Lord Rothschild has revived the question, till now discussed only (for fear of libel proceedings) behind closed curtains, of whether he was the sinister Soviet agent, hitherto unrevealed, who, on instruction, moved the subordinate figures – Philby, Burgess, Maclean, Blunt – about the board. Was Rothschild the 'Fifth Man'?

No, he was not. He was, in sober fact, the 277th Man, and I should know, because I was the 276th. My job was to steal the butter from the kitchen in the Foreign Office. Rothschild, who reported to me, was charged with the task of sprinkling large quantities of salt on it (his scientific knowledge came in handy here); then I put it back. The plan (hatched in the fertile brain of Professor Lindemann, who was, of course, the 275th Man), was to make the FO sandwiches so salty that the staff would be forever running to the canteen for a cup of tea, thus leaving vital documents unguarded, whereupon the then Bishop of Chichester, who was the 278th Man, would slip in and purloin them; his clerical garb disarmed suspicion, and if he was challenged he would say he thought this was the most direct way to Westminster Abbey.

The documents thus acquired, it was the task of Lord Reith (the 279th Man), to get them into Russian hands; this presented no difficulty, because the man who cleaned the windows of the Soviet embassy was the 280th Man. (For reasons I cannot disclose – viz., that I have made the whole thing up – I cannot name him; I can say, however, from my certain knowledge, that he was *not*, as has been rumoured, the 281st Man.)

Have I done enough of this? Or, to put it another way, has there ever been in all history, anywhere in the world, a literary genre as shallow, implausible, unsourced, revenge-seeking, ill-written, money-grubbing, tedious and fraudulent as the now immense corpus of books claiming to reveal the final truth about the British security services before, during and after the second world war? Spy and double-spy and triple-spy, traitor and pseudo-traitor, nest of homo-sexuals and ring of fascists, blackmailed politicians and destabilised prime ministers, literary agents, serial rights, six-figure advances, television adaptations, ghost-writers, typing agencies, photo-copiers, off-shore bank accounts – entire careers have been built from such shoddy cardboard, and writers who know absolutely nothing that you and I do not know have become immensely rich on the public's gulli-bility, the newspapers' lack of imagination, the impossibility of disproof and – perhaps the most absurd aspect of a subject well supplied with absurdity – the ululations produced by all the participants simultaneously shouting their wares as the only true gospel and denouncing their rivals as ignorant charlatans.

Since most of them *are* ignorant charlatans, there is a certain rough justice about the business, or at least there would be if it were not for them keeping us up half the night with the appalling din they make. There are not half a dozen books in the vast library they now comprise which are worth reading (Andrew Boyle's *The Climate of Treason* is one, but, significantly, it was written very early in the business, before the thimble-riggers got into the game).

It may be safely assumed that everyone in the business of espionage or counter-espionage is mad. Some go into the business *because* they are mad, and the rest go mad fairly soon after they join, but there is no known exception to the rule. It follows, then, that whether, say, Sir Roger Hollis was or was not a homosexual, and indeed whether he was or was not a traitor, is irrelevant; the only thing necessary to be borne in mind is that he was a lunatic.

This is not just a fancy of my own. It is impossible for anyone in the business of spying to stay sane (let alone recover his sanity if he was mad to start with), because the work is done in a world which is made of nothing but unreality. If you shut up a man in a cell made entirely – walls, ceiling, floor – of trick mirrors, he will, quite certainly, go off his head. The analogy is exact; if you are in the spy business, half your time is spent in endeavouring to discover whether your colleagues are working for the enemy. And they are spending half *their* time trying to find out whether you are. Meanwhile, of course, the enemy is doing exactly the same as we are; obviously, the other side is every bit as mad as ours.

But that does not exhaust the fundamental lunacy on which the world of 'spooks' rests. Suppose that agent X3GZ5 (familiarly known as Boris) has supplied you, through the usual channels, with some sensational material, which might, handled properly, alter the entire balance of power. A high-level meeting is arranged, the purpose being to put into action the knowledge just gained. But nothing happens, because before any decision can be taken, an insuperable objection is raised; how do we know that X3GZ5 (or Boris) is really on our side, and not a double agent? We do not know; indeed, we cannot know. It is therefore impossible to evaluate the material he has supplied, and, *a fortiori*, to act upon it.

I am not playing games; what I have described is precisely what happens in spy circles. Again and again in the past 50 or 60 years, crucial information has been passed by agents at the risk of their lives, and ignored.

Sometimes it ought to be. For all the hysteria about the 'atom-traitors' (Fuchs, Nunn May, Pontecorvo, Rosenberg), I do not believe they hastened the Soviet acquisition of the atom-bomb by more than a fortnight. (Those who insist that, on the contrary, they gave Stalin anything up to a year, are the spooks themselves, defending themselves from the fully justified charge of irrelevance. And, in any case, what was

Stalin supposed to have done with the year that he could not have done without it?)

I will go further. I do not believe that more than half a dozen espionage coups have actually altered, in a significant manner, the course of modern history. I will go further still; if all the spying and counter-spying – British, American, French, German, Russian, the lot – of the period leading up to the second world war, of the war itself, and of the decades of the Cold War that followed, had never taken place, the war would not have been avoided or fought in any other way, the years which followed would not have been any more or less tense and dangerous, and the world today would be no different.

That, of course, is not a claim which will commend itself to the secret services of this country or of any other; face the truth, and Othello's occupation is gone. So, of course, is the spurious, dropsical industry which has grown up to accommodate the mendacious memoirs of the spooks themselves and the fictional accounts of their doings by the outsiders.

Lord Rothschild was not the Fifth Man. Nor was he the 277th. Nor was I his 'control'. Nor was Professor Lindemann mine. Nor is there any sign that the torrent of spy books is likely to cease, or even to flow less copiously. Nor will any of the new ones be any better or more truthful than the previous thousands.

The Times April 9th, 1990

The Big worm-eaten Apple

IF YOU WANT a comprehensive definition of the way the world is going, together with accurate readings of its speed, you may find it in New York, from where so many notable innovations have emerged. It comes in two parts, and I must stress that the picture is not complete without both.

There, the number of murders since the beginning of the year has just passed 2,000; the figure constitutes a 'first' for the city, and in view of the fact that 1990 has some days to run, it is clear that 1991 will have to look to its laurels if it is to have a chance of breaking the newly established record. Stand by, as the chimes of the new year prepare to sound, for a cascade of corpses, generously provided by citizens of New York who understandably want their city to hold the proud standard high.

Well done, Big Apple! But I promised you a vivid glimpse of the future, and made clear that the widespread incidence of insomnia in New York, caused by the nightlong rattle of musketry and screams as the neighbours are being shot or stabbed, cannot alone be sure to typify what is coming. Here, then, is Part Two.

The mayor, presumably raising his voice to be heard above the gunfire and bleeding, recently announced that 83 more policemen have been deployed across the city; most of its citizens, it is true, would have thought the number insufficient for their protection by at least a couple of noughts, but no doubt the more sanguine New Yorkers agreed that it was a start. The next news, though, would have startled even the most laid-back: the additional squad is not to be a back-up for the homicide division, nor even for the burglary-watch. The sole job of its members is to inspect the city's dustbins to see whether the newly promulgated decrees requiring every citizen to sort his or her rubbish into separate piles, according to its nature, are being observed.

If they are not, a fine of $30 looms, a sum that will grow steeply for unrepentant scofflaws who thumb (or, I suppose, hold) their noses at the new laws, until the officer whose duty it is to demand and enforce the fine announces that it has reached $20,000 – long before which point, I imagine, it must be cheaper and easier to murder the policeman.

Some of the garbage police (officially the Sanitation Department's Enforcement Task Force) have been talking to the *Sunday Times*, and mucky talk it must have been.

. . . the foul stench of stale spaghetti sauce, rotten eggs and other odious forms of waste can be overpowering . . . as they trawl through bags of foul-smelling, rotten food and disposable nappies, the officers hope to find an envelope addressed to the offending citizens so that they can charge them . . . 'Sometimes it can be difficult to pinpoint exactly whose garbage is whose . . . But we try to be as fair as we can, especially if it seems to be a genuine mistake that people have thrown out newspapers or something with their regular trash' . . . Money for the . . . programme has run out . . . As a result, the newspapers and tins that have been collected now languish in warehouses all over the city . . .

In New York City, in every span of 48 hours, 11 people are murdered. And all day and much of the night, while the death-count mounts, 83 trained policemen, all armed and fully expert in the pursuit of criminals, are spending their entire time on the beat, by order of the city, searching through the city's dustbins not for spent bullets, bloodstained knives and half-empty vials of poison, but to bring to book those careless citizens who do not with sufficient diligence sort out their domestic rubbish into separate containers (kindly supplied by the city), viz., paper, cardboard, tins and bottles, under penalty of law.

Have I not summed up our world and the way it is going? New York is a bankrupt city with a murder-rate of 2,000 a year and a mayor without a thought in his head, yet its police force must spare 83 officers to poke their noses, literally, into the city's rubbish, and fine the rubbish-creators if they leave the *New York Times* in the receptacle dedicated to used Coca-Cola tins, or vice versa.

You will not need a member of the New York Sanitation Department's Enforcement Task Force to sniff out what lies at the bottom of this lunacy. It is, of course, the fashion of the day. The new brand of confidence tricksters, who would never do anything as improper as selling Brooklyn Bridge to an out-of-town innocent, think it is very proper indeed to sell the decaying city their fashionable green nostrums, for all that these are every bit as fraudulent as the certificate of sale that the thimble-rigger of yore used to hand over when the Brooklyn Bridge transaction was complete.

The poor, muddled, well-meaning, hapless, dazed mayor, approached (or perhaps threatened) by the fanatics in Kensal Green, has been persuaded to promulgate the Rubbish Decree, though anyone of any sense at all, if there is such a figure left in New York, could have told him that the imposed fad was not only useless for its presumed purpose, but would be ignored throughout the city before a month had passed, or even sooner – if only because the faddists can don new nostrums as fast as a dustbin-lid can be raised.

The joy I felt at seeing the Green party get so notable a drubbing in the recent German elections can hardly be expressed in words, and I hope – oh, how fervently I hope – that this wonderful sign of the world coming to its senses is only the harbinger of a tide (can a tide have harbingers? probably not, but I can't stop for a couple of mixed metaphors) that will sweep the world clear of the whole business; indeed, I now promise that I will publicly eat an entire dolphin without salt, when the last Green is stuffed with broccoli, spinach, lettuce and dandelion-leaves, and boiled in a very large bio-degradable iron cauldron, not that anyone would notice a difference in the nonsense he would be spouting, boiled or raw.

The only success of which the Greens can boast is their ability to set back the important and serious work of ecological conservation, to which their monkeyshines contribute nothing but obstruction, partly because of their fanaticism and partly because the nonsense they talk tars the real thing with their useless brush. And so craven are the New York authorities in the face of the bullying and swaggering of these people that as the city moves towards a murder-rate of six corpses a day, they hire 83 more policemen (whom in any case they cannot pay) to ensure that such few citizens as survive shall be prosecuted for not distinguishing a bottle from a tin can and a pile of newspapers from a heap of chicken-bones.

Incidentally, into which city-provided receptacle (they can't pay the bill for them, either) do you suppose that a dead body should be put, and are there different bins according to whether the body was murdered, died of old age, or succumbed to a surfeit of Green propaganda?

The Times December 13th, 1990

Evening dress strongly recommended

WHEN, AND HOW, did the word 'elite' learn to stand on its head? More precisely, when, and how, was it deliberately stood on its head, and by whom? More precisely still, whoever it was who stood it on its head, what did he think he was doing?

This is not an exercise in philology or semantics, but let us continue a little while longer as though it were. The *OED*, after some now obsolete meanings, comes down unambiguously on elite with: 'The choice part or flower (of society, or any body or class of persons)'.

The *Shorter* – the one that should be called the Scandal of Lexicography, for its omission of 'ambivalent' – dispenses with the body and class of persons, although only to save space; there is no hint of a pejorative sense. On to the *Concise*; mine is the 1976 edition, and it gives: 'The choice part, the best (of a group)'; in addition, it records 'elitism' for the first time, but the word is still the right way up, as witness: 'advocacy of or reliance on leadership or dominance of a select group'.

I turn to the four-volume *Supplement*, steeling myself against the likelihood that the wicked Dr Burchfield has yet again opened the dikes to disorder, impurities and chaos. Not a bit of it; he even restores the 'body and class of persons'. Moreover, he has a good deal of fun with the citations, quoting Carew Hunt's *Guide to Communist Jargon* and the *New Left Review* for uses of 'elitism', and a straight-faced lift from the *Listener*, reading: 'the *New Statesman* was, and remains, an elite paper, a "quality" paper.'

So then what happened?

A short story by Ray Bradbury is set in a future which looks and sounds uncomfortably like the present; in the story, a crowd has assembled for a purpose known to them, but not to the reader. Very gradually, the reader begins to realise that what is afoot is the destruction, at a given signal, of an object around which passions run high; the mob, united in hatred of it, are looking forward to tearing it apart. The signal unleashes the passions, and the doomed thing is indeed ripped to pieces; only in the last sentence (characteristic of the tantalising Bradbury) do we discover what has been destroyed, when one of the crowd makes off with a piece of canvas on which is a painted smile: the ceremony had consisted of the destruction of the *Mona Lisa*.

The story is a powerful metaphor for our times, in which striving for excellence is cried down, uniqueness is denied or derided, Jack is as good as his master, and decent envy has no place in the dead ashes of the world the yahoos want to make. What makes it all the worse is the cowardice, and even treachery, displayed by those who should be first in the fight against this levelling: universities, the arts, politics.

We must amend Shakespeare:

'Hang out our banners on the outward walls,
The cry is still "Me too".'

You want proof? Go back to my opening theme; in *not more than a dozen years* the word elite has ceased to mean the best – an elite regiment, an elite of thinkers, an elite centre of learning, an elite circle of sages who understand and care for the finest qualities in every area of life – and has become, along with its repulsive ism, something to be mocked, hunted out and destroyed. And instead of a defence, manned by those to whom we would instinctively look for one, we have seen an instant capitulation. If you deny it, tell me when and where you last saw the word in print with the meaning it originally bore, and while you are about it, tell me at what dinner table you last used it, again with its real meaning, without occasioning surprise.

That, you will allow, is an introduction as mournful as it is long; be of cheer, for this page is not labelled 'Enthusiasms' for nothing. My tirade against the haters of the best was but scene-setting for the lovers of it, for there is in England a place which is truly elite in the original sense; the house that dominates the demesnes, the gardens that surround it in wonderfully varied profusion, the unspoilt perfection of the proportions, the combination of water and greensward, the noble trees (sprouting anew as saplings after the massacre wrought by the hurricane), the fitting meals with the finely chosen wines, the joyful, joy-giving couple who reign over this elite vision, and above all, the meaning and purpose of the whole place, a meaning and purpose that themselves constitute an elite so rare, so complete, so brave, so defiant of the wretched levellers and their word-twisting that they deserve to have an honour hung round their necks. Well, here to hand is the beautiful, worthy bauble: let that élite have its acute accent back.

This place is called Glyndebourne, and it is very elitist indeed, thank God. I have never plucked up the courage to ask George Christie (who inherited the whole thing from his father) whether he really wanted to spend his life continuing the place, the purpose and the preservation of the tradition; it does not follow that, because a man invents a magic carpet and a means of propulsion for it, his son will want to continue keeping it in the air, and for all I know George might have had ambitions to be a champion motor-racer, a Member of Parliament, an actor or a door-to-door carpet salesman.

If so, I can only say that his decision was as splendidly and courageously elitist as the place itself, for he has never wavered in his loyalty and devotion to Glyndebourne, and with Mary, perfect chatelaine, at his side, they have reigned for all but 30 years over this élite paradise, a paradise of music taken seriously and surroundings designed to spread happiness. Wherever you look, you can see the fruits of elitism: rejoice. For instance, it is the custom for many Glyndebourne-goers to picnic in the grounds during the long supper interval; in the programme-book picnickers are required not to leave litter – the debris of a picnic can strew a formidable trail.

Now there is nothing special about a request to visitors to be tidy. In this case, however, the request is a perfect demonstration of the very finest elitism: *there are no litter baskets of any kind* in the grounds or the buildings. That élite charge to the picnicking audience is based on an even more elitist principle: Glyndebourne is the private house of the Christies, and just because a wonderful opera festival takes place annually in the grounds of their home there is no reason to forget that fact. If you bring gnawed chicken legs, empty wine bottles and lots of crumpled greaseproof paper into somebody's house, it is not particularly remarkable if they politely ask you to take it away when you go.

The Glyndebourne picnickers invariably do; I have *never* seen the debris of a picnic anywhere in the place, in all my 37 years of Glyndebourne-going, which suggests that not only is the lack of unsightly litter baskets elitist, but it further encourages an elitist outlook.

Then there is the matter of dress. The legend which says no one may enter *diese heil'gen Hallen* clad in anything other than evening dress is a legend indeed; right from the start, although dinner jackets were encouraged, there has never been a requirement for them, and the programme-book went no further than to say 'Evening dress is strongly recommended'. Even this attitude is rooted in a splendidly practical elitism; John Christie's principle was that because all those on the stage and in the orchestra pit and behind the scenes were doing their best to bring the evening as close as possible to perfection, the audience should help them to do so – not by playing the oboe or singing the role of Figaro, but by wearing clothes of a fitting nature.

But once you start on the catalogue of Glyndebourne elitisms, I am happy to say, there is no end to it. From the start, for instance, all the operas performed were sung in the original language, and on top of that Fritz Busch, Glyndebourne's first conductor, forbade any use of appoggiaturas. (The tradition was followed until only the other day, when Glyndebourne succumbed to the 'original instruments' nonsense, and Simon Rattle let slip the leash of appoggiaturas – damned silly ones they were, too.)

Glyndebourne gets no subsidy from the Arts Council or any other public source, except for the work of its touring company; I rather think that for an opera house to have no recourse to the taxpayer is the most tremendous act of elitism in history. True, it is the devil's own job to get tickets, so huge is the demand – the demand being, in my delighted opinion, itself a sign of residual elitism, happily not yet stamped out. To forbid late-comers to enter the tiny auditorium until the interval is hardly elitism, for any serious opera house does as much; but the lavishness of the room where those shut out of paradise can hear the music transmitted is most elitely fitting. Nor should we forget the three restaurants, taking their élite names from villages in the area where the family comes from: Over Wallop, Middle Wallop and Nether Wallop.

Perhaps it will last for ever; perhaps, indeed, when the world comes to its senses, Glyndebourne's élite standing will lead the way back to sanity and beauty and the relentless quest for perfection. But at Glyndebourne, even to think about the world, mad or sane, comes close to lèse-elitism: the whole point of the place and its defiant stance is that it rejects with scorn the surrenders going on all round. Long may it live to show us the elite qualities that were once rife, and could be again.

Glyndebourne, if it wants a motto, can have a Shakespearian one: as Falstaff nearly said, 'I am not only elitist myself, but I am the cause that elitism is in other men'.

The Times (Saturday Review), July 27th, 1991

More out than in

HERE'S A SPLENDID wheeze. Recently, in India, a gentleman went to court with a novel request; he was seeking an order to have the then Prime Minister's sanity tested, under the provisions of the Lunacy Act.

The petitioner argued that there were sufficient grounds for such an order to be granted, citing the fact that the Prime Minister had made contradictory statements, and adding that the minority government could hold office only because it was supported by fringe parties, though these were of both left and right, and of the extreme left and right at that. Nevertheless, the order was refused; the judge went so far as to say that the request was frivolous.

I'm not so sure. We can dismiss the assertion that for a politician to make irreconcilably opposite statements is in itself a sign of *dementia praecox*; if it were so, the whole boiling lot of them would be on the wrong side of a set of exceptionally high walls. Nor can a loss of marbles be deduced from an alliance with ideologues united only in mutual hatred; since when was fastidiousness a quality useful for political advancement?

However, it would be wise for us to assume, in the absence of conclusive evidence one way or the other, that all politicians, and not just prime ministers, are certifiable. You may think I jest, and to some extent of course I do, but some years ago I learned that a highly qualified psychiatrist had spent, in the course of a serious study, many hours in the House of Commons, by no means all in the public gallery, studying the members, and had concluded at the end of his researches that no fewer than 40 per cent were unmistakably deranged. (The proportion must be a good deal higher today.)

As far as I know, there is only one politician who admits, indeed proclaims, his disability, and that is Screaming Lord Sutch of the Monster Raving Loony party, who makes much play with his willingness to agree that he is indeed a lunatic. Yet it is Screaming Lord Sutch whom I wish to salute today. I do not intend to join his party, because I long ago made a rule that I would not join anything, and unless he goes through with his proposal to stand for all 650 seats at the next general election, I fear that I shall not even be in a position to vote for him. He is never for long out of the public eye; no one could call him shy, and not only because he is in the habit of appearing in public wearing nothing but an off-the-shoulder leopard-skin, calf-length boots and a top hat. But his most recent dose of publicity is more richly deserved than usual: he has at last equalled the record for the largest number of parliamentary elections fought; the next one he contests will give him the crown that was worn for so long by the late Commander Bill Boakes.

Boakes, who scored 29 to the new victor's 30 (as it will be), was in his way a figure scarcely less striking than Lord Sutch himself. His obsession was road safety, and in his cause he would march about the streets of London, well-stubbled and pushing a kind of bicycle-cart, sandwich-boarded with the sinister message: 'I stop-watch cars'. One of his regular beats was Gray's Inn Road, where *The Times* used to be, and I occasionally tried to engage him in conversation, though it was a fruitless task, partly because it was impossible to understand what he was talking about and partly because, to put it plainly, he was a miserable old sod, which can certainly not be said of his successor. (No doubt Boakes was genuinely dismayed by the incidence of road accidents, but it is hard to believe that anything he said or did about it had any effect. By a truly tragic irony, he himself died after a road accident.)

Boakes was no less devoted to putting up for Parliament; his record, as I say, was 29 shies at the coconuts; he was the first to entertain the thought of standing in every constituency at once (oddly enough, it is constitutionally possible and legal to do so, though a candidate who is multiply successful cannot take his seat for more than one constituency), but he could not raise the money for the deposits.

It is the fashion at the moment to sneer at Lord Sutch, to profess boredom with his antics and to claim that they are performed only for publicity, though if you can show me any MP who rejects with horror the very idea of seeking publicity I will eat my head unbuttered. The point is, his Lordship is a genuine addition to the nation's mirth, which can be said of very few MPs, mad or sane. Who would begrudge him his sensational victory in the Bootle by-election in May? (I mean, apart from David Owen.) It was, of course, a special kind of victory: Labour galloped home, but the real excitement lay in the fact that his Lordship, with 418 votes, beat the SDP's candidate by better than two to one. And in Bootle's second by-election of the year, last Thursday, his vote was well over 10 per cent of that of the second-placed Tory, and he beat two other candidates, one of whom called himself a Liberal.

I have never jeopardised my feelings for his Lordship by going to any of his pop-concerts, but I do not disdain them as his means of livelihood; it is at least more wholesome than selling your name for the letter-heads of transparently fraudulent bucket-shops, which is the favoured method of many a well-established MP. In addition, his Lordship is clear as to his political aims; when he is in power his first action will be to put Big Ben on the other side of the river.

The idea of laughter at the hustings is in general a horrible thought. The laboured jokes provided by the speech-writers invariably put the listeners in mind of coffins, so ghastly are they, though most of the spontaneous ones generated by the candidates themselves are actually worse; the last time

I laughed out loud at an election meeting the candidate was Disraeli, and the time before that it was Charles James Fox.

Then along comes Screaming Lord Sutch, whereupon the latest by-election ceases to be only a mournful parade of po-faced mendacities, and becomes a mournful parade of po-faced mendacities enlivened by a colourful figure who not only *is* mad, but who seizes the nearest loud-hailer to announce the news of his lunacy to the four corners of the earth.

The value of Screaming Lord Sutch is the same as that of Arnold Bennett's Card; he is devoted to the cause of cheering us all up. So I am sorry that that spoilsport of a judge in India refused to sanction an examination of the Prime Minister, in the cause of discovering whether or not he was mad within the terms of the legislation. Though perhaps the judge was wiser than we think, and the all-encompassing serenity of India more powerful than we would like to admit. Is it not possible that the judge's decision was based on the conviction that whether the Prime Minister was mad or sane it would make no difference? If so, it is clear that India has at least caught up with Screaming Lord Sutch.

The Times November 12th, 1990

Waiting for Godot

KINDLY SETTLE DOWN, preferably with a stiffish drink in hand, and listen to this extraordinary account: I took it, word for word, from *The Times* Diary.

> . . . he is reckoned to have spent at least £100,000 a year on his unofficial campaign since he stalked out of the cabinet in June 1986 . . . he often addresses four Conservative associations a week, sometimes at opposite ends of the country . . . Friday evenings, a favourite for Tory meetings, are booked up 12 months in advance and he does not have a spare lunch-time date till February. Every weekday evening throughout parliamentary sessions is booked for dinners with backbench colleagues or Tory pressure groups . . .

Obviously, it is Mr Heseltine who is being described, if only because it is unlikely that any other MP could afford £100,000 a year on any kind of campaign, let alone one that is as likely to fail as to succeed, and indeed much likelier.

Leave the money out of it; Mr Heseltine can easily afford it. (His fortune, reckoned in tens of millions, he made himself.) But just look at the life he leads. How would you like it, *it* being four constituency parties addressed in a week, every Friday booked a year ahead, dinner to useful colleagues and pressure groups every weekday evening in the session and no empty lunch-time spaces in your diary till February?

It is impossible. No human being could stand it; the mayors' greetings alone would have killed him years ago, never mind the travel. Either he is one of identical triplets who secretly share the burden, or he is a Thing from Outer Space. Whichever it is, we must probe further. However the trick is done, the important question is: what is it done *for*?

We have all known the answer for many years, not least because he has never attempted to disguise his ambition. Very well; I don't want to be prime minister, and I dare say you don't either, if you have any sense, but Mr Heseltine is entitled – he is a politician, after all, and few politicians can resist advancement – to follow his star, and to do so with all the fervour he can summon up, which, in view of the schedule he follows, must be considerable. He has measured the ground; but what kind of a life must he lead in his chase after this unreal and all but worthless quarry, a jack-o'lantern that has led so many ambitious men (and at least one woman I know of) into the woods, there to quench their burning hopes in the slime of the quicksand which is all that can be found at the end of the trail?

Well, *what* kind of a life? When did he last spend a long weekend in Rome, just for pleasure? When did he last go to the theatre? When did he last cancel an engagement, on a whim, to take his wife out to dinner?

Easily answered, those questions, are they? More important things . . . never was much of a playgoer . . . Anne doesn't care for restaurants. Try a few more, starting with those four Tory associations addressed week in and week out. These must comprise, as to perhaps 97 per cent of their number, bores so dreadful, so implacable, so clinging, so monomaniac, so vacant of mind, face and bearing, that any man with even the slightest residue of sensitivity left in his make-up would, after half an hour of them, go to the lavatory, lock himself in, and cut his throat. (Note that I say nothing of the unimaginable filth that passes for food at such gatherings, together with wine that can take the enamel off your teeth with the first sip.)

As for those backbenchers who feed nightly at his cost

throughout the parliamentary year, it must be worse still. Imagine being obliged to be not just polite, but attentive, sympathetic and admiring to creatures that have *not* crawled out of the woodwork because no self-respecting woodwork would have allowed them to crawl in in the first place. Imagine laughing at their jokes, remembering the names of their wives and mistresses, pretending not to notice that they are drunk, shoving expensive cigars into their faces. Surely a hook, a noose and a kitchen chair would be preferable to such waking nightmares?

It is not enough to say that he doesn't agree, and there's nowt so queer as folks. Heseltine is an intelligent and far-seeing man, and he knows that the horrors a prime minister has to embrace are much worse than what he has had to endure in the cause of his advancement. Yet he wants the job so badly that he has put up with that punishing routine for years, and is plainly willing to put up with a far more gruelling one.

Why? To stand next to the Queen at the Cenotaph? To mingle with his opposite numbers at European conferences more boring than the Tory associations and to shake hands with delegates more dreadful than his own backbenchers? To unveil statues which would have been much better left veiled? To – my hands hover over the keyboard, unwilling to descend – to get into the history books? Dear God, when did he last *read* a history book?

And what about her? She has had 11 years of it, *and she wants more*. In that decade she has certainly experienced every atom of the disillusion that comes to those who imagined ('Can I do this, and cannot get a crown? Tut, were it farther off, I'd pluck it down') that the view from 10 Downing Street would be utterly different from anything the tenant had hitherto seen, filled with vistas of a world new-made. Well, now she knows, as her predecessors found out, that the only vista she can see is the roof of the Foreign Office.

*

Harold Macmillan, whose elevation was achieved by a brutality, cunning and greed for power normally met only in conclaves of Mafia *capi*, said, after he had climbed the greasy pole and pushed all his rivals off (*takes out handkerchief containing concealed onion*) that the whole thing was Dead Sea Fruit. Even he, who had revelled in the post more than any other prime minister since Disraeli, found that the glittering prizes were made not of diamonds, nor even convincing paste, but glass.

And yet she will slug it out with Heseltine, and if it goes to a second round, Hurd will push his nose in, and so will half a dozen more people almost as terrible as he, who know they have no chance but think they are putting down markers for the next round a few years hence.

I ask again: what is it for? To acquire power? They can have none that merits the word. To garner the admiration of the masses? Even hers ran out a year or two ago. To have Britain shake the world? As well expect Botswana to do so. To find their memoirs and diaries serialised in the *Sunday Times*? We have long since learned how to skip.

I return to Mr Heseltine, where I started. Suppose she beats him, but not by a knockout. Suppose, therefore, he continues to pursue the ambition he has nursed with such grisly assiduity. Suppose he is in opposition after the next election. Can he really go on with that dreadful self-torture in the hope that his time will – after yet another one or two administrations – come at last? Suppose it doesn't, and he realises it has all been wasted? Worse, suppose it does, and he inherits the crown, and *then* realises that it has all been wasted?

The Times November 20th, 1990

Going Nap

I AM NOT much of a film-goer; a year or even more can go by without my entering a cinema. Long, long ago, I used to go to the Cannes Film Festival, to enjoy the mad circus of producers who did not have a film selling it to renters who did not have a cinema, with hundreds of pretty girls wiggling their bottoms along the Croisette, hoping to be discovered like Brigitte Bardot. When my more earnest colleagues looked at their watches and announced that I simply must come with them to the latest four-hour Japanese epic, already internationally famous for the beautiful 20-minute disembowelling scene, I said I would rather sit on the terrace of the Carlton Hotel and go on drinking, if they didn't mind. As far as I recall, I went to only one film there, Peter Brook's *Lord of the Flies*, and that was only because Peter is a friend of mine. (Mind you, I did persuade one of my more gullible *copains* that there was a stunning proto-Bardot staying at the Martinez, and if he hurried he could get the first interview. I even remember the name I gave her: Quiche Lorraine.)

So when, in 1980, I learnt that there was a film about Napoleon, made in 1927 by a French director whose name I had never heard, and that the film in question was about to be screened in London, I took little interest; when I discovered in addition that it was a silent film and went on for some five and a half hours, I made clear that I had better things to do. But I had not. Oh, indeed I had not.

The story of the making of Abel Gance's *Napoléon* and its subsequent fate has been written by Kevin Brownlow; the book is also the story of a quest almost as magnificent as that of the Knights of the Round Table but far more mad. Brownlow has spent much of his adult life hunting down the material of Gance's tattered masterpiece, reel by reel, fragment by fragment, frame by frame, and putting this stupendous jigsaw puzzle together. All the king's horses and all the king's men confessed themselves baffled by the task of reassembling Humpty Dumpty, but Brownlow's achievement will live in the annals of art, fidelity and civilisation while any of these three exists.

But why was Gance's glory lost, for Brownlow to find again? One reason was that it was so far ahead of its time that it puzzled those who saw it. The principal reason, though, is that only a few months after it was first seen in France the talkies arrived, and the silent film was dead for ever, or at least until Brownlow the Resurrection Man stumbled across the story that was to absorb 25 years of his life.

At that first experience of *Napoléon*, I was not ten minutes into the film when I knew I was going to stay to the end; I have seen it twice since, and I am going to see it once more on July 4th, in the Barbican again. I do not know whether it is already sold out there, but if it is not, let me say this to any of my readers who have not seen it on the full screen: Abel Gance's film is not just a gigantic, beautiful, daring, original, absorbing, heroic, tremendous and unique masterpiece: it is one of the most completely satisfying and memorable encounters with art I have ever had in my life.

The film, obviously, is romantic; this Napoleon is a hero so heroic that we instantly fall under his spell and forget all the history we ever knew; considering that the first part of the film shows Napoleon as a boy, and it is *that* Napoleon we fall in love with, it is clear that what we have here is a myth of giant stature. But then, the film is of giant stature, the events of it are of giant stature, the crowds are of giant stature, the battles, the seas, the chases, the Revolution, the Terror, the casting, the actors, the music, are all of giant stature, and our minds and feelings are on tiptoe throughout, as we try to match our imagination to the giant stature of Gance's own.

Take the music first. The score is by Carl Davis, who was set a task that would have daunted Wagner; indeed, it is considerably longer than *Götterdämmerung*. Mr Davis, wisely, has not attempted to write the lot himself; he has ransacked Haydn, Mozart and above all Beethoven, and fitted their work to his so skilfully that the seams are truly imperceptible. On an ocean of C major the silent film floats, sounding depths and breadths that anyone would have thought impossible in a two-dimensional medium.

We start with Napoleon as the rebellious schoolboy; flung out of the academy, he and his guardian eagle defy the world and everything it can do to them. The boy becomes the man; the transition is lit by the flames of the Revolution; we are off on one of the world's most tremendous journeys.

One of Gance's greatest strengths was numbers; again and again, he must have ransacked all Paris for his crowd scenes, and none is more exciting than the seething Convention, dominated by the Jacobins, acted by men full of blood and understanding. We can see, raging before our eyes, a world being created; soon afterwards we see the struggles which are to make or destroy that world. The Battle of Toulon is hideously reminiscent of the first world war, down to its unforgettable symbol: the hand of a corpse sticking up through the mud.

Not only has Gance stripped Paris of its crowds; he has also stolen some of the most striking and eloquent faces in all France. Marat, for instance (played by Antonin Artaud, of all people), and Tristan Fleuri, and Josephine; once seen, you would recognise them again anywhere. Moreover, Gance scorns backcloths; his huge armies are deployed on hugely real terrain. I believe that no other film in history has registered so many casualties in the making. Inevitably, some of the scene-linking is crude by today's standards, but there is no sense of isolated episodes loosely tied; within half an hour, we are moving purposefully through a seamless narrative.

And that is to say nothing of the great physical triumphs

which again and again make us gasp. Take, for instance, the escape from Corsica. It is preceded by a breathstopping horseback chase, but that is only the overture; the principal scene has him alone in a tiny boat. The mountainous seas fling this cockleshell up and down; Gance begins to cross-cut between the sea and the Convention. Then he plays his finest card; the whole Convention, not just the players but the entire auditorium, starts to swing like a pendulum, to match the swing of the waves Napoleon is fighting.

There are scenes, too, so replete with imagination that they must make today's cinema envious. After Thermidor, Napoleon goes to the silent empty Convention; gradually, it fills with ghosts, dominated by the five pillars of the Revolution: Robespierre, Danton, Marat, Saint-Just and Couthon. There, before them, he renews his pledge to make France the greatest nation on earth. Soon after, we see him setting out for Italy, at the head of the Beggars of Glory; I defy even the most self-controlled member of the audience not to find tears in his eyes when we come to the speech before Italy.

It is difficult, but necessary, to remember that this film is significantly incomplete. What is more difficult still to comprehend is that at its full length it was intended to be only the first of a series built to the same dimensions. After all, the Italian campaign was the beginning, not the end.

What we shall see in the Barbican on July 4th is something we shall never forget; the sight of genius setting out on its journey, driven by an indomitable will to succeed, and succeeding so tremendously that the achievement adds one more item to the world's rarest stock: an artistic creation that can never be forgotten, and will endure as long as art does.

The Times (Saturday Review), June 23rd, 1990

Black tragedy

IF WISHES WERE horses, beggars would ride. So says the ancient wisdom. But what if wishes *were* horses? The question arises because President Mobutu of Zaire has been in the news: he says that his country ('his country' is a phrase with more than one meaning, and I shall touch upon the less obvious one in a moment) is going to become a democracy. It is not true, of course, and nobody in Zaire or anywhere else believes it, so nobody will be disappointed, let alone surprised, when things continue as before.

Yet the promise is significant, and it is being repeated all over Africa. Even Mengistu, the bloodiest savage in the continent (a remarkable title, considering how many have contended for it) will shortly announce his intention to join the Social and Liberal Democrats and become a vegetarian, followed by Field–Marshal (*ci-devant* Sergeant) Doe of Liberia, though he, happily, will probably be hanged first. Kaunda has got the thing the wrong way round; hitherto he has not had much blood on his hands, but he is now in the same panic as the others, and has taken to a little weekend shooting of those who displease him, whereas Moi (as in *l'état c'est*) has been at it longer and more enthusiastically.

Let us get back to Mobutu, for he is the clue to the whole thing. He is almost certainly the greatest thief in the entire history of the world, at least as measured by the magnitude of his thefts. Serious attempts have been made by experts to establish just how much money he has stolen and stashed away in Swiss bank accounts and property abroad; most of it (apart from the amount looted from his bitterly poor country, whose people have an average annual income of much less than £100, and steadily falling) consists of the stupendous sums in western aid diverted wholesale to Mobutu's safe-deposit boxes. The consensus puts his loot at around *five billion* American dollars. The usual African irony rules: when Zaire was the Belgian Congo, it was ruled abominably, but not even the most contemptuous colonial officer treated the people as badly as Mobutu has, and not even the poorest of its subjects was as poor as Mobutu's helots.

Is there any example, either from antiquity or modern times, to match his looting? He collects *châteaux* as other folk collect Victorian jam-spoons. Mobutu, it can be said, not only rules his country but owns it outright. (Many regard him as a comic figure, but it is a serious mistake; his rule has been corrupt and murderous, probably second only to that of Mengistu.) Whence, though, the promises of reform, almost throughout the whole continent?

The devil a monk would be . . . When Mussolini was shot by partisans towards the end of the war, his body was taken to Milan and exhibited, hung upside down; whereupon some enterprising citizen cut off the Duce's genitals and stuffed them in his mouth. Mobutu may not have heard of Mussolini, though Mengistu must have done, but even if no African despot can make the connection, the shrewder ones realise that a real wind of change is blowing throughout Africa (doubtless raised by the collapse of the Soviet empire) and a hideous fate is in store for them unless they can give their people something to assuage their rising anger and determination. Whence the promises of reform, however illusory.

What went wrong with Africa? A popular response is that blacks are incapable of ruling themselves because they are in some way congenitally inferior to whites. If you reject this thesis, as I do, you are still left with the question: what went wrong with Africa?

That something did go wrong cannot be denied. In the entire continent there are only two states which truly respect human rights – Botswana and Senegal – while the rest of Africa is divided among poor, bad and worse. Much the same, obviously, could be said about Asia, and until recently the whole of Eastern Europe, too. But to African repression there has been added African economic failure, and what can best be described as African fatalism. Certainly, there have been scores, if not hundreds, of uprisings against brutal African rulers since independence, but almost without exception the purpose was to replace one half-mad and evil tyrant with another. Why, I suppose I am asking, has democracy not taken root in Africa?

It had every chance. The debate on the merits and drawbacks of colonialism will never end, but it would be difficult to deny that the British, at least, did not go home before ensuring that those who were to rule the newly independent nations had been taught the rudiments of democracy.

It did not last: genuine self-rule in Africa vanished in a tragically short time. The weasel explanation given by those who cannot face the truth is that democracy does continue to flourish, though in a different form. Whenever I hear the words 'Westminster-style democracy', I know a lie is coming up, to disguise the fact that there is almost no sub-Saharan African state which has a genuine multiplicity of parties and gives its people a genuine opportunity to choose their rulers. All sorts of excuses are made; 'tribalism' is the favourite, though it explains nothing.

Ideology would be a better target, though the excusers would never fire at it. Nyerere, for instance, never pocketed a single Tanzanian shilling by way of a backhander, but the Great Humbug none the less comprehensively ruined his country, by demanding that it advance immediately upon the socialist millennium, and not pause till it got there.

Perhaps, too, we spent too much time shaking our heads in rueful admiration at the way many African rulers – not just Mobutu – stole most of the money lavished in 'aid'; we would have done better to stop the aid completely, or better still never to have given it in the first place. A choice between swimming and sinking concentrates the mind wonderfully, and indeed such a choice has frequently led to an instant grasp of the technique of the breast-stroke.

There must be somebody who would argue that the best thing we could do for Africa is to recolonise it and start all over again, with both sides having learned the necessary lessons. I dare say that some of Mobutu's citizens would prefer the Belgians to him, even if Leopold II's atrocities were thrown in, and I am quite sure that any Ugandans left alive (there won't be many soon, what with rival butcheries on the one hand and Aids on the other) would be delighted to have a British governor running their country, though presumably not in the person of Lord Hatch.

The mystery remains: unfortunately, so does the lack of an explanation. Sooner or later, unless he is very lucky, someone will murder Mobutu, even if only for his money; the 'scramble for Africa' will then mean something very different, as the din of floorboards being prised up fills the air. But when he is gone, we shall be no wiser than before. *Ex Africa aliquid semper novi*, said Pliny. How wrong he was!

The Times July 16th, 1990

Ten years hard

ONE OF RENÉ Magritte's most striking and memorable paintings is a picture of a pipe; there is nothing surrealist about it – bowl and stem are perfectly in proportion, and the viewer can almost see the smoke gently ascending. The only troubling thing about the picture is that at the bottom, in very large letters, the artist has painted the words '*Cela n'est pas une pipe*'.

I find myself today in a somewhat similar situation, for I now propose to spend some 1,500 words writing about a book, very recently published, which is not at all surrealistic, though at the bottom of my assessment of it I am obliged to write, in very large letters, the words '*Cela n'est pas un* book review'.

Well, it isn't. It is a shout of triumph for the conclusion of an almost inhuman endeavour, a plaudit for a man who has defied years, ink, wearisome labour and a wide range of multiple jealousies, a thunderous cheer for the raising of a monument that will stand all the tests of time and weather, a salute to a colossal task at last completed. Which is to say that I have just finished reading the third and last volume of Michael Holroyd's biography of Bernard Shaw.

When the first volume of 463 pages appeared, I devoured it at a sitting and, so hungry was I for more, I prevailed upon the publishers to pass me a contraband copy of the typescript of Vol. 2; that, too, went down in one huge gulp.

There I paused, as a shadow fell on the last page of the second instalment. It was obvious to me, and must have been even more obvious to Holroyd, that the third, concluding, volume would be the most difficult to write, and that the difficulty would increase exponentially towards the end; moreover, the difficulty would be the mortal danger of boring the readers – not because Holroyd's powers were waning (though heaven knows he must frequently have had to fight off several bad attacks of the wanes) but because as Shaw got closer to the end of his immense life, he was doing fewer and fewer interesting things. So before I embarked on Vol. 3, I took care to make the sign of the Evil Eye.

Let me dwell upon that Evil Eye for a moment. It is now very well known that the advance for Mr Holroyd's monumental work was £625,000. I shall come to the comments in a moment, but first let us see what the publishers, Chatto, are getting for their money. The biography itself runs to 1,378 pages in three volumes, comprising more than 600,000 words. In addition, and quite apart from the 16 years of his life Holroyd is giving, the price includes three more volumes. One is devoted entirely to the *apparatus criticus*, the second is a concise version of the biography, and the third takes the form of a commentary on the plays; on top of all that the deal includes the entire paperback series. And, of course, 10 per cent to his literary agents. (But I must pause here to make sure Mr Holroyd is listening. If, when the volume with the sources and references appears, it does not include one complete alphabetical index of the whole three biographical volumes, with the same thoroughness, detail and clarity of the indexes that have been appearing one by one, I shall go to his house – I know where he lives – and ring the doorbell, and when he opens the door I shall bow politely, draw from my breast pocket a small but serviceable revolver, and shoot him dead.)

But now to those critics who snarled at Holroyd's bounty (which was less, incidentally, by £175,000, than the advance for Frederick Forsyth's next scholarly work). I have just read a packet of such comments, and the stench of envy was so overpowering that I sent my valet out to buy a half a pound of the strongest snuff; there was even a suggestion that Carmen Callil of Chatto bumped the sum up to its height because she had had a *tendresse* for Holroyd, while there was a fierce struggle to be the first sour grape to use the inevitable word 'obscene' about the Shaw advance; the winner was Hunter Davies.

As for John Carey, though I cannot believe that he was moved by envy, he seemed to have had, while reading Vol. 1, a fit of the vapours so extreme that he said of Holroyd's photograph on the back jacket that he looked 'glum and costive . . . '. I have the picture propped up in front of me as I write, and I can assure you that in it Holroyd is his usual reflective self; what colony of giant ants have got into Carey's pants and bitten him so savagely that he manages to see what is not there? Mind you, judging by his review of Vol. 3 (' . . . tedium . . . narcotic . . . ') it must have been scorpions rather than ants this time, or possibly the final jacket-photo, in which Holroyd is actually smiling. (Carey must have had a fit when he saw the *Sunday Times* with his review in it; it was illustrated with yet another picture of Holroyd, and in this one he is *laughing*.)

Which reminds me; several hundred words ago I was worrying about Holroyd's problem with Vol. 3. As his subject moves further into the shadows there is less and less activity, but the apparent ease with which Holroyd overcomes this handicap is the perfect paradigm of the whole work, which for all its massive length never flags.

Holroyd's mastery of the material (would *you*, making notes all the way, go through at least 10 million words for a lousy £625,000? – I'm damned if I would) is astonishing; it never clogs and it never sprawls, nothing is crammed and nothing is spread too thin. Holroyd is so confident of his talent that he can afford a delightful tease; Chapter Four ends with these words:

No trumpets had sounded for Shaw's fellow playwright Pinero whose death on 23 November 1934 'passed almost unnoticed'. Few people noticed either when the following day, in the middle of a telephone conversation, Shaw himself suddenly dropped down dead . . .

There is another 32 pages to wait for the truth about this startling news; while the reader is in amazed suspense, Holroyd is calmly discussing *The Simpleton of the Unexpected Isles*.

Holroyd's industry is as scrupulous as it is prodigious; he has collated in the most meticulous detail the biographies by Archibald Henderson and Hesketh Pearson, and gone through the alterations and additions to these that Shaw had demanded for the published works; he has then disentangled the bits which Shaw faked from the bits he only corrected; by the end Holroyd must have been the only person in the world, other than Blanche Patch, who could read Shaw's handwriting with ease.

He is also a master of chronology and – much more important – a master of where to put things out of time's order, so that he can dwell properly on a matter of significance, while the lesser question is put aside, though never forgotten. There is hardly a page of the 1,378 that does not deserve its space, and there is hardly a moment when the reader feels that something has been omitted.

But of course there are greater questions to be answered, and Holroyd has to face them; in a word, he has to judge. Now no man, or even superman, could spend 16 years on such a subject without acquiring an immense affection for him, and Holroyd is no exception. It is a further tribute to him that although he softens the indictments that can be levelled with powerful evidence at Shaw (try him on Stalin) he fudges nothing and hides nothing. In a different context, he leans frequently on Shaw's infant nickname, 'Sonny', deducing all sorts of things from those very early years and the soubriquet; perhaps he leans too hard and too often, but there is no force-feeding for the reader, who never feels that he is being manoeuvred.

Perhaps there will be more biographies of Shaw, though I cannot imagine why anyone would bother now; certainly there will be none for a good many years, though Holroyd, generous to the end, carefully records in his bibliographical notes and acknowledgments the books that have appeared while Jacob served Laban (for two years less than Holroyd, incidentally). There will, alas, be special studies; I dread the appearance of 'Shaw and Knickerbockers' and no doubt 'Shaw and Beards: a Freudian elucidation'. But no one will ever surpass Holroyd's achievement: it is a balanced, muscular, comprehensive, explanatory, beautifully written life story, composed with an unfaltering integrity, a firm elegance, a shrewd wisdom, and – by the end of 16 years – a warm and warily admiring understanding of Shaw that no one could improve upon. Michael Holroyd can well afford to wink at the Evil Eye.

The Times (*Saturday Review*), October 26th, 1991

Mr Wilson forgives God

MR A.N. WILSON, the well-known person, has recently written a biography of Jesus Christ, to be published next year, and he has kindly been giving a preview of his findings – or perhaps it should be tidings – to the world. Presumably to allay the qualms that the news must have aroused, he has come out with a ringing endorsement of his subject: 'I am sure', he says, 'I would like Jesus.'

Now that, you will allow, should stand your man in pretty good stead. I mean, being crucified must be a really rotten business, but to know that you have the A.N. Wilson seal of approval would go far in the way of making the nails less painful. He has much more to say about Jesus, and I have much more to say about *him*, but I must first get one pressing matter out of the way. Mr A.N. ('put it there if it weighs a ton') Wilson is sure that he would like Jesus, but what I want to know, and I suppose most of you want to know also, is: would Jesus like Mr Wilson?

The omens are not good. First, there is no specific statement anywhere in the words of Jesus indicating a liking for our author. Negative evidence, you will say; well, perhaps, but you can build a formidable case on it. Take, for instance, the best-known roster of Jesus's friends; he went out of his way to count the circle of his really close buddies – the poor in spirit, they that mourn, the meek (well, there's damn little meek about Mr Wilson), they which do hunger and thirst after righteousness, the merciful, the pure in heart, the peacemakers and they which are persecuted for righteousness' sake (catch Mr Wilson allowing himself to be persecuted for anybody's sake, starting with his own). A pretty eclectic bunch, it is clear, and a pretty big bunch, too; he must have had a massive Christmas-card list, *but not a word about 'blessed be the biographers'*.

Nor can it be that Jesus thought biography too vulgar a trade (a tabloid journalist, perhaps, but not a man whose books are published by Chatto & Windus); his closest mates included several fishermen and a tax-collector (well, he was a carpenter himself, remember) and a lot more riff-raff of the kind. Yet he was not above entertaining the lot of them at supper; you will remember that when he and his pals turned up at a wedding reception – the easiest kind of junket to gatecrash – and he turned the water into wine, it was all over the front page of the *Cana News*, but there was no mention of Mr Wilson, not even in the 'and many others, including . . . ' bit at the end of the guest list.

Never mind: if Mr Wilson is feeling a bit miffed about his cordiality being spurned, I have good news for him; your man is famous for liking practically everybody, including publicans and sinners, and somewhere in his big heart there is a corner for Mr Wilson, I am sure. Indeed, I can recall only two occasions on which he really expressed dislike; the first was when he got his dander up and for some reason went round the West End throwing the staffs of the Bureaux de Change out of their kiosks (even the American Express in the Haymarket), and the other was when he was talking about child-abuse, and said anyone practising it would be better off tying all Mr Wilson's books round his neck and jumping off Brighton pier.

But Mr Wilson has more important fish to fry (and loaves to bake, I imagine). He makes it clear that his biography will be very wide-ranging; for instance, he wants to know what hobbies Jesus had, whether he got married and whether, if he did, he had children.

The hobbies question has him stumped; presumably he can find no evidence. Well, I can help him here. I know for a fact that Jesus was a real Scrabble expert; moreover, he was a whiz at petit-point, and for good measure he collected matchbox-labels. Mr Wilson is hardly more confident on the marriage and family question; he says no more than 'probably'. Again, I can fill in; Jesus was indeed married, and had two children, a girl called Tracy and a boy, Kevin.

There is more to come; Jesus, for instance, was born not in Bethlehem, as has hitherto been supposed, but Nazareth; Luke made up ('a straight fib . . . ') the bit about Pontius Pilate washing his hands; Mr Wilson tells us that he 'dislikes Luke's gospel very, very much', which should settle Luke's hash for good, eh? Moreover, Jesus was crucified by the Romans because they thought he was politically dangerous, which I can confirm – there was a vital by-election going on, and Jesus was on the stump night and day, campaigning for Paddy Ashdown. And finally – this'll make you gasp for the daring of the man Wilson – he declares that Jesus was not born of a virgin, was not the Son of God, and did not rise from the dead.

I suppose that by now I have offended practically everybody, though I set out only to offend Mr Wilson. For the fourteen thousandth time, I am not a Christian, partly because I do not think myself worthy to be one; but it is really beyond patience for a man who loves very profoundly the person, words and message of Christ, and among that loving finds Mr Wilson arsing about and squeaking, the squeaks being composed of the same tired old arguments, deployed in a quality not quite as high as that of the schoolboy who tries to embarrass teacher by drawing attention to Isaiah 36, verse 12, or who explains to his friends while they are playing conkers that his dad says that it was impossible for Sarah to leave a baby under a gooseberry-bush at the age of 90, though dad wouldn't explain exactly why.

Come; let us suppose that Christ was born neither in Bethlehem, as the Christians believe, nor in Nazareth, as Mr Wilson believes, but in Tunbridge Wells. Suppose, even, that Mr Wilson, rather than the Christian religion, is right about virgin births and resurrections; will those tremendous metaphors – is there anything in all history to touch them? – wither and die? Is not the nature of Christ, in the words of the New Testament, enough to pierce to the soul anyone with a soul to be pierced?

Mr Wilson will no doubt assure us that there is no such thing as a soul; after all, he has recently made plain, in a pamphlet, that *all* religion is bogus and should be ignored. I suppose the pamphlet was a herald of the forthcoming book, which will knock down Christianity and bury it. Well, its founder was very thoroughly knocked down and ever so buried, and whether he rose from the grave or whether he was playing possum, he still looms over the world, his message still clear, his pity still infinite, his consolation still effective, his words still full of glory, wisdom and love.

Mr Wilson says that he has not yet decided on the title of his book. Perhaps I may suggest 'Gawd 'elp us', or possibly 'Christ Almighty!'. Or better still: 'How I Set Out to Demolish the Christian Religion, and Succeeded only in Making a Right Nana of Myself'.

The Times June 6th, 1991

A man's a man for a' that

THE THING ABOUT a circle is that if you keep going round it in the same direction, you inevitably return to where you started. It took a lot of hard work, disappointment, anger and throat lozenges to convince Parliament that the employment of women and children as coalminers ought to be stopped; it was eventually ended in 1842, largely through the work of Lord Shaftesbury.

Now, following an advertisement for 'young people aged 18 and over' to work at the coalface, British Coal has received a number of applications for the jobs from young ladies; suitable candidates, after a successful medical examination, will shortly be winched down into the pits, 148 years after Shaftesbury's task was done. (It is almost eerie to realise that for this notable advance in civilisation, Shaftesbury's Mines Act had to be repealed.)

Very well, we shall have female coalminers, and after a time we shall cease to think them odd, though what Lord Shaftesbury might think is another matter. But assuredly I at least shall never cease to wonder at the thought of women prizefighters.

Perhaps you did not know that there *were* any women prizefighters; I certainly didn't. I discovered the fact from a vivid article by Glenys Roberts in a recent *Sunday Telegraph*. Listen to this: 'American fighters usually wear glassfibre breast plates. Not Sue Atkins, who believes them to be more dangerous to the wearer if they split, than a blow to the soft tissue itself which, though vulnerable, will yield.'

I'll say it will yield; it's supposed to, after all. I don't want to be descriptive, let alone indelicate, much less still anecdotal, but I can say, and I do, that by the end of the article I needed a glass of something stronger than milk. Hark.

> . . . no woman purposefully targets another's breasts when the object is to win a match by knocking her senseless . . . one hundred men paid £3 each to watch the two girl contenders . . . go the full eight rounds . . . Some girls went up North on what is called the tough girls' circuit . . . fighting, wrestling, kicking . . . often topless. Atkins has fought topless opponents just to get a fight, but she herself will not strip off . . . once, sitting in a bar, she accepted a fight from a girl on the next stool . . . she was 6ft 2in tall and weighed 11 stone. The British girl came away with some bad bruising and a headache but a lesson in life . . . And that is the whole point of boxing, she says . . . that it is real.

There was an American novel called *They Shoot Horses, Don't They?* It was set in the years of the Depression, and based on what was called 'marathon dancing' in which the dancers who were still moving when the others had given up or collapsed won a cash prize. At much the same time, women were induced to wrestle with one another in a ring a foot deep in mud. But these people were living in financial despair; they had no jobs and no hopes of any, and such repellent practices at least offered them a chance of winning a substantial sum of money.

No such constraint is suffered by Ms Atkins and her fellow prizefighteresses. Nor, manifestly, do they feel in any way oppressed or degraded; they want to knock other women senseless not because they are starving, but simply because they enjoy the experience, because 'it is real', because (in Sue Atkins' case) 'She likes to call herself "hard . . . and one of the lads".' (One obvious explanation is conclusively ruled out by Glenys Roberts: these women are not butch lesbians, or any other kind of lesbians.)

Now *I* think that this is about as disgusting a notion as I have heard for many a long day, and I also think that the women who take part in it, sexually normal though they be, are truly denatured. The women coalminers, after all, are not going back into the conditions which ruled in our mines before 1842; their labour will be demanding, but – with so much of the work today being done by machinery – not brutalising. The women fighters, whether they wear glassfibre breast protectors or not, are in a category entirely different. But my mere assertion is not enough, nor is an appeal to my feelings; *why* is the idea of women slugging it out over eight rounds before a crowd so sordid?

Well, male boxing is pretty sordid, too, at least nowadays. Among my childhood heroes were men like Len Harvey and Tommy Farr (who went the distance with Joe Louis) – real boxers, who relied on their skill, their speed, their cunning, their intelligence. Since the Brown Bomber, I don't think there has been a world heavyweight champion you would allow to walk your dog, and that goes for the contenders, too. Today, the top weight is fought out by two huge Neanderthal lumps, bashing each other in slow motion until one falls over. (Yes, I know Frank Bruno is not a Neanderthal lump but a true gentleman, and a witty one too. But that is the point: he has no business in a ring with Things like Tyson, and if he tries it once too often he will emerge with his brains turned to goulash soup.)

Still, why do some men, including me, always open a door for a lady, give her our seat on a bus, pick up something she has dropped, refrain from swearing in her presence? Skin-deep, you may say; but these gestures denote instincts, and the deepest instinct here is the one most central to the argument. The Almighty might have made men and women identical, and their roles in procreation likewise. But he didn't; he differentiated the sexes in many ways, but one was crucial. It was given only to women to bear and suckle children, and I know of no evolutionary development which has yet issued in women growing glassfibre breast plates.

It is no answer to say that many women do not want children and have no interest in procreation. I certainly would not argue that such women are betraying their sex, are unfeminine, or wasting their lives. But their bodies, and much more than their bodies, are different from men's, and that would remain true even if they all insisted on double mastectomies.

That would solve the glassfibre argument, but nothing else. For any woman to use her body in a way which invites, *pace* Ms Atkins' logic, the battering of her breasts, signals something far more deeply shocking than the inevitably seedy surroundings and conditions in which female fighting takes place. For here the sexes meet; what is the only part of the body, in *male* boxing, which may not be hit? Testicles are specific to men, as milk-giving breasts are to women; what use they are put to, if any, makes no difference to that overwhelmingly significant truth.

Women kill in wars, drive buses, run huge businesses, become prime ministers or bishops; why, then, should they not beat each other to pulp in the boxing ring? Because creation, or evolution, built their bodies, and the purpose of their bodies, differently from those of men. Let Sue Atkins and her kind wait until men give suck, and only then put on the gloves.

The Times July 23rd, 1990

Silent night

A FRENCH GENTLEMAN I met the other day gave me some alarming news. The Catholic hierarchy in France, he said, had banned all secular music from their churches. When I asked the reason, he said that the use of non-liturgical accompaniments to the service had been getting out of hand, and the *dernière paille* was reached when *le hard rock* was heard resounding from High Mass in a provincial cathedral, to the infinite scandal of the devout.

Name of a pipe; though one takes the point. But this, if it is true, must surely rank high among instances of throwing out the baby, or at the very least the soap, with the bathwater. 'Make a joyful noise unto the Lord, all the earth,' says Psalm 98, and who would wish to deny the Lord the sweet sounds of music? Better than the scent of burnt offerings in His nostrils, I'll be bound.

Some time ago, I had occasion to rebuke an English clergyman for banning applause in his church – applause, that is, for a piano recital, the programme being wholly secular, but not in the least irreverent; surely that should be the test. I cannot believe that the walls of French churches have been resounding with whatever is the French for 'Daisy, Daisy, give me your answer, do,' as the nuptial knot was being tied, or 'Massa's in de cold, cold ground,' at a funeral, though I have to say that I would not myself think either out of place in the circumstances.

After the horrors of my earliest introduction to music, which I have recounted elsewhere, the next exposure to the loveliest of the arts was the music in chapel at my boarding school. If my infant attempts to learn the violin brought on a savage rejection of the whole idea of music, the things we had to sing there did nothing but confirm my belief that it was an unqualified pestilence.

Mind; the hymns I greatly enjoyed, and the psalms only a little less. It was the more substantial items that made me shudder. Surely children – innocent children who have done no harm – are not still suffering Stanford's *Magnificat*? If they are, there should be prosecutions under the laws against baby-battering. As for Parry's *Nunc Dimittis*, I suspect that it was not the Lord who guided his pen, but His Satanic Majesty, the Father of Mischief.

Shaw, in his music-critic days, once started an article 'Parry is sickening for another oratorio,' and the image was perfect. There was a performance of Parry's *Job* a few years ago in London, and I went to it, having long since taken music to my heart and even forgiven both him and Stanford for postponing my entry into the heaven of *die holde Kunst*. I longed to discover that I had misjudged him all those years ago, but I hadn't; it was perfectly awful from beginning to end.

The musical director at my school was C.S. Lang; 'Doc' we called him. He must long ago have been gathered to Handel's bosom in heaven for organising an annual performance of *Messiah* in the chapel, with the whole school as chorus. As far as I know, he wrote only one work, its title sufficiently descriptive: *Tuba Tune*. I shall never cease to blush with shame when I recall the occasion, on *Face the Music*, when I was given it to identify, and failed. (I hadn't heard it for nearly 40 years, but that was no excuse.)

There must have been, some time during the centuries, a pope or two who was expert in music; I wouldn't be surprised if there was one who wrote some. (The nice thing about sentences like that is that there is bound to be a reader who knows the answer, and takes the trouble to enlighten me.) I fear that there must have been many who thought it at least distracting and at worst devilish. But then, you see,

you are stuck good and proper when you get to Rossini's
Petite Messe Solennelle.

I last heard it in, of all places, Adelaide Cathedral, and
I wish I had known at the time about the French decree,
because I could have blown the cruel edict out of the water
with a single shot. Rossini was, presumably, a faithful son
of the Church; faithful enough, anyway, to write a mass.
Well, little it may be, but he could not have been solemn in
a torture-dungeon; it sparkles along as merrily as one of his
second Act endings. Now if you ban, say, *Vapensiero* from
the order of service because it is not sufficiently reverent
(though it is as reverent as any music ever written), how
can you accommodate Rossini's Mass, which has everybody
smiling throughout and occasionally laughing uproariously
as well?

The performance in Adelaide, incidentally, had more than
Rossini to cheer up the congregation. Half-way through, a
lunatic lady left her seat and clambered on to the conductor's podium. The baton was in the hand of Myer Fredman,
who kept his nerve magnificently, even when the intruder,
having studied his technique, began to wave her arms about
in a most commendable impersonation, though her beat
was rather more in the misty style of Furtwängler than
the crisper technique of Mr Fredman. She was led away,
gently.

Does the Three Choirs Festival still go on? I hope so,
though I wouldn't be surprised if somebody had pulled
down Hereford Cathedral because it was getting in the way
of the traffic. I cannot now remember whether the festival
was entirely liturgical, but even if it was (and is) there could
surely be no total ban.

Of course, Hereford and Adelaide, and for that matter
my school, are Anglican centres, and it is the Catholics who
are down on extra-curricular music-making. More precisely,
perhaps, it is the *French* Catholics; I cannot believe that the
Italians, decrees or no decrees, would exclude beautiful and
fitting music merely because it was uncanonical; dammit, the

Verdi *Requiem* is more operatic than *Un Ballo in Maschera* itself.

Some religions are severe on the pictorial arts, presumably because of the Lord's insistence that graven images are forbidden by the second commandment. Is there any religion that bans music altogether, sacred as well as profane? Surely not, though I have never been to a Quaker service (meeting, I should have said), and they may eschew it as they eschew other forms of adornment which could disturb the directness with which they approach their God.

The Old Testament is full of music, though that cannot be the reason why every Jewish mother is convinced that her infant son is going to be a violin virtuoso. Mind you, there must be an explanation for the astonishing fact that almost all the world's great violinists have been Jews, and the phenomenon continues. Did Jesus say anything about music? Off-hand, I know of no reference to it, and that can hardly be because the violin did not then exist, for Jewish mothers certainly did. All the arts, through the centuries, have laid their tributes at Christ's feet, and assuredly the tributes have not been spurned, references or no references; how terribly bare and cold the world would be if Christian art had never been born. Presumably, music was enlisted very early in the service of religion, which is hardly surprising, in view of its enormous potency. (Sound is more powerful than sight.)

Perhaps, though, it is the potency which disturbed the French Catholic hierarchy as more and more secular music was heard in their churches. I do not suppose anyone ever dared to mount *Tristan* in Notre Dame, though on the other hand *Parsifal* might have been thought suitable, despite its unorthodoxy. I hope my French acquaintance was mistaken, and if he was not, I hope that the ban will soon be lifted.

The Times May 28th, 1990

Oriental Express

W E KNOW WHICH is the highest mountain, and where is the deepest part of the sea; we know that there is no object hotter than the sun, no genius greater than Shakespeare. But in some categories, it is impossible to point to one supreme example that dwarfs all the others. Come: who is the greatest living violinist, who are the happiest married couple, which the worst High Court judge? We cannot say, at least without facing a dozen immediate challenges, particularly from the judges. So we have to admit personal prejudices and choices.

Very well; but we must be prepared to defend our choices, for our *ipse dixit* is not enough. That said, I propose to put in a claim and defend it. *I* think that the greatest hotel in the world is the Mandarin, Hong Kong. (Alas, I must pause here to report that there are terrible rumours circulating about it; the word is that it is going to be transformed from the haven of wonderful peace that it is into a glitzy simulacrum of the worst kind of American monster hotel. In all my life, I have never wanted more passionately to be proved wrong.)

We shall see. Meanwhile, it starts at the airport. You emerge and say, to nobody in particular, 'Mandarin'. A young man in whites materialises from the pavement, followed by a more senior figure in pinstripes. You open your mouth to give your name; it is already known. The young man takes your luggage away, his elder summons a car: the car is a Rolls, a Daimler or a very large Mercedes. The driver has a carphone; when you near the hotel, he announces your imminent arrival. You arrive, and get out of the car. Before your second foot has touched the pavement, the welcome committee is on the steps. A phalanx, led by an assistant manager, welcomes you. Nonsense like checking in is unknown; you may be asked for a signature, but nothing else, and if you are a regular or frequent visitor, not even that.

If you are a newcomer, you may feel uneasy about your luggage, which was taken from your hands but not put in the boot of your car. The assistant manager shows you to your room, bows, leaves you. Seconds later, the doorbell rings – oh, no, they do not *knock* at the Mandarin – and there is your luggage.

I begin to unpack; I am a regular visitor, and at the Mandarin they like to make their friends happy. The doorbell rings, a procession enters. It is headed by a senior manager, who is profuse in welcome. Behind him comes a waiter with champagne; the glass on the tray is of the finest Waterford. Next comes another waiter bearing a tray with a large tin of the very finest chocolates. Next is a chambermaid who proffers yet another tray, this one laden with huge tablets of the finest bath soap. All but the manager leave; to him falls the last part of the ceremony. He draws back the curtains; outside is the most moving view in the world – Hong Kong harbour, and the Star Ferry going back and forth, back and forth, back and forth, across it. A last bow, and I am alone. I am in the Mandarin Hotel; I am happy; I am home.

There are 33 handsome wooden coat hangers in my wardrobe; there are colour-coded bags for laundry, pressing, dry-cleaning, all made of the finest material, beautiful and opaque; there is, of course, a brand-new umbrella, and a shoehorn 2-foot long. (Oh, no; the Mandarin's guests must not bend down to put their shoes on.) There are 17 drawers in my suite; there are seven gigantic glass ashtrays, together with two china ones; the dressing-table is 8ft long, and the bowl of fruit on a sideboard would feed an army, which could then take a bath in the fingerbowl. There are orchid petals floating on the water in it. The vases in the room contain orchids, too.

The furniture is handsome, not ornate. The drawers roll, not slide; they *never* stick. The décor is soothing, friendly, unobtrusive; there are charming prints on the walls. The mirrors are large and well-placed, the lights are where they are needed, there are tiny nightlights, and a single master switch that can be thrown without getting out of bed. The pillows are huge, lulling; there are extra ones in the wardrobe.

To the bathroom; on every visit I find that the Mandarin has added something to its hospitality, and this time it is a lavatory flush that goes on for a full minute and a half, foaming with a pleasantly scented detergent. There is the usual range of bath gel and toiletries; not content with that, the Mandarin has added bath-salts, in a pretty, decorated jug. There are three taps at the basin, not two: hot, cold and iced. The bathrobe could wrap the entire aforesaid army, and keep it warm throughout the Retreat from Moscow.

The doorbell rings again: it is the 'roomboy'. I do not like the word, and do not use it, but I have never seen any steward seem offended by it. He wants to replace the fruit bowl; I have eaten a banana and half an apple, but replace the fruit bowl he must and will (and does). I have kicked off my shoes; he leaps at them; I decline a struggle. He takes them away, brings them back highly polished, heedless of the fact that they were highly polished already.

There is a susurration; for years now I have not needed to tell anyone that I want the *The Times*; today's just arrives under the door, together, for good measure, with the *Wall Street Journal* and the *International Herald Tribune*. On the table there is the handsome leather folder that holds the stationery; I know what is coming, for many hotels now play the same charming trick. My name is neatly printed at the bottom of every sheet of writing-paper. But no; I do *not* know what is coming. This is the Mandarin; my name is not printed on the writing-paper; it is *engraved*.

It is things like that – small and unimportant – which mark this place as one where continuing thought is brought to bear on the task of keeping old hands happy and making newcomers determined to return. (Every evening, a steward enters with a tray bearing a delicious *amuse-gueule*; he, too, removes and replaces the fruit bowl, even if it has not been touched.)

You feel it in the atmosphere; the staff are neither frigidly correct nor ingratiatingly familiar, neither surly nor obsequious. It is plain that the Mandarin's staff are trained (there must be a huge school for new recruits somewhere) to believe that although they serve they are not servants, let alone servile. In all the years, I have never encountered a member of the staff, from the room-maids to the senior managers, who lacked character, who seemed to have been bought ready-made.

After that, it comes as no surprise to find that the breakfast order comes not within the usual time-band – a quarter of an hour each way, say – but on the *exact* minute specified on the doorknob menu.

Ah, but the Mandarin can do better than that. Once, a year or two ago, I had had my breakfast and was contemplating getting up, postponing the resolve by sending some laundry to be done. I put it in the bag, with the appropriately colour-coded slip, and rang the bell for my steward. I was not consciously timing him, but I was sitting on the edge of my bed, and my little travelling clock was on the bedside table, in my eyeline, so that when the doorbell rang, I saw that he had taken exactly *three* minutes, no more, to arrive. He opened the door, entered, bowed, and said, 'Sorry for delay.'

Of course, it is expensive; how could it not be, with the quality it offers to its guests? But if you can afford it, you will realise that it truly is different from other hotels, even the finest; the Mandarin aims at perfection, and reaches it. At any rate – and it is perhaps the best test there is – I know no hotel harder to leave than the Mandarin, none that makes the traveller yearn so powerfully for the next visit. And it goes on to the last moment; the limousine takes you back to the airport, your luggage is brought and put on a trolley, and as you take one step towards the check-in desk, your ticket and passport are gently taken from your hands; no, Mandarin guests do not do their own checking-in. It would not surprise me in the least to find a bevy of Mandarin employees at my elbow throughout the flight – indeed, I dare say that there are more of them up front, flying the aeroplane.

But I have a complaint; it concerns the Great Kipper Horror. Many years ago, seeing kippers on the breakfast menu, I ordered one. Even I, a seasoned Mandarinist, was astonished to find the real thing under the silver cover, the backbone gently curling up. Ever since, I have breakfasted with a kipper at least once on every stay, and every time it has been the real succulent thing. Last year, to my dismay, it was the feeble filleted, packaged object that you get in Other Hotels.

Homer, it is said, nodded from time to time. But the Mandarin may not. Bring back real kippers, my dear home from home, and you shall have a rating on the Levin Scale not just of 99, which you had before, but of 99½. Do not be upset if I rate one other hotel at 100; it is, after all, the Hotel Heaven, that great resting-place where Mandarin staffers and Mandarin guests mingle now indistinguishably, for ever.

The Times (Saturday Review), April 20th, 1991

Dead men talk no sense

THERE IS A jolly row going on concerning the will of the late Philip Larkin, and since rows are my speciality, I shall do my best this morning to make matters worse.

For those who have not followed the story – it began when Larkin died – I summarise the course of the dispute. Larkin, in many ways a reclusive figure, gave instructions in his will that on his death his diaries should be destroyed. That was done; but he also gave instructions about the unpublished remainder of his work, including poetry, short stories and matter forming part of unfinished novels, and this is where the trouble started.

His executors insisted they were in a difficulty over Larkin's wishes in the matter of these remains. To some eyes it has seemed clear that he wanted them all to be destroyed, as with the diaries; other eyes – those of the executors – have seen what to them were ambiguities in the will, and deduced that that was not so. In the event, the executors are plainly bent on publishing some of the unfinished *oeuvre* and leaving other works unseen, though whether they propose to destroy the matter they are not intending to publish is not clear.

The row has been bubbling along since Larkin's will was read, and it has just boiled over. The executors (they include Anthony Thwaite, whose integrity none, I think, would question), mindful of the argument over the apparent ambiguities in the will, called in a lawyer to study the wording and give an opinion. Here, I feel, they were being a touch disingenuous. True, the lawyer opined that the wording of the will permitted them to publish what they wished, and I suppose they were entitled to rely on his expertise, but they knew perfectly well that by tea-time on the same day they could have assembled 40 lawyers to give an entirely contrary view, and by lunch the day after another 50 to back up the first opinion, and indeed before the weekend another 77 who would unanimously say that on the one hand it was clear that they could publish, and on the other hand that it was plain that they could not.

'Dead men tell no tales,' says a judge in one of A.P. Herbert's *Misleading Cases*, adding, 'and it were better that they made no wills.' It is not clear whether Larkin composed his entirely unaided, or whether he sought legal assistance; if the latter, he should have known that the chances of post-humous chaos were thereby substantially enhanced. (So far, there has been no litigation, but that happy state of affairs may not last.)

But even if Larkin had made it quite impossible for anyone to misinterpret his wishes, saying plainly and in capital letters that he wanted every unpublished word he ever wrote summarily burned, there would have been a body of opinion, including, I am quite sure, some of his literary executors, who would have objected to what they would have seen as failing in their duty to posterity rather than to the poet. (History is littered with such disputes; James Joyce died in 1941, but his descendants are still kicking up rough about his literary remains, not necessarily because the copyright is about to run out.)

As it happens, when the Larkin row caught fire I was read-ing the *Diaries* of H.L. Mencken, my hero since boyhood; the editor and Mencken's literary executors had faced a similar problem. Mencken had stipulated that his diaries should be sealed for 25 years, and the ban had been faithfully observed. He died in 1956, which is considerably longer than 25 years ago, but publication was held up by a dispute over another item in his will; apparently, he had no objection to letting scholars and students see the diaries when the quarter-century was up, but jibbed at any wider circulation. The deadlock was broken when a lawyer (I bet you didn't know that they have lawyers in America, too) studied Mencken's will and opined that it would be all right by him (him the lawyer, not necessarily him Mencken) for general reading to take place.

For my part, I am grateful to the American lawyer; Mencken in the original cloth could be candid enough, but Mencken 34 years dead, his cackles clearly audible from the afterworld, fair takes away the breath, with no suggestion of ever bringing it back. Even now, the editor thinks it politic from time to time to replace a name or identification with a few discreet suspension points, but I would not have missed the ripeness of Mencken unchained for all the lawyers and all their bills.

There is a real dilemma in this business. Many people, particularly artists, have left instructions that certain works of theirs should be destroyed at their death; sometimes, the stipulation is for everything left unfinished to go. But suppose Schubert had left such instructions, to his brother Ferdinand, say, or Grillparzer. Would you have applauded them for their fidelity to his instructions as they fed the bonfire with all those unpublished songs? I'm damned if I would; I would have called them criminals of the lowest degree. And if Hüttenbrenner, his memory jogged at last by the news of Schubert's death, had trotted round with the MS of the Unfinished, which Schubert had entrusted to him years before, and tossed it on the flames, would not the very universe have demanded vengeance? Dear God – suppose Mendelssohn had gone to Carter-Ruck for advice on what to do with the MS of the C major Symphony and been told that Schubert's children might sue if it were not destroyed? (Schubert did not have any children, but Carter-Ruck might not have known that.)

Nor, though, can we take refuge in the artist's choice of what to keep and what to throw out; artists are notorious for misjudging their own work. Larkin did leave some poetry which was plainly inferior to his best work (and he was not one of those who cannot tell their best from their worst – he was merciless to his failures, as witness the scores of extant versions of some of his poems). It could be said that the executors are ignoring the implications of his refusal to publish poems left, years ago, in manuscript. But that does not settle the matter either; if, in my hypothesis, Schubert's instructions had gone unheeded in the greater cause of preserving his genius for posterity, who am I to say that Larkin's should have been rigidly followed? No doubt Schubert was a greater genius than Larkin, but that cannot be the test – we should have missed much pleasure and solace if the Great McGonagall's verses had not been preserved, even (which is extremely unlikely) if he did not wish them to be.

In law, there is a remedy from the courts if a legacy is given to someone other than the stipulated legatee; perhaps there is a law that testamentary provisions that do not allocate money or money's worth cannot be enforced. But that still leaves the Larkin problem where it was, for whatever the courts may decide, the argument is not a legal one but a moral one, and the argument over should/shouldn't would still not be resolved.

I don't suppose it ever will be. For my part, I have made no provision for the testamentary disposition of my literary remains; not because I think them too insignificant but because I have no intention of dying. And that is all I have to say this morning.

The Times November 1st, 1990

A bite and a sup

NOT LONG AGO, I found myself in Basle at lunch-time. No, let me start again. As I know from much past experience, this article will inevitably cause the most frightful uproar, and I had better not invite any more lightning than I am going to get anyway.

I lied; I did *not* 'find myself' in Basle at lunch-time. I went there quite deliberately, changing trains twice each way. It is true that it was lunch-time, but that was not irrelevant: I was there for lunch.

In Basle there is a restaurant called Stücki, in the Bruderholz Allee. The Gault-Millau guide to good food gives it the second highest rating in Switzerland; Frédy Girardet gets 19½ out of 20 (no establishment has yet got the full 20), and Stücki gets 19. I was going to lunch at Stücki. I lunch there whenever I can; if I am within one or two hundred miles of it and there are suitable trains, I *always* eat there. If I am staying overnight in Basle, I take dinner, always remembering that for dinner it is necessary to book much earlier than for lunch, though lunch, of course, has one advantage over dinner – there is much additional pleasure to be had from sitting in the sunny garden sipping an aperitif while studying the menu.

The menu is immense, which usually casts suspicion on a restaurant, or ought to, because very few can really provide dozens of dishes without the lavish aid of the freezer, and some of the Hotel Splendide types can even sink to the boil-in-the-bag.

An infallible clue is the offer of items that are out of

season. But nothing like that happens at Stücki; oh, nothing like that. No, no, no, not Stücki; their gold is absolutely pure 24 carat. (Well, in reality there is no absolutely pure gold, so nobody scores 24. Let us say that Girardet gets 23½, and Stücki 23.)

At some stage of your meal, your host, Hans Stücki, makes his rounds. Far be it from me, a notorious paladin of moderate speech, to call another gentleman fat, or even plump; but it is quite impossible to describe Hans as looking thin, svelte, lean, slim or willowy, much less emaciated. For one glance is enough to show that he eats his own food, and enjoys it.

So do we, Hans, so do we. At which point my trouble begins, because I can hardly sing the praises of a marvellous meal without saying what I ate at it. Strictly, what *we* ate at it, for I am damned if I am going to be pelted in the streets all alone; there are limits to how far even Chivalrous Jack Levin will go, and the truth is that 'the woman whom thou gavest to be with me, she gave me of the tree, and I did eat'. (If you meet her, she will say: 'The serpent beguiled me, and I did eat.' Don't believe a word of it.) Here goes.

We drank a bottle of Laurent-Perrier – NV, but in magnificent condition – to start with, and felt we might as well go on with the same all through; the menus we compiled lent themselves to it. *Here* goes.

The *amuse-gueule* was a button of monkfish, crammed with taste, on a crispy bed. The lady then started with caviare and smoked salmon on blinis. The salmon was rolled into a cornet stuffed with a mild, fresh-grated horse-radish; the caviare was Oscietre and the blinis firm and light. I took the truffle and broad-bean soup; it had a dice of vegetables, and the velvety richness of the whole thing, to say nothing of its scent, was quite miraculous.

For the next course, I had an escalope of *foie gras de canard*, poached with a mild raspberry vinegar; the lady had the terrine of *pâté de foie d'oie*, accompanied by a mass of fine-sliced truffles.

I must pause here to mention that of course we each shared of the other's plenty throughout; I have always felt that those who keep rigidly to their own plates are missing something very important in the art and pleasure of eating well.

Next, the lady fancied the grilled lobster with a basil and tomato coulis; basil can be obtrusive, but here it was perfectly discreet. I asked for the loup de mer, but there was none to be had; the maître recommended as an alternative the dorade in a mustard sauce, and a fine alternative it made. Again, the mustard was carefully tamed.

Cheese next. I will have you know that I am a *Chevalier de la Confrérie des Tastes-Fromages de France*, and I know a good cheese-board (cheese-wagon, actually) when I see it. The lady is not well up in cheese, but eager to learn; she does not care for *chèvre* (sad, sad), so I proposed a Reblochon (nothing like the mass-produced version now found everywhere), a Sbrinz, also the real thing (it is a cheese I like more and more, a kind of cousin to Parmesan), an Epuisse and a Tête de Moine, which is not only delicious but fun, if it is sliced by that ingenious machine. I regret to say that I was so happily engaged in trying hers that I forgot to make a note of the four goat-cheeses I picked.

Next, ordered in advance, came a quince soufflé, for both of us; it was magically light, the sharpness of the fruit clearly there but not too powerful. We noticed that although it had been ordered at the beginning of the meal, and we had not mentioned cheese at that time, the soufflé came perfectly on time, as indeed did every course.

After that, we examined the chariot des desserts; the lady chose the *île flottante*, and I, mindful of my reputation as an ascetic, feasted only on a mixture of fresh raspberries and blueberries. Then there was nothing but some delicately delicious petits fours, particularly a tiny tartlet of fraises des bois, to accompany in her case a mint tea, and in mine some black coffee, powerful and gloriously bitter. (I have always asked what the point of coffee is, if it doesn't give you palpitations of the heart.) The second bottle of Laurent-Perrier ended perfectly on time.

I must now explain the hints of trouble I have been dropping. I believe most profoundly that eating well is itself an art. It is a lesser art, to be sure; nobody would put it with music or literature or painting. But an art it is, and a meal such as ours at Stücki provides a resonant pleasure that is recognisably of the same stuff as the pleasure of the greater arts.

Some people would deny that claim; so be it. But some – I have had the experience every time I have described the pleasure of eating – are thrown into a terrible rage at the very thought of good food and the describing of it. I have asked again and again why that should be; after all, if someone has no ear for music, he simply doesn't go to concerts, and turns the page when I am revelling in Mozart or Schubert. And he who is always bored at the theatre shuns it – but he does not write me hysterical and abusive letters denouncing my pleasure in *Hamlet*. Food and drink, however, considered as an art, set off the most appalling behaviour. I know very well, for instance, that my references to champagne will be condemned with special savagery; but if we had drunk a fine old claret with the foie gras, or a noble white burgundy with the fish, let alone both, the savagery would be even greater.

I have, as I say, asked why; but truth to tell, I have long since stopped caring. Art, in all its forms and however it grew into the world, is second only to love for the solace and harmony it gives to the human soul; assuredly, it was no accident that the universe had to encompass it. They also serve, these lesser arts. Why, the French think it no shame to speak of *les arts ménagers*, and it is they, of all nations, who have made an art not only of cooking, but of savouring what has been cooked. I do not envy the French very much; but I wish we had something of their attitude to the art and pleasure of the kitchen, and of the moment when the kitchen door swings open and the meal is brought to the table.

Funny: neither of us felt like dinner that evening.

The Times (Saturday Review), October 20th, 1990

Here and there

I LOVED THE sight of a 747 flying from New York to London with only three passengers on board. And what a chorus of 'Yah-boo, yellow-bellies!' has greeted the decision of most of the population of the United States to forgo planned visits to Britain and other European countries. But I want to put a different complexion on the wholesale cancellations – one that does not accept cowardice as the reason. The problem is not funk, but geography.

Over many years of travelling in America and scores of other lands, I have come to the conclusion that God's Own Country is, by a very wide margin indeed, the most insular nation on earth. What is more, the insularity is not of the kind which has for centuries been attributed (with a good deal of reason) to us, and in a somewhat different way to the French. Our insularity is partly boasting, partly contempt for other countries' different customs, and partly the conviction that every other country is out to swindle us.

On the whole, the Americans are refreshingly free of such attitudes; indeed, they are so trusting that they are probably the number one suckers for con-men throughout the world, and their reaction when they meet a situation unknown back home is touchingly bewildered rather than angry. No; American insularity, and hence the present headlong flight from flying, is based on a truly stupefying ignorance. Americans know that if they go far enough westward in their own country they will come to the Pacific Ocean, and if they go to the limit eastwards they will find the Atlantic. *And that is practically all most of them do know.*

Well, they know about Canada, because it is sitting on top of them, and they know there is a thing called Latin America, because it is attached to them; they know there is another thing called Asia (though few of them know where it is), because the Vietnam war took place there. They have heard of Africa, but they think it is near to the said Asia; they have only a hazy idea where the Soviet Union is located. And the whole of the rest of the world, including the Middle East, the Antipodes and Scandinavia, are located in a place called Yerp. I tell you, and I am not joking, that most Americans truly believe that Baghdad is a couple of hours' drive from London.

Landing at Heathrow from New York some years ago, there being no vacant 'stands', we had to deplane and be bussed to the terminal. An elderly American gentleman, as the vehicle lumbered off, could be heard plaintively enquiring: 'Does this bus go to the *Savoy*, does this bus go to the *Savoy*, does this bus go to the *Savoy*?' I got near enough to him to point out that before he could check in at the *Savoy*, he would have to go through immigration and customs procedures, but I might have saved my breath, for all he could understand. He was, obviously, used to flying within the United States, where indeed you walk off the plane without any formalities, and it had not crossed his mind that when visiting other countries, other rules apply.

You wave such ideas irritably away. Very well, but then tell me whether there is any other country in the world whose citizens, wherever they are, so frequently proffer their own currency in hotels and shops and are first amazed, then become truly alarmed, when told they will have to change their dollars for the local money. I must insist that this attitude is not based on any theory of the Master Race, of which I have found very little evidence in America. It is, I say again, their implacably total ignorance of where the rest of the world is, let alone how it lives. The very idea of distance is alien to them: when the Gulf war started, a Los Angeles store that sold gas-masks was cleaned out of its entire stock of several thousands within two days. The customers were not cowards; since Kuwait was almost certainly a few miles off the Californian coast, it was only prudent to take precautions.

Do not believe that such attitudes exist only in times of war or other crises. Read the American newspapers, even the few 'quality' ones, and you will find that you can turn several hundred pages without finding any reference to anything that is happening in Yerp. Again, this is not contempt for lesser breeds; it is the knowledge in the mind of the editor that none of his readers (or, to be fair, he) would have any idea at all, however approximate, where to find, on a map of Yerp, London, Riyadh, Durex, Sydney, Helsinki, Bovril, Edinburgh, Tahiti, Amman, Paris, Gitanes, Brussels, Tehran, Xerox, Qom, Amsterdam, Esperanto, Warsaw, Beirut, Aquavit, Cairo, Horlicks, Berlin, Athens, Marmite, Prague, Tapioca, Oslo or Harrods. But although none of them could point to these places on the map, there would be agreement that every city in the list could be found in Yerp, within 200 miles of London.

In those circumstances, it is only reasonable that people should stay away from the war-zone if their presence there is not urgently needed; it is obvious that any attempt to assure stay-at-home Americans that the map is not quite like that is bound to fail.

What we should be asking, though only out of curiosity, is how this bizarre hole in American knowledge came to be there. I suppose the very size of the United States militates against knowing or caring that there is a world elsewhere. Particularly in Yerp (the real Yerp), we feel frontiers all round us; even Britain, whose frontiers are in the sea, does not think herself a separate continent. But that is not only because we are all part of Yerp; it is because from the Irish Republic to the western borders of the Soviet Union, each sovereign state, measured by area, could be amply accommodated by two or three of the States of the Union.

Those who live in a country which has half-a-dozen time-zones, and demands, if you want to cross it from one side to the other, much the same number of hours as it takes to fly across the Atlantic, will inevitably come to think that their country is the world. This does not necessarily lead to a contempt for smaller nations, but it must certainly lead to a belief that the United States contains so much of the world that there is no need to examine, much less learn about, the rest of it.

Whence the man on the airport bus; whence the conviction that if this is Tuesday it must be Belgium; whence the consternation displayed by Americans in London wanting to go by Underground and unable to understand that our method of doing so is different from that in New York. And whence the charges of cowardice.

This leads to an intriguing question which I must ask, risking charges of bad taste as I do so. No one could possibly think that the American soldiers, sailors and airmen in the Gulf are cowards. But – er – do *they* know exactly where they are?

The Times February 4th, 1991

This little piggy stayed at home

THERE WAS I, only a few weeks ago, vigorously rebutting the charge of cowardice levelled at all those American tourists who decided to stay at home for their holidays while the Gulf war was going on (I argued that it was ignorance of geography rather than fear that held them back), and blow me, here comes the news that the Philadelphia Orchestra, booked to play in London, have cried off, giving as an excuse that they are a bunch of poltroons afraid to fly to Britain in case unmusical persons might put a bomb on their plane, or – much worse – might hijack them and keep them for as long as 48 hours in one of those Middle East countries (Australia, for instance, or Portugal) where it is an offence to sell, buy or drink alcohol.

My parody of their excuse falls short of the reality: the Philadelphia says the decision 'will help to reduce the anxieties of our musicians, anxieties that, if left unabated, could seriously inhibit their ability to perform'.

Shucks. What would Stokowski say? He was its principal conductor from 1912 to 1938, and it was he who created the 'Philadelphia sound', which was certainly not the sound of teeth chattering and knees knocking. Stokes had a sharp tongue and he used it; a pioneer of concerts with unfamiliar ingredients (he gave the first American performance of Mahler's Eighth), he was in the habit of denouncing from the podium those who jeered at new music, and he would surely have had the skin off the backs of such craven musicians.

But it is not only Stokes who is turning in his grave; the musical life of Philadelphia has a long pedigree, and if the

Philadelphia weaklings are capable of shame, let them feel it in remembering that the first musical ensemble of their city to be called the Philadelphia Orchestra was founded by a man with the magnificent name of Henry Gordon Thunder.

Come; let me be serious. Have the milksops of the Philadelphia ever heard of a place called Terizen? It was one of the Nazi concentration camps, from which the population was regularly removed to the gas-chambers; the number of Jews was kept steady by an equal inward flow of the condemned. These transient unfortunates included a considerable number of musicians, who banded together in a makeshift orchestra. They knew where they were going, and they knew they were going there soon. Yet they played on, not only for their fellow-prisoners but for the personnel and guards of the camp; art knows no discrimination.

These musicians would have liked to be given the option of staying away, and I dare say that many of them were afraid of what was going to happen to them – *was* going to happen, not *might*. But in the accounts of their performances there is no suggestion that they played wrong notes in their fear, or indeed that they played wrong notes at all.

Yet the yellow-bellies of the Philadelphia Orchestra maintain that if their anxieties about travelling to Britain were 'left unabated', they would get into such a state of terror that it 'could seriously inhibit their ability to perform'. One of the Philadelphia's managerial figures said he is 'very embarrassed and frustrated' by the cancellation but cannot override the decision of the orchestra, who are 'scared of flying on a US or British airline'. (Well, Philadelphia is a mere 45 minutes' flying time to New York, from which city they could fly to London by El Al or Kuwait Airways, both of which are most knowledgeable about the Middle East and might be persuaded – because the orchestra would obviously have the plane to themselves – to give them, *en route*, a spin over Baghdad, just for the hell of it.)

★

But important though the long musical tradition in Philadelphia is, the City of Brotherly Piddlepants is notable for
something much more significant to history. I presume –
one cannot be quite sure – that the faintheart members of
the Philadelphia Orchestra know what is commemorated in
the United States every Fourth of July. Many of them, I am sure,
know not only what happened on that day in 1776, but where
it happened: it was the well-named Independence Hall, in Philadelphia, from which the magnificent prose of Jefferson blew
a trumpet-blast of liberty to the world. These were his words.

> We hold these truths to be self-evident, that all men
> are created equal, that they are endowed by their Creator
> with certain inalienable Rights, that among these are Life,
> Liberty and the pursuit of Happiness, and – in the case of
> members of the Philadelphia Orchestra – to run away and
> hide in case King George comes and hits them on the head
> with his sceptre.

It was, of course, Benjamin Franklin who mediated between the Continental Congress and the lily-livered Orchestra; the latter had gone on strike when the Liberty Bell was
rung, saying that it was a musical instrument and therefore
only to be used by accredited members of the Musicians
Union. But Franklin said something else on that memorable day, something even more apposite to the Casper
Milquetoasts of the Philadelphia Orchestra. As he signed
the Declaration, he murmured to John Hancock, 'We must
indeed all hang together, or, most assuredly, we shall all
hang separately.' Franklin was a wit, and wittily made light
of what they were doing, but his jest, as he and all the other
signatories knew, was nothing but the plain truth. In the eyes
of the British government, these men were rebels who were
committing treason, and if the War of Independence had been
lost, they would have died for that noble document.

*

Stands Philadelphia where it did? Apparently not, at least among the chicken-hearted members of its orchestra. It is not necessarily far-fetched to think that among its fraidicat ranks there may be descendants of some of the signatories; at least it is quite likely that a wheyface or two among the orchestra's players can trace their families back to 1776, and possibly to this very city. What would such ancestors think of the line they had begotten? What would they say?

What they *ought* to say is, 'Don't give yourself airs.' It is clear that the quitters of the Philadelphia Orchestra are convinced that if they put one foot on British soil, or even a plane going there, they will immediately be murdered by a syndicate consisting of Brian Boru, Parnell, Cyril Cusack, Des O'Connor, Sean O'Casey, Sir Roger Casement and Dave Allen, and no amount of reasoning will dispel their terror.

Indeed, it gets steadily worse; the tympanist has been made redundant because all items including strokes of the drum which might be confused with pistol-shots have been dropped from the repertoire, as has Ravel's *Mother Goose*, on the grounds that they cannot find a member of the orchestra brave enough to say Boo to it.

I am wasting my time; if the Philadelphia cry-babies could be scorned out of their pusillanimity they would never have taken refuge in it in the first place. We can only hope that the next time the orchestra's programme includes Beethoven's *Eroica* the audience will see the joke.

The Times April 25th, 1991

The reason why

O N MY LEFT, on the desk, lies a slim pamphlet, the text of two recently delivered lectures, hardly 50 pages in all; the print is large, and the layout lavish, as befits our well-designed day. The date of publication is 1990.

On the other side of my desk is a work in two volumes; the first comprises some 320 pages, whereof 120 are footnotes, collected for ease of reference at the back of the book. The second volume is of 370 pages, 90 of these being notes, again removed to the end. The print is small, especially the notes, the margins crowded; I wouldn't be surprised to learn that the paper was recycled, for the first edition of the book was published in 1945 (when paper rationing was still in force).

Worlds have come and gone in the interval of the two publications, yet the older one still holds sway, its thesis inexhaustible, perhaps eternal. The younger is spritely, adventurous, iconoclastic, penetrating. Between the two works and the two dates I sit, quietly contemplating eternity and other grave matters. But a fierce and shining gratitude pours from me, as I salute the author – one and the same – of both.

Can a book, a single book, shape – even make – a man's life? Milton seemed to think so:

> Books are not absolutely dead things, but do contain a potency of life in them to be as active as that soul was whose progeny they are; nay they do preserve as in a vial the purest efficacy and extraction of that living intellect that bred them.

Perhaps, then; but it is more likely that a combination of

a book and a teacher will embed in the pupil precepts which will thereafter never change, never be doubted, never fail. At any rate, it was thus with me.

I was politically precocious; indeed, I held views on the nationalisation of the means of production, distribution and exchange when my years were hardly in double figures. At that time – I blush to own it – I professed an admiration of all things Soviet, Stalin being the great hero, the steadfast ally in the wartime ranks of democracy. This phase lasted through my public schooldays; in the 1945 general election I hung a red flag out of the window on polling day, to the infinite scandalisation of the authorities, made all the more delightful for me as the results came in. (I rather think that any young person who is not on the left when growing up has missed something important.)

When I became a student the colour had already begun to fade a little for me, but I was still on the left; those further left than I began to sing a parody of the 'Red Flag', signalling disillusion with the Attlee government, which began, to the familiar tune, 'The People's Flag is turning pink, Much nicer colour, don't you think?'

In those days, the London School of Economics degree, for everybody, was half economics; the other half was chosen by the student. My subject was government, so I went to the appropriate lectures, which were compulsory. (Imagine compulsory lectures anywhere nowadays; there would be revolution!) But, as in any sensible university, we were encouraged to seek knowledge and understanding outside our particular fields.

One day I wandered into an unfamiliar lecture room and began to listen to a kind of discourse I had never heard before, to follow the speaker into realms of thought and ways of thinking utterly new to me, to face concepts that stretched my mental powers further than I feared they would go, to be provoked into challenging and reconsidering ideas and beliefs I thought I would carry proudly to the grave. (It was not, I must say, an entirely smooth passage into enlightenment;

our guru had a sharp tongue. One day, at a seminar, a fellow student offered an opinion couched in terms greatly lacking in coherence. The sage frowned and said bluntly: 'I don't understand what you are talking about.' My hapless colleague flushed, and rephrased his comment. 'Ah,' said teacher, 'now I understand what you are saying, and I think it's nonsense.')

And now at last, dear reader, you are about to discover what I am talking about. Karl Popper – he has been Sir Karl these many years – taught me, and many hundreds of others, to think; more precisely, he taught us the mechanics of thinking. Determinism and historicism were, and still are, his enemies, and he has fought them all his immensely long life (he has just passed his 88th birthday); trial and error have been his beloved companions, and indeed the slim booklet I referred to, with the lectures, ends with this quotation from Dürer: 'But I shall let the little I have learnt go forth into the day in order that someone better than I may guess the truth, and in his work may prove and rebuke my error. At this I shall rejoice that I was yet the means whereby this truth has come to light.'

Sir Karl (I really can't call him just 'Popper' – would a devout Christian writing about St John Chrysostom call him 'Chris'?), when I sat at his feet, was not yet a professor; but he lectured on logic and scientific method, and that was his title when he donned the senior gown. If he had to be defined in a word, I suppose he is a philosopher. But although his electrifying words and thoughts in his lectures and seminars constituted the most refreshing and fruitful effect he had on me and my mind, it is the two-volume work which lies beside me that cut out for me a pattern to which I have tried to be true all my life.

When I finished *The Open Society and its Enemies*, I knew that I had been inoculated for ever against accepting any political position, any pragmatism, any sophistry, any excuse, any compromise, any doubt, which would allow me to contemplate adhering to even the mildest form of autocracy, the most plausible argument from determinism, the smallest moment of sympathy for any closed system, political or philosophical.

The very titles of the two volumes speak with devastating clarity. Vol.I: *The Spell of Plato*. Vol.II: *The High Tide of Prophecy – Hegel and Marx*. The book, its argument closely packed and formidably supported (do not succumb to the temptation of skipping those hundreds of pages of notes), slaughters great herds of the oxen of politico-philosophical necessity; necessity means inevitability, and anyone who has read or heard Sir Karl even on the subject of coin-tossing (the first of the two lectures in the new publication brings him back to the subject in splendid form) knows what inevitability means in his lexicon. The Great Satans are the enemies in the war against freedom, but he knows that there is an even more terrible struggle going on: the war on understanding. In a sense, the most important part of the book is Chapter 24, entitled 'Oracular philosophy and the revolt against reason'.

'Man is born free, and everywhere he is in chains.' The only criticism of this masterpiece that I have ever had – I have expressed it occasionally – is that Rousseau is let off with extraordinary and unnecessary lightness; I have always maintained, on the contrary, that Rousseau is the greatest villain in the entire list of the open society's enemies. I am convinced that the 'General Will' is the key which unlocked the seven and seventy hells our century has burned in; I do not suppose that Stalin and Hitler ever read Rousseau, but once his poison had escaped into the atmosphere, the rest led remorselessly to the piled pyramids of the innocent dead.

There, then, is my hero and my hero's heroic book, and my conviction that, in great measure, between them they made me what I am. If so, it must be true that a great number of men and women have had the same stamp of freedom embossed for ever upon their minds, hearts and very lives, simply because Karl Popper lived, taught and wrote.

He has written a great deal; but for reasons unknown he also has a considerable store of work that he has never published. He has pursued knowledge, wisdom, and above all understanding, throughout his long and majestic career, and he seeks his quarries still. There is a passage in Forster's *The Longest Journey* that somehow brings him to mind: 'He seemed transfigured into a Hebrew prophet passionate for satire and the truth.' It is indeed truth that he has chased, the most elusive and the most rewarding of game; truth, mind, not certainty. His *Who's Who* entry should be set to music by Beethoven, no less; all over the world his former students remember him with gratitude, awe and affection. How glad I am to be one of them!

The Times (Saturday Review), September 29th, 1990

And half a pound of liver

I MUST RETURN yet again to the Fallacy of the Altered Standpoint. A recent visit to the theme concerned the 'breakthrough' in transplant surgery, by which a pig's kidney was transplanted into a human being. Whatever next, I murmured in the course of a couple of thousand words, but the trouble with that question, I have found by long experience, is that my imagination is not lurid enough to make a useful guess; could I – could you? – have thought that a Dutch doctor would have been reported to the equivalent of the BMA because he failed to practise euthanasia on one of his patients who had asked for it?

For those reading me today who have not followed my discovery and examination of the Fallacy of the Altered Standpoint, let me define it. It is the belief that, because some action or attitude is universally considered abhorrent, it will always remain so; the fallacy lies in what happens when the standpoint from which that belief derives is altered. The view changes; from the new standpoint it is possible to believe that what was once unthinkable can now be thought; all too often, what *can* be thought *is* thought, and shortly afterwards what is thought is put into practice.

Some years ago, a Bill was introduced into Parliament; the purpose was to provide a special card which would indicate that, if the holder was fatally injured, his or her organs were to be made available for transplant. I said then that in time, the onus in the legislation would be reversed, so that the organs could be used unless the owner of them bore a card specifically forbidding his or her innards to be used for such a purpose. I was roundly hooted for my prophecy; well, that day comes ever closer. But stop reading for a moment, and answer a question with as much exactitude as your memory, or that of those around you, can provide.

Here is the question. How long ago would you have dismissed as absurd, repellent and obviously untrue, a claim that in this country's hospitals doctors have taken to keeping dying patients, with no hope of recovery, on artificial life-support machines, and making withdrawals from these living but moribund organ-banks when a patient who needs a replacement lung, say, or heart, is ready to receive it?

Yet I tell you that that is happening now, and the doctors do not deny it. Indeed, there was an exquisite comment, recorded in the *Sunday Times*, from the president of the British Transplantation Society, Dr Douglas Briggs: 'It is not the sort of thing we go public on,' he said, 'but I don't feel we should cover it up in any way.' Another medical enthusiast for the practice said that it 'provided a new pool of donors'; I must repeat, though I have no great hope of getting it into the heads of more than half a dozen people, the fact that a body on a ventilator is *not* a donor, because a donor is one who gives, not one who is taken from. (That particular linguistic perversion has always struck me as significant; if doctors have to pretend that an organ was given to them, rather than removed from a patient incapable of giving permission, it can only mean that they are not nearly as certain of their rectitude as they would like to be thought.)

It gets worse. Referring to the patients who provide the organ-bank, one of the doctors said: 'Previously, these patients were simply cared for and kept comfortable until they died. Instead, we are approaching the relatives of such patients to tell them that, unfortunately, there is nothing we can do for them and to ask them to consider the possibility of organ donation for when their relative stops breathing.'

Roughly *when* and exactly *why* did the doctors decide that their previous custom – '. . . these patients were simply cared for and kept comfortable until they died' – should be abandoned? I do not suppose that the doctors enjoy asking for the parts of somebody's loved ones, and I am sure they make their requests tactfully and with sympathy; nevertheless, the argument that someone else can benefit from the organs of a relative who will never again have a use for them gives a powerful – I think too powerful – tilt to the feelings of those who are soon to be bereaved.

At this point, I fear that many people, not just the doctors engaged in the organ-bank system, are saying that they cannot understand what I am talking about. If there are proper safeguards (and I have no doubt that there are) to ensure that only those who have no possibility of recovery are used as repositories of spare parts, and that the relatives are willing, what possible objection can there be?

There are three. In my previous comment, on the matter of the pig's kidneys in human beings (did they, incidentally, ask permission of the pig's relatives?), I discussed the opportunity-cost: how many less glamorous treatments – the familiar hip operation, or the one for cataract, or for hernia or prostate – could be done dozens or hundreds of times for what one heart transplant costs in medical equipment, personnel, resources, time, skill and attention? I never got an answer, and do not expect one now; but I am quite sure that if the transplant craze had never taken hold, there would now be a massive credit balance of pain relieved, mobility restored, sight saved and research pursued.

The second objection is that the practice reinforces, rather than (as it should do) corrects, one of the most extraordinary and distorting notions of our time: the widespread belief that it is possible to live for ever, and certainly that if it is not possible it should be made so at once, by Act of Parliament.

I sometimes think that the *timor mortis* of today takes the form of a *resentment* of death, and certainly the maddest but most representative form of this attitude so far has been the grotesque phenomenon called 'cryonics'; certain charlatans claim (it started, of course, in California) that they can preserve a dead body until a cure for the disease which killed the client is found, whereupon the preserved corpse will be treated with the appropriate remedy, and in no time will be sitting up and singing. I know no more pitiful example of our greatest delusion: the boast that we have shrugged off all belief outside our senses, and have created an entirely materialistic universe.

And the third objection is, of course, the Fallacy of the Altered Standpoint. I do not envisage the mad scientists of fiction kidnapping perfectly healthy people to stock their organ-banks, although there is a horrid and uncomfortably memorable precedent:

> Up the close and down the stair,
> Round the town with Burke and Hare;
> Burke the butcher, Hare the thief,
> Knox the boy who buys the beef.

But the point of the Fallacy is that until the standpoint has been altered, no one can safely predict what the view from the new one will be. Nevertheless, there is a clue. So far as I know, there is not one example of a new standpoint being less disturbing than its predecessor; the alteration *invariably* goes further, in the matter of actions that had previously been ruled out, towards danger.

I have no doubt that some lives will be saved by transplants from the new organ-banks. I have cast doubt on the relative cost of such projects. But there is another kind of cost, not involving money, and this kind may be leading us to a new, and by no means welcome, moral bankruptcy.

The Times April 19th, 1990

The keys and the Kingdom

EVERYBODY ASKS THE wrong question about Lord Longford, viz., is he barmy? The question is not worth asking: of *course* he is barmy. What we should be discussing is something quite different: is he right?

Right about what? For an explanation we must turn to his recent appearance in the criminal courts at Winchester. There, a gangster, Eddie Richardson, was on trial for his part in a drug-smuggling plot; it was said in evidence that the coup would have netted £75 million. (All estimates of booty mentioned in courts trying cases of alleged drug-dealing, whatever the context, should be divided by five if any serious approximation is to be had. All sums expressed as 'street value' should be divided by nine. I digress.)

The judge, who seems to have been reading some of the less expensive Sunday newspapers, said the potential harm done by the offence was like 'spraying bullets into a crowd'. He then sent Richardson down for 25 years. (Five more, if he does not pay a third of a million in confiscation charges.)

Eddie Richardson is no stranger to iron bars. In the 1960s, he was part of a brotherhood of crime based on extortion rackets; a good deal of hideous violence was involved. Richardson then collected a total of 15 years. It is not necessary to weep for him.

Nevertheless, tears were shed, almost literally. When sentence was to be pronounced, the judge heard a plea for mercy from Lord Longford, who had travelled to Winchester to make it. This is what he said:

I have a great liking for Eddie. There is another side to him, there is much good in him. If he is sentenced to prison, and I hope not, I will go and see him there and visit his wife and two daughters if they want to see me. I plead for mercy.

Lord Longford's eloquence had no effect. The obvious unworldliness of it is demonstrated not just by the plea, but more particularly by his 'I hope not' in reference to the possibility of his friend being imprisoned. Did he really imagine that Richardson, after being convicted of so serious an offence, would get off with a caution, or perhaps 90 days of community service? But Lord Longford's naïvety is not the point; it is subsumed in his barminess, but still leaves out the really interesting and important question, which is why does he do it, and should we applaud him for doing it?

I have not had the pleasure of Eddie Richardson's company (which may explain why I still have all my toenails), but a man who has been given nearly half a century of bird, without anyone seriously suggesting that he was innocent, and for crimes as dire as any in the calendar, can rightly be categorised as a hardened villain. Yet Lord Longford calls him friend. He calls Myra Hindley friend, too, and by now he must think that he knows her very well, to judge by the frequency of his visits to her in prison. Possibly there are many other men and women, in prison for atrocious crimes, whom Lord Longford would also speak well of.

He is subject, whenever he speaks up for Miss Hindley, to much jeering and not a little fierce abuse. He will get more over the Richardson episode. His forbearance is remarkable; I know of no instance of his losing his temper or even replying, let alone harshly replying, to his tormentors.

Somewhat to my own surprise, I find myself much in agreement with him. I am obviously in no position to judge whether Miss Hindley has, as he claims (and to be fair, as others close to her claim), entirely repented of her wickedness and become a transformed woman. Nor can I evaluate the good he sees in Eddie Richardson, or measure it against the evil. But I am not astonished, nor moved to mirth or indignation, when Lord Longford says that there is another side to Eddie Richardson, and much good in him, nor when I hear him say that Myra Hindley, from being an abominably wicked woman, has now become a good one.

Really, it is not I who should be conducting a defence of Lord Longford in his role as spokesman for sinners; where is the church – either his or the Anglican one – whose pastors are willing to speak in his tones? Nowhere, apparently; yet if there is one dominant theme in Christian scripture, it is surely that no one, no one at all, is past hope of redemption and forgiveness. (Only the Calvinists, I think, have believed in predestinate damnation, and surely they don't still hold that belief?)

The secular form of this argument is grounded in a phenomenon that is rarely recognised, though it is one of the most remarkable qualities of the human race. It is summed up by Lord Longford in his comment on Eddie Richardson: 'There is another side to him, there is much good in him.' The claim points out that very few human beings – astonishingly few – are entirely bad. I am therefore perfectly willing to believe Lord Longford on the subject, though he gave no examples of his friend's good side; I am no less willing to believe that it is at least possible that Myra Hindley has changed as he insists.

If I did not believe in such possibilities, the universe would be empty around me; indeed, life would be pointless. For it would mean that there can be no true development in a human being, that when Christ said to the woman taken in adultery, 'Go, and sin no more', she went, but continued to sin. Perhaps she did; but if Lord Longford's accusers are right, she *certainly* continued to sin, which I cannot and will not believe, though the entire cohorts of the Manichee come against me.

*

In that faith, Lord Longford – and as far as I can see nobody else – preaches the doctrine of redemption, and preaches it, moreover, in much the same terms as Christ did. It is argued, of course, that he is too easily deceived, that his innocence leads him to swallow an unreformed Myra Hindley's calculated plan to be released on his coat-tails, and that Eddie Richardson, when Lord Longford is about, makes a point of helping lame dogs over stiles, even though they are lame only because he kicked them. But I prefer – oh, *how* I prefer – Lord Longford's rashness to the Home Office's cowardice.

For the crimes of which Eddie Richardson was rightly convicted, severe punishment is certainly proper. For the crimes of Myra Hindley, who has already spent 26 years in prison, likewise. But neither sentences nor expiation touch the central core of the argument, which is: whatever they were and whatever they are, are they beyond salvation?

No, says Lord Longford, and he is right. From all I know of him, he does not feel the need of support; convinced of his mission, he suffers ridicule and hostility in the true Christian manner. But should his faith waver, and to shore it up he seeks an authority somewhat higher than my commendation of him, he will find it in the Ninth Beatitude, and to save him (or rather my readers) the trouble of looking it up, here it is:

Blessed are ye when men shall revile you, and persecute you, and shall say all manner of evil against you falsely, for my sake. Rejoice, and be exceedingly glad: for great is your reward in heaven; for so persecuted they the prophets which were before you.

The Times October 15th, 1990

Patience on a monument

O F ALL THE nations of Europe, surely the greatest burden of suffering has been laid upon the back of Poland. Fought over countless times, torn into pieces again and again, endlessly crushed by foes and tyrants, betrayed by those it trusted, the nadir of its torment was reached in the half century between Hitler's invasion of the Polish lands from the west and their final liberation from their equally evil ideology in the east; only since then, a mere eye-blink as history measures, has it been free to wrestle with its own destiny.

The indomitable spirit of Poland can be summed up by the extraordinary occasion I shall be attending at lunch-time today: a party for the 100th birthday of Count Edward Raczynski, whose long and immensely full life, dedicated entirely to the service of his native land, epitomises that spirit. *Na zdrowie!*

But there is another nation, or rather a group of three nations, whose history is perhaps even stranger: the Baltic states, Latvia, Estonia and Lithuania.

Of the three, Lithuania has by far the most imposing history. The country goes back to the 13th century, and by the 14th had a gigantic empire which stretched from Moscow to the Black Sea. All three, in modern times, have had a tragic fate. Lenin signed a treaty with the Baltic states, guaranteeing their independence, and even after Stalin ascended the throne, they were left in peace, until in 1939 he forced them to cede territory for Soviet bases. The following year they were swallowed whole by the Soviet empire.

Those words 'swallowed whole' denote far more than the

incorporation of the Baltic states. The three nations brought
with them their baggage of independence, self-identification,
culture and language, and Stalin could not bear the thought
that in his empire there were free spirits with free ways.
There followed a crime which in its wickedness was little
short of Hitler's.

In any close-knit community there will be leaders, respect-
ed and trusted for their professions. Destroy the leaders,
Stalin reckoned, and the nation will vanish. The round-up
began: schoolteachers, dons, clergymen, doctors, lawyers,
businessmen, artists, musicians, skilled artisans – these were
sorted out, arrested, packed into wagons for the endless
journey to the east, and decanted (those who survived) into
the wastes of the Gulag. I have in my library a book of 677
pages; apart from a brief introduction, it contains *nothing* but
a list, in alphabetical order, of some 30,000 names, the names
of people 'reported missing' by those who, at the peril of
their lives, compiled the information and smuggled it out of
the Soviet Union to Sweden, where it was published. And
that list, I must point out, includes only the vanished souls
of Latvia; Estonia and Lithuania could have drawn up their
own lists with numbers as great if not greater.

Yet Stalin (and no less his successors) discovered that
even the terrible cull did not suffice to destroy the cohesion
of the Baltic peoples trapped in an alien and hated rule. So
the next move was 'Russianisation': until the emergence of
Gorbachev, a substantial flow of Russian immigrants, enticed
or compelled, poured into the Baltic states. The reasoning
was that dilution of the Baltic peoples in a test-tube filled
with Russians, together with the ceaseless propaganda and
multiple indignities piled on the Estonians, Lithuanians and
Latvians, would in time erase the folk-memory of the days
of independence and difference.

'If I forget thee, O Jerusalem, let my right hand forget
her cunning.' Because of course all the attempts to extinguish
in the Baltic peoples the sense of belonging elsewhere were
doomed to fail, as all such attempts throughout the centuries

have failed (look at the Jews). The more pressure was exerted on the Balts, the greater was the resistance with which it was met. From mouth to ear, from *samizdat* to smuggled-in books, from a fading photograph to a determination to be revenged, the idea of a nation is more powerful than any repression (look at the Kurds).

This history is leading somewhere, and it offers to those who can grasp its meaning a meed of joy and justice going hand in hand. In addition it means that we have a splendid opportunity to give determinism another black eye; however many times the coin turns up tails, sooner or later it will turn up heads.

With which I introduce Vincas Balickas. He is 87 years old, and by profession a diplomat; long may he live to grace his postings. For this is no ordinary plenipotentiary.

Fifty-three years ago, Mr Balickas came to London as a *chargé d'affaires* in the Lithuanian embassy; he was very new to the work. A year later, his country was annexed by the Soviet Union, whereupon some of the staff of the Lithuanian diplomatic legation stayed in Britain in preference to being murdered in their own country. Although the *de facto* incorporation of the Baltic states could not be reversed, Britain and other countries refused to give the annexation approval *de jure*, and Britain never did give the Soviet Union the imprimatur for its three engorged nations.

And the years went by, more and more of them. Death claimed, one by one, the remaining members of the Lithuanian legation; Mr Balickas's last colleague, the Ambassador, died after some 30 years *en poste*, and from then on Mr Balickas *was* the Lithuanian legation. Some 19,000 times the world revolved, and Mr Balickas doubtless had a twinge of rheumatism here, a fallen arch there, a gentle thinning of his hair; he was fortunate that his wife was with him as they grew older together. But he did not despair.

And rightly; for the world revolved once more, and lo!, after a grudging struggle, Gorbachev realised he had no option but to give back to the Baltic states their identity, their lands, their languages and their opinions, all of which had been stolen long years ago. And when the formalities were over, and the structure of the phoenix Lithuanian state completed, the Lithuanian foreign office appointed His Excellency the Hon. Mr Vincas Balickas Ambassador to the Court of St James's.

Is that not a story to warm the heart? If you think not, your heart is chilled indeed. For the story tells us that nothing is hopeless, nothing is impossible, nothing is cause for giving up. For half a century Mr Balickas has kept the faith, and his faith has been rewarded. But I mustn't delay him; he is about to go out on an important errand. Every year, on the anniversary of Lithuanian independence, he was wont to raise his country's flag, and over those years it became worn and faded. He is off to get the materials for a new one, but something tells me that when the spanking new flag flies proudly and in freedom from the Lithuanian embassy in London, he will not throw away the old one.

The Times December 12th, 1991

How long is a piece of rope?

WHENCE COMES THE extraordinary and apparently implacable desire among Members of Parliament (mostly Conservative) to have people strangled or, at the least, have their necks broken? There are one or two people I would love to strangle, and a few whose necks I would be happy to break, but it is all pretty metaphorical; given the chance, I dare say I would make a lordly gesture of forgiveness and go my way. Not these; necks are for stretching, they never tire of saying, and despite the countless disappointments they have had to face in their decades of fruitless yearning for a rope, a trap door and three rousing cheers, their loving dream is with them still.

I know some of them; indeed, one, before he became an MP, could be found shoulder to shoulder with me, as we filibustered away in the mad hope of trying to make the National Union of Journalists a body that could be taken seriously. (We did not succeed, of course, but that was hardly our fault; when I asked Hercules to help he said: 'You must be joking, mate.') But what I am saying is that in those days he exhibited no such interest in necks and their breaking; what bug has so severely bitten a calm, logical and agreeable man that he lives in the hope, however far it has receded, of giving the National Union of Neckstretchers a shot in the arm?

This business is much odder than you might think. Capital punishment was abolished in Britain in 1965; since then, no fewer than 15 parliamentary attempts have been made to restore it to the statute book, all of which have failed. When

Labour was in office, there was really no serious chance of a restoration of neckbreaking; the great majority of Labour MPs were (and still are) against it, and there was always a substantial number of Tories willing to go into the No lobby as well.

Nevertheless, there were regular attempts, presumably for demonstration purposes; by keeping the death cell warm until a Tory majority could be assembled, they would be ready for the lovely sight of the black cap. When Labour fell, in 1979, the Tory advocates of capital punishment retired to the Hanging Gardens of Babycham to toast success; to their surprise and dismay the first attempt failed, and every attempt since then has been defeated, usually by a larger majority than the previous tally, despite the fact that the ensuing Conservative governments had much bigger majorities than in 1979.

The hangers have tried every path into their beautiful dream; hanging only for premeditated murder, for the murder of children or policemen – every form of ruse has been rebuffed. The most recent attempt was made only two and a half years ago; the trick was to give juries trying murder cases the right to recommend (only recommend) capital punishment. Yet even that plea was defeated, in a free vote on both sides of the House, by a majority of 123.

It should surely be plain that the longer the span of time since capital punishment was abolished, the weaker will become the passion for its restoration. After all, an entire generation has been born and grown up in a land where (like almost all European lands, incidentally) capital punishment is unknown. I am sure there are many MPs who think that capital punishment might help to keep down the murder-rate (it will not) but who would recoil in mingled embarrassment and revulsion at the very idea of passing a bill through all its stages and then advertising for hangmen, training them (*quis custodiet?*), building scaffolds and finally watching the first poor devil to draw the short straw.

Of course, we are told that MPs' postbags are stuffed to bursting with demands from their constituents for the restoration; certainly, the Tory party in conference is so given to screaming – literally screaming – for the stretching of necks that the organisers of the conference (the rule was imposed some years ago) have to make sure that the hanging debate is fixed for a time which makes it difficult for the television companies to show more than a few moments, if that, of the eldritch howling for the compression of windpipes, so revolting is the sight and sound. As it happens, I already knew Waddington was an inadequate Home Secretary, but if I had not I would have deduced it at once from his shallow, stale, sycophantic speech on crime and punishment, which had the howlers and screamers on their feet, particularly when he announced that there would be another parliamentary chance for the restoration of the Bourbons.

Now, happily, we have a new man in the Home Office, one who voted against capital punishment last time round – as did the new prime minister, while his predecessor voted for it, as indeed she had consistently done. As before, the neckstretchers have tried to find the easiest path to their goal; apart from the special categories mentioned above, they propose a cumbersome and meaningless system of special consideration by the Court of Appeal when a capital sentence has been handed down; some have also, rather less attractively, kept the word 'hanging' out of their proposal, though hanging is what they are after.

They will be defeated, as they must know, and they will be defeated by a larger majority next time, and a yet larger one the time after that. This passion for a lost cause, therefore, seems to need a psychological explanation, which I am in no position to supply. But when you think of the astonishingly small number of murders in Britain, even including the sectarian and terrorist ones in Northern Ireland, does it not seem very strange that so many MPs, who have many more pressing and important matters to attend to, are obsessed by this one – obsessed to the extent of repeatedly courting defeat with an ever-diminishing chance of achieving success?

Moreover, when the figures are examined, a very substantial proportion of murders turn out to be of a kind that even most of Waddington's harpies would not wish to visit with the extreme penalty: the murder of a brutal, drunken, wife-beater, say, by a woman driven beyond endurance, or a mother on the edge of breakdown who kills a child born hideously deformed both physically and mentally. These killings are murder under our law, but few, I think, would want hanging for them. The result is that the number of what might be called exemplary hangees shrinks to practically nothing; is it not strange, as I say, that so many Tory MPs are still implacably determined that Mahomet shall one day come to the mountain, no matter that the mountain has long ago been razed to the ground?

And what about those postbags? If the Tory conference has to be gerrymandered to prevent the nation seeing it, fangs bared, baying for blood, and the parliamentary timetable hurried along so as to get the hanging debate forgotten long before the election, does not that suggest that the nation as a whole is by no means as rope-loving as the rope's parliamentary supporters claim?

Perhaps we could enshrine the hanging debate (and what about flogging – why don't the floggers even get a discussion, let alone a debate?) in one of those bits of parliamentary procedure still lying about from centuries ago (such as the rule that an MP wanting to raise a point of order during a division must do so sitting down and wearing a hat), their purpose long since forgotten, but their quaintness protecting them from complete abolition.

Let the scaffold-lovers have their debate, and let them be defeated. But to show that there are no hard feelings, let us join them, after the division, in a drink at the Neckstretchers' Arms.

The Times December 17th, 1990

Eating people is wrong

I HAVE A rather curious request to make today; though odd, it would not be difficult to grant, and I would be very grateful. The trouble is that I am really making my plea worldwide, and I can hardly flatter myself that the entire world is listening. Still, I must start somewhere.

It all began with the film *The Silence of the Lambs*; I have not seen it – I see very few films, and was not drawn to this one – and I know little more than that it is about a man who kills and eats women, and that the film has been hugely successful both in the United States and Britain, and for all I know everywhere else. So it seems that my plaint, if it is to be answered, must be answered soon or never answered at all.

In the film, the name of the cannibalistic murderer is Hannibal Lecter, and – obviously because of the rhyme – Hannibal and cannibal look as though they will shortly be intertwined for ever. Indeed, when a couple of weeks ago a very real cannibalistic murderer was apprehended in the United States, his refrigerator crammed with human heads and pots on his stove bubbling away with other parts of bodies, he was immediately dubbed 'Hannibal'. His name is Jeffrey Dahmer, but whatever happens to him he will be known as Hannibal for ever, and every time another mass murderer, even without cannibalistic tendencies, is suspected the name of Hannibal will be fastened upon him.

But not if I can help it, though I suspect I can't. For I want to rescue the name of Hannibal from the infamy of horrible and inexplicable murder.

Those readers who have done me the honour of reading my book *Hannibal's Footsteps*, or who have seen my television series of the same title, will know that Hannibal was a boyhood hero of mine, and the idea that led to both book and films was in turn conceived very many years before, when I came upon the tenth satire of Juvenal:

Weigh the dust of Hannibal; what do the mighty commander's ashes amount to now? Yet for him Africa was too small . . . he added Spain to his Empire, then he crossed the Pyrenees. Before him lay the Alps, drenched in snow . . . Italy lies prostrate; on he goes. 'It is nothing,' he cries, 'until we are through the gates of Rome, until we pierce with the standards of Carthage the very heart of our foe. On, on, you madman! Onwards across these murderous Alps! Thrill schoolboys with your exploits, so that they may have a fit subject for their mock orations!'

The point is that Juvenal was right; he guessed that the name and fame of Hannibal would endure where and while audacity, courage and steadfastness were admired. Indeed, he proved it then and there, for he was writing something like 300 years after Hannibal's death, and from the tone of his words it was clear that he assumed his readers would be familiar with the great name and exploits of the great general.

Hannibal knew, as anyone who understood power and dominance knew, that 'Two stars keep not their motion in one sphere'; sooner or later either Rome or Carthage would have to be destroyed. In the end, it was Rome that conquered; but Hannibal made it a close-run thing; if he had listened to his cavalry commander after Cannae and gone straight for Rome, world history might have been very different.

Never mind what might have happened; let us look at what did. The first characteristic vignette of Hannibal we have comes from Livy – a citizen, after all, of a nation which fought Carthage for centuries.

He woke and slept not according to the time of day

or night but according to the demands of his work, and when he did finally go to his rest . . . his troops became familiar with the sight of their commander lying on the bare earth among the guards and sentinels, wrapped only in his cloak. On horse or on foot . . . he was the first to charge, the last to leave the battlefield.

You may argue that Hannibal's principal achievements – practically all his achievements – consisted of a series of battles, in almost all of which he was victorious; a great general, then, but what else? Well, a devoted servant of his country, which (it is a theme that runs through history) repeatedly let him down, her leaders preferring to squabble for power at home while he fought their battles abroad. He was also a man who, in a time when consideration had hardly been invented, thought of his men day and night; when they finally got down on to the Italian plain, looking and feeling, as Polybius says, more like animals than men, Hannibal gave them fresh heart, and more to the point, fresh food. And there is another, and overwhelming, clue: although his army was made up mainly of mercenaries, there is no record of any of his soldiers deserting.

What does all this amount to? It can be put in a word: leadership. We usually think of that in terms of war, and particularly of course in the case of Hannibal. But the truth is that his character was far broader; in any walk of life, he would have been a man who inspired devotion and to whom a lifelong allegiance would be sworn by all those who recognised his qualities.

Of course, the elephants have adorned the story; Hannibal buffs have mis-spent many hours arguing about whether they were African or Indian ones, and even more time arguing about which pass he took over the Alps, but the magical thought of those tremendous beasts lumbering up the foothills, up the steeps, finally up the crest, has captured the imagination of the world for centuries, and rightly.

*

Yet there is more to him even than that. After the final defeat of Carthage, he went into exile, hunted by an implacable Rome longing to show him, defeated and bowed, to the multitude. But in one of the cities in which he came to rest, he met his great opponent and ultimate conqueror: Scipio? Who can fail to cheer at the marvellous compliment – one of the most beautifully couched in all history – that Hannibal paid to Scipio? Of course their talk was of soldiers and battles, and as they talked Scipio asked Hannibal whom he would name as the greatest of all generals. 'Alexander,' was the inevitable reply. And who, said Scipio, would he put second? 'Pyrrhus,' said Hannibal. And third? 'Myself.'

Scipio had a final question: 'What would you have said if you had beaten me?' 'Ah, then,' said Hannibal, 'I would have thought myself the greatest of them all.'

Now do you see why it pains me to see the noble name of Hannibal dragged through the blood of real and fictional murderers? As I said when I began, he was my boyhood hero, but the more I contemplate him and his qualities, the more I admire him, and the more I grieve for a world in which there are very few men of such stature, knowing that soon there will be none. Please, oh please, do not let Rome have the last word.

The Times August 12th, 1991

Caliban's mirror

L OOK HERE UPON this picture, and on this. This country's idiotic law of vacant possession permits anyone to break into unoccupied premises, knowing that they cannot be summarily ejected; the law actually protects them from their theft of the beneficial owners' living space, until an application to a judge to make an order for their removal is successful. (And who has ever known the law to hurry?)

Very well, very well; there are homeless people for whom the line between 'buy' and 'steal' has become invisible. A modicum of sympathy is in order, at least until someone remembers that most homeless people do not steal or break in. An uneasy makeshift truce rules this battle, or until recently has done so. But now there is another aspect to consider. Let us consider it.

Not long ago, in Weybridge, a secluded part of Surrey, where despite the falling-off in the market, property prices are still high, a large and handsome ten-room mansion fell vacant. A gang broke into it; there is no evidence that its members were without shelter, nor that they had homes which they thought too cramped or in other ways inadequate, nor even that they had insufficient means to find reasonable lodging. What, then, did they want the place for?

This.

They tore up the carpets, smashed the mirrors, ripped out cupboards, covered the walls with obscene graffiti. They hauled out the ornamental banisters and burnt them; they did the same with the elegant furniture. A handsome four-poster

bed was torn apart, leaving nothing but the frame, the
mattress having been slashed into pieces. There were seven
bathrooms; every basin was smashed. Fittings were torn
out of the walls, whereupon water poured out and went
through to the rooms below. A handsome chandelier was
dragged from its moorings and destroyed; rubble and filth
were thrown into the swimming pool. Human excrement
and puddles of urine lay everywhere in the rooms. The cost
of the devastation has been put at £100,000.

Nihilism, we think, is a word to be applied to a group
of mad Russians who lived in the 19th century; to think
of it in our comfortable semi-detached British lives is to
think the absurd. But then what word, and more urgently
what understanding, would you apply to the vandals of
Weybridge?

Let us pause here to describe the fate of a quite different
mansion. A Mr and Mrs Edward and Joyce Widdup (a
splendidly English surname, don't you think?) have owned
for some 40 years a 19th-century cottage near Bradford,
bought for £4,500. The cottage, all those years ago, came
with a smallholding of some eight acres; that amounts to
some 200 yards each way, which could not be classified as
a rolling prairie. On this scrap of land, the Widdups have,
all that time, raised horses, goats, chickens and cattle, and
have clearly found, or rather have made for themselves, a
happy, beneficial and productive life.

The Widdups have now been offered *four million pounds*
for their patch; it was wanted for 'development' (*recte* 'ruina-
tion'). They turned the offer down without hesitation, saying, among other things, 'What on earth would we do with
four million anyway? It is a ludicrous amount of money.'

Having made their position clear, they went on to make
it clearer, saying, 'This place is not for sale . . . You can't
put a price on your friends and your way of life. There has
been too much development here anyway . . . there is a lot
of wildlife including partridges, owls and squirrels. This is
a lovely spot – much too nice to spoil . . .'

Hurrah for the owls and squirrels, beasties I love too. (Alas, I eat the partridges.) But go back to the very different dwelling with which I started. Is it time to turn Tennyson upside down and say, 'We needs must hate the highest when we see it'? There *is* a strain in mankind that cannot bear the thought of beauty, let alone the real thing, just as there are people who cannot bear the thought of God, and for exactly the same reason: that, measuring themselves against perfection, they fall so far short in their own estimation that they must destroy the thing that tells them so.

There are two terrible tragedies in that attitude, and both of them are obvious, or should be. One is that if you have cause to hate yourself, for whatever reason, you will not improve your circumstances by hating yourself even more. The other is that we *all* fall short of both God and perfection, which is why God and perfection exist: to teach us that if we can get but one answer right out of a hundred questions on the paper, we can, with enough struggle, get two, and with even more of a struggle, three, and . . . (Don't take my word for it; go to Colmar and look at the Issenheim Altar, then go to Milan and see Michelangelo's Rondanini Pieta, and then tell me whether you think your journey and what you found at the end of it were worth the struggle.)

That, perhaps, is a little too elevated for the people who took a thing of beauty ('Beauty is truth, truth beauty,' – that is all Ye know on earth, and all ye need to know'), and dunged upon it, before smashing it, or perhaps after. No doubt, when they sober up (it is said that when the police finally arrived with the dispossession order, the stenches included a powerful one of cannabis), they will start to whine about a capitalist society which owns great houses when others have only small flats; certainly there are enough voices – teachers and books and dotty clergymen and a thousand *groupuscules* – to tell them so, and some (well, not many of the clergymen) to urge them on to the violent expropriation of the houses of the rich, or more exactly the richer.

Yes, but that still does not face the real problem. There are people like the Widdups, who have a house they love and a way of life they take joy in; there are also people with a way of life which is very different, though presumably satisfactory to them, who break into others' dwellings. But why did they want the destruction they achieved?

Assuming there is a soul, the vandals have no less of one than do the Widdups. The latter live in theirs, the former want to destroy theirs. Mistily, an answer takes shape. They *are* nihilists, real ones, and the clue is the smashing of the mirrors; dozens to one that when in their orgy they came to these (the mirrors were ceiling-to-floor ones) their howls were the loudest.

Self-hate has only one provenance; see Caliban. These filthy fools deny their humanity precisely because it will not let them deny it. They plan to go to the grave in their state of nihilism, and indeed they might. But the horizon to which they are afraid to lift their eyes will not go away, and one careless blink, even as they are burning beautiful furniture, could transfix and save them. If they are caught and prosecuted, prison won't help; is there a judge wise enough to sentence them to go and look at the Widdups?

The Times December 30th, 1991

It's a jingle out there

RIDER HAGGARD HAS a lot to answer for. It is possible that if he had not written such books as *King Solomon's Mines* and *Allan Quatermain*, Edgar Wallace might not have written *Sanders of the River*, and modern anthropology might never have existed. That suggests a considerable burden of guilt, but he must bear it, because it was he who invented, or at least established, the vogue for finding lost tribes in impenetrable jungles.

The practice goes on, though today it is put on a supposed scientific basis; the lost tribes in question, when the jungle drums beat out the depressing news that another lot of idiots from Princeton are on the way to study their customs, either rapidly pack up their gear and get even loster, or stay to sell the visitors medicinal bark, pigskin belts, runes carved on wood, bits of rock with magic properties and the like, all of it imported from supermarkets in Miami. This junk is taken back and exhibited, and a few months later the book is published, whereupon the lost tribe – they weren't as lost as all *that* – hires a Californian lawyer to demand a hefty slice of the royalties.

Here comes another lost tribe, this one very lost indeed, called the Hasupuweteri, who still live as did their ancestors in the Stone Age. They had got lost in the interior of Venezuela, but an intrepid American anthropologist found them again (where you and I would immediately have sought them as soon as we heard they had been lost, viz., in the heart of the Amazon rainforest, which by now must be strewn with neatly painted metal signposts reading 'This way to the lost tribes') and stayed with them for 12 years; the quantity of medicinal bark, pigskin belts, etc., he must have acquired doesn't bear thinking about.

But he also acquired a wife, Yarima, which is where the trouble started. His betrothal was at first a symbolic one only. But as the years passed, he fell in love with her, and after immense efforts and hardship he brought her to the United States as a legal spouse; when last heard of, they were living happily ever after.

I turn now, however, to the excerpts from the book (yes, of course there is a book – *Into the Heart*, published by Hamish Hamilton for £15.99 or a lot of medicinal bark, pigskin belts, etc., whichever shall be the dearer) and to the interview with the happy couple by June Southworth for the *Daily Mail*. And it was at this point that I found the subtle worm of doubt twitching its whiskers. The doubt was not for the authenticity of the tale; I am willing to accept every word of it, runes, magic rocks, the lot. No, I blanched only when I came to passages like these:

> Today the girl who walked the jungle nude, with bones through her nose, wears the US uniform of jeans, sweat-shirt and trainers. Her hair is permed in tight black curls and ear-rings dangle against her coppery skin. She eats Kentucky fried chicken, drinks Coke and screams with delight when Madonna appears on TV . . . Yarima loves to see herself on video . . . But her son David, now four, scowls at the screen and mutters 'no more jungle!' He cheers up when the video is replaced by *The Flintstones* . . . Already David is running to his father complaining that he said 'Thank you' and 'Mommy didn't say "You're welcome".'

You see the problem. I am touched – who would not be? – by this story of a modern American and a wife from 10,000 years ago. But I cannot help wondering whether she might not do better to get lost again, and this time permanently, if what she has exchanged for her wretched jungle existence, bones through her nose and all, is a perm, a pair of dangling ear-rings, jeans, sweatshirt, trainers, her image on video, *The Flintstones*, Kentucky fried chicken, Coke, 'You're welcome' and Madonna.

Here, surely, her husband seems to have displayed a remarkable lack of imagination. No one would have wanted him – and he surely would not want – to use his wife as an object of study. But she came to him and his country as an absolute *tabula rasa*. He could, with enough patience (and the years among the Hasupuweteri suggest that he had a good deal of it), have taught her practically anything about anything. Just think of what faced her; everything was new, different, unfathomable – language, customs, clothes, other races, sights and sounds, cooking, the streets (when she saw her first motor car she thought it was an animal), machinery, artificial light and heat, music, the printed word, metal, glass, everything was as a Martian would find it.

Yarima could have been taught as a child is taught; and it is up to the teacher to map out the syllabus, which can range over an infinity of knowledge, from art to traffic, from good food to colours, from words to things. But what did teacher provide?

Ken translates as she says: 'I did not know what music was. My people have no musical instruments. All is chanting. When I first heard your music I hated it. Then I started snapping my fingers and tapping my toes. Madonna has a good voice and I like the way Michael Jackson moves.'

Let us think for a moment about that Martian. When he got back to Mars everybody would have wanted to know what it was like on earth. He would have brought back a range of goods and products, a vast collection of books in many languages, art and artefacts of every kind, every type of clothing, food and entertainment, a comprehensive range of all the varieties of earthly worship, studies of our medicine, communications, government – everything, that is, which would help the people of Mars understand the people of Earth, not forgetting those things that the Martians would puzzle over for ever, like the attachment in expensive penknives for taking stones out of horses' hooves.

The Martians would naturally be eager to know what he had seen, to examine the things he had brought back. Imagine their disappointment if he were to declare that he had left all the luggage behind and could only remember that Madonna had a good voice and he liked the way Michael Jackson moved.

No doubt, when the whole touching story is told, there will spring up, in America at least, groups insisting, to the point of demonstrations and marches, that any attempt to widen Yarima's horizons with vistas of the modern world would be racist, sexist, elitist, northernhemispherist and indeed Stone Ageist. After all, in the United States it is already a serious criminal offence (or it will be very soon) to suggest that there is any difference between Michael Jackson and Beethoven, let alone that the latter is a greater composer than the former. It follows, *a fortiori*, that a woman who has known no culture (in the widest sense of the word) other than that which governed the Stone Age, must at all costs be prevented from moving out of a milieu last heard of 10,000 years ago. Indeed, Yarima will be lucky not to be kidnapped and forcibly repatriated to the land of the Hasupuweteri, there to resume her Stone Age life and live it until she dies. A grim fate; that will teach her to answer damn fool questions from anthropologists in search of lost tribes.

The Times March 7th, 1991

One man in his time plays many parts

IT IS FAR too long since anyone hit a theatre critic; nowadays they don't even get banned. And the argument they have been having is most unlikely to lead to grievous bodily harm. Still, it is quite an interesting argument.

I think it began in the *Daily Telegraph*, which has scores of theatre critics, for some reason all called Charles. Some of these urged the theatre managers to adopt the reviewing practice of the critics in New York, which is that they are allowed to see one of the last two or three previews, and write their notices from that performance, on the condition that these are under embargo until the morning after the official opening night. The reason for this indulgence is the difficulty experienced by the critics in getting their overnight reviews into the paper; the Broadway critics complain that a considered judgment is impossible with such deadlines, and theatre people endorse the complaint most heartily. Our Critics' Circle considered going over to the New York pattern, but has decided, for the present, not to.

I think I am uniquely placed to take part in the debate. I have in my time been a theatre critic for more than 10 years all told – successively on the *Daily Express* and the *Daily Mail*, on both of which I invariably wrote overnight, immediately after the opening, and later on I was a Sabbath critic, on the *Sunday Times*, when of course (plays never open on a Saturday, or at least they never did when I was in the business) I had leisure to compose my review.

Curiously enough, the problem is substantially an economic one at heart. When I was a critic, plays destined for London were tried out in rough form, being polished as they went, in the provinces; whence the familiar cry of managements who had flopped in Shaftesbury Avenue, 'They loved us in Harrogate!' Some years ago, it became virtually impossible to tour before opening, as it had become prohibitively expensive, particularly for a big play or a musical. Reduced-price previews therefore replaced the tour, and somehow the fact that many playgoers had seen the play before it officially opened lessened the status of the First Night. At about the same time, the social atmosphere of the London theatre changed dramatically, when and because the plays did.

I have lived through several theatrical revolutions, but none was as dramatic as the one ushered in by John Osborne's *Look Back in Anger*; from then on, for those who had eyes to see, the old theatre, which had survived into the post-war world, was doomed; there was a beautiful irony in the fact that the first play written jointly by Hugh and Margaret Williams, who represented the past, was produced in 1956, the same year as Osborne's sensation. (Margaret Williams said: 'We like to see people on the stage looking clean and well-dressed'; alas, she said it at the moment when the customers, never mind the cast, had ceased to look either clean *or* well-dressed, let alone both, and the very idea of plays with smart characters was unthinkable.)

Anyway, the point of all this is that as the nature of the theatre changed, so did that of the theatre-goers. First Nights (they really did use both capitals) glittered with the *beau monde* then; Charles Morgan, when he was the theatre critic for this newspaper, wore tails and a topper, and even I, when first a critic, donned a dinner-jacket for significant openings, though very few of my colleagues did.

Once, in the stalls, I overheard a member of the audience declaring that he would never again read the *Evening News* because its critic, Felix Barker, a very jolly fellow and a good friend of mine, had arrived at a First Night not only clad in a jacket that did not match his trousers, but *with a rolled-up newspaper sticking out of his pocket.* (Many years later, when First Nights had become very down-market occasions, I occasionally wore a dinner-jacket to, of all places, the Royal Court, but only to annoy Lindsay Anderson.)

When First Nights were still what they had been, every-body – my dear, *everybody* – went on to the old Caprice for dinner, and bitched the playwright, the director and every-body in the cast, especially those whose dressing-rooms they had crowded at curtain-fall with cries of 'Darling, you were wonderful!' True, it was not all roses. Noël Coward once told me the story of what happened to him after the First Night of a musical of his called *Pacific 1860*; this was the first show to be put on at Drury Lane after the war, during which it had been dark (tut! in theatrical parlance, 'dark' only means closed), and Coward was the obvious choice for the reopening of the oldest and most splendid of London's playhouses.

Unfortunately, on this occasion the Master had lost his touch rather comprehensively, and when he emerged from the stage door, he found something uncomfortably like a lynch mob outside; the detail that stuck in my mind, as well it might, was that the cleaners to which he sent his dinner-jacket found that all their skill was unavailing, so spat-upon had it been. When the show closed, it was followed by *Oklahoma!* which ushered in the years of the great American musicals; not long after that, at the Coliseum, I was madly in love with Dolores Gray, in *Annie Get Your Gun*, and I still am. I don't reckon much to Lloyd Webber.

I am just too young for the days when the playwright, as well as the players, took a bow after the curtain fell, but I certainly remember booing. It died out when galleries did – it survives, oddly, only at the opera – and I remember the gallery well, from long before I became a journalist, let alone a critic. You would put down a curious wooden stool outside the gallery entrance, a cheat-proof form of queueing, because your stool had a number stuck to it. The most uncomfortable gallery seats were those at Covent Garden; the runner-up was the New, which is now the Albery. There was a Gallery First-Nighters Club, but the president of it invariably sat in the stalls.

Gradually, the insurgents conquered; gradually, therefore, the romance of the First Night faded and died. By then I had been a critic for some years, and some memorably hairy evenings had etched themselves on my soul. I recall very clearly indeed one of the very hairiest, not so much because it was bad (though in fact it was terrible), but because of its sequel; I have written about the play elsewhere, but never, I think, about what happened afterwards.

The star, now dead (*de mortuis . . .*) was returning to the legitimate stage after some years on the musical stage. Understandably nervous about this début, he had, before curtain-up, fortified himself with, I guessed, at least a bottle of the hard stuff, almost certainly not diluted with soda. He managed to get through Act One, though somewhat unsteady on his pins and more than somewhat slurred in speech, but shortly after the curtain rose on Act Two, he subsided gently to the floor, and did not rise again. After a strained pause, the curtain fell, and a member of the management came before it to announce that the unfortunate actor had been taken ill, and the remainder of the performance was cancelled. Rejoicing in the thought of an early night, I left; I was just getting into the taxi when I recalled that Philip Hope-Wallace, then the critic of the *Guardian*, had fled the theatre at the interval, maintaining that he had seen quite enough on which to review it.

Now Philip also was a good friend, and one of the funniest and most interesting men alive; that, plus *noblesse oblige*, meant that I could not possibly let him walk into catastrophe. I nipped into a call-box (this was so long ago that they worked) and rang the paper, asking to be put through to Mr Hope-Wallace. To my horror, the operator refused to comply; no, I could not speak to Mr Hope-Wallace, who *never* took calls when he was writing his notice. But Mr

Hope-Wallace would *want*, I said, to be interrupted with the news I brought; nay, he *needed* to hear it for his own sake. No dice. I began to scream, rant and swear, and finally Mr Cerberus-Jobsworth put me through to an understandably tetchy Philip, who rapidly became much less tetchy; it was the only time I have ever *heard* a man go white.

There was a similar case, this one concerning an actor who had been in America for many years, in films, and was therefore similarly making a second début on the London stage. The play was set at Christmas time, and again, it was clear from Act One that the star had been gargling before curtain-up. He, too, got through the first half; when the curtain went up on Act Two, however, the play called for him to be fixing the lights on the Christmas tree, and he was therefore, reasonably enough, prone on the carpet, understood to be fiddling with the socket and plug. But what we actually *saw* as the curtain rose was not the details of the scene, but our hero lying on the ground, and eleven hundred people simultaneously hissed 'He's passed out!'

Mind you, the critics were not all tee-totallers; I don't suppose my other old mate Alan Brien will sue me if I recall a First Night when he arrived so monumentally plastered that he began, loudly, to add lines to the play. It needed some, I can tell you.

With all these memories intruding, I seem to have wandered away from the argument, now over for the moment: should critics review 'live' overnight, or go to previews and store their notices against the Press Night, as it is now feebly called? Well, I have written overnight, and also overweek. For an overnight reviewer, the time at his disposal is measured by two barriers, neither of which he can move. The first is, of course, the length of the play, and the second is the size of that night's paper (the fatter the paper the earlier the edition goes to bed). It so chanced that when I was first a critic, on a daily paper, the early weeks had plays which were almost all long, and the papers were almost all plump;

I therefore found that I had some 25 minutes in which to embed the play in the crystal of my prose.

Now as any real journalist will tell you, the time you take in writing your article is the time between when you start and the deadline, *whenever the deadline happens to be*. If I had had 15 minutes to write my notice instead of 25, it would have been written in 15 minutes, and if I had had 17 seconds, it would have been written in 17 seconds. (I am frightfully sorry if I am shocking some of you, and I am quite prepared for a flood of letters from actors and playwrights whom I handled roughly in those days – there can't be many left – denouncing me for scamping their masterpieces, but the truth is the truth.) But the point is that when shorter plays and thinner papers left me not 25 minutes to write but, say, 45, or even an hour, I was quite unable to start writing until the 25-minute mark had arrived; I spent the spare time wandering about the office eating digestive biscuits and interfering with my colleagues.

From that, you will deduce which side I was on. But I recognise that in this matter I am living in a nostalgic past, and in any case it is so long since I was a critic I really have no right to give an opinion. Anyway, I have run out of space, and even if I had more, I would not continue with the argument, but instead tell you the story of how, many years ago, I saved the then critic of *The Times* from choking to death.

The Times May 7th, 1990

Picking up the pieces

NO GAME HAS bred more metaphors than chess, the royal game. Indeed, no game has a literature a thousandth the size of it. That is not really surprising; from the moment the board is set up, chess mimics humankind in countless ways. War, cunning, power, flight, struggle, attack, defence, capture, contrast: all these can be read into the ensuing battle before a piece has been moved. Then, in action, one player sets traps (another) and his opponent feints (yet another). No wonder the knight looks like a horse, the rook a castle, the bishop a mitre; no wonder a lowly figure in human strife, useful and even necessary but little regarded, is called a pawn.

That is all very well, and has been for centuries. But this very day marks another, and very different, aspect of chess; the chess championship of the world is being fought for in New York and Lyons, between Gary Kasparov and Anatoly Karpov, and on the 64 squares a shadow falls. Another parallel with reality has been drawn, yet for once there is no metaphor to stand between the board and the spectators. Here is momentous reality, full-fledged and undisguised, and though the two contestants have eyes and thoughts only for the white and black they face, a starker colour-contrast surrounds the players, board, pieces and game alike.

I have long made it clear that as soon as I become prime minister my first item of legislation will be a measure to prohibit any actor, on pain of being summarily hanged, from expressing in public any political opinion. It might therefore be thought that I would have the same attitude to chess-players, and so, in ordinary circumstances, I would. But these circumstances are very much out of the ordinary.

It is tempting to see Kasparov and Karpov as black and white in terms of what is happening in the Soviet Union (the very name now sounds absurd), and the temptation is strong. Kasparov, who rejects entirely the system he lives under, Gorbachev's reforms and all, is 27 years old; Karpov, who is still loyal to the regime, insofar as there is one, is 39. Across the board, these two are fighting out the future of their country amid the ruins of its dying empire.

The temptation should be resisted. A few days ago I read an account of the potato harvest in the Soviet Union; the writer was talking to an official whose job entailed knowing about such things. With the food shops empty from one end of the country to the other, and the peasants, as wily as peasants have been since the first cavemen cultivated the first growing plant, keeping their produce for the black market, potatoes are going to be the staple fare of most of the population most of the coming winter. The official, gazing at a field of potatoes that would never be harvested (because there was no machinery in a fit condition to be operated and anyway no one willing to do the operating), said that 500,000 tons of potatoes would be needed to stave off widespread famine. And how many tons had been gathered, now that winter is coming on? The answer was 38,000.

That, then, is the reality that hovers over the chessboard. And it is also the reality that stays my hand from the noose and trap when Kasparov speaks. He speaks in tones which, whatever else can be said of them, are unambiguous. Glasnost is not for him; he is a leading figure in the Democratic party, which says plainly that it is an anti-communist organisation; more, he has refused to play under the Soviet flag, and at his elbow during the sessions there will be the flag of the Russian Federation.

But in all that he is only getting into his stride; hark: 'I am terribly pained and distracted by the chaos and misery in my homeland, the result of 73 years of communist dictatorship . . . my fellow citizens must struggle each day to find food . . . I have decided not to play this match under the communist flag which, to me, represents oppression and tyranny.' As for Gorbachev, the heroic figure he cuts with the free world is to Kasparov quite outrageous, in view of 'his flagrant use of force to crush independent democratic movements from the Baltic republics to the Transcaucasus'.

This, then, is no metaphorical struggle, and when winter comes and starvation hovers over the ruined land, it will not matter very much which of the contestants has emerged as world chess champion. I have been amazed at the cautiousness displayed in much of the current analysis of the dying giant; I shall be much more amazed if the country exists in any real sense by next March, unless providence sends the mildest winter in all Russian history, and why should providence do so?

There is no way out now. It is all very well for Gorbachev's Professor Shatalin to proclaim his 500-day dash for a market economy, but to have a market economy you need a market, and in a few months' time the only market will be the black one. Moreover, when a couple of hundred million people discover that the immediate effect of the economic upheaval that has followed the political one is that most of them are redundant, without anything like unemployment pay to stand between them and beggary, they are likely to cut up rough. Even I shall refrain from saying 'I told you so', though as a matter of fact I have been telling you so since the 1950s, and if anybody is entitled to crow, I am.

Stalin's man-made famine killed millions; just how many millions is still debated. The Soviet Union is heading for another famine, this one brought about not by deliberate, murderous intent but by decades of incompetence and lies, together with the healthy response of a workforce that sees no point in working for a handful of roubles that can buy nothing, because there is nothing to buy.

I cannot recall any instance in modern times, or indeed

in any times for a good many centuries back, in which a huge and mighty state crumbled into dust. Some small ones have done so – Cambodia under Pol Pot, for instance – but when and where did a state that counted in the world fall apart altogether? (Well, perhaps the Ottoman empire; the Austro-Hungarian was a much less coherent state from the beginning.) The American Civil War was a terrible wound, but there was no danger of disintegration; the ruined Germany after the second world war put itself together in no time; the Bolsheviks had Russia in their grip long before the Whites were finally defeated; at no time during the French Revolution, even at the height of the Terror, was there any sign that France would break in pieces. But the greatest and wickedest empire the world has known is now facing not just decline but extinction, and if famine does fall upon the Soviet Union, I can see nothing that would hold it together.

What that would mean for the constituent parts, and what it would mean for the rest of the world, is almost impossible to guess. There might be a series of civil wars, or the rapid construction of some kind of federation, or the one followed by the other. But there will be no return to the metaphor; the chessboard cannot turn into chaos. Kasparov or Karpov; Gorbachev or Yeltsin; sooner or later; the end must come. In Moscow, I learn, it is already snowing.

The Times October 8th, 1990

Sororicides of the world, unite

HERE IS A simple sentence of only 24 words, beginning the newspaper report of a criminal case, and if it doesn't make your hair stand on end, you must use a singularly powerful brilliantine. 'Muslims in Britain', it runs, 'have been divided by the murder of Sharifan Bibi, 18, by members of her own family as a punishment for adultery.'

Savour the word 'punishment' for a moment; does it not suggest something like a trial, with a prosecution and a defence, with witnesses and evidence and a jury listening to a judge's summing up, and an appropriate sentence at the end of the proceedings, followed perhaps by an appeal?

That is what the defendants got, but not their sister. These two murderous hitmen, stinking of self-righteousness, killed the girl and her lover; they apparently dismembered the bodies and threw the remains into a pit in a cellar. Meanwhile, the family 'appeared unhelpful and unconcerned'.

If I have only made your flesh creep, you have missed the point. Go back and find the crucial words in the opening paragraph: 'Muslims in Britain have been divided by the murder . . .'

Oh, they have, have they? And in what proportions? For although only a small number of mad fanatics would act similarly, and not many more would applaud from the wings, the very fact that such murder most foul can be condoned in Britain or any civilised country is surely a cause for shuddering, and – more important than any shudder – action.

Harmonious relations between races in a country as small

as Britain are very important; on the whole, they have here been good, or at least peaceful. Mr Enoch Powell's wild vision of 'the Tiber, foaming with much blood', as he foresaw a dreadful *Kulturkampf* between the indigenous and the incomers (forgetting, among many other things, that we were all incomers once), has not come to pass, God be thanked and Allah be praised and sensible men and women be applauded.

It has been argued that the newcomers should for a time have the seesaw tilted towards them rather than to the host population; if we are serious about assimilation, we must encourage as many immigrants as possible to take on the lineaments of the rest of us. Besides, there are lots of potential black Tory votes in Bradford.

The seesaw, inevitably, is very delicately balanced, and it is easy for the authorities – local and central – to smile at the quaint habits of the erstwhile foreigners, confident that the quaintness will fade along with the erstwhileness. There was a nasty moment a few years ago when a gentleman from the Middle East took it into his head to slaughter a sheep outside his front door, and seemed surprised, just as he had finished cutting the beast's throat and was getting on with emptying the blood into the gutter, to be told by a passing policeman that such customs, however familiar where he came from, are on the whole frowned upon in the more fashionable parts of London, and would he therefore kindly desist. (There is also Dr Siddiqui and his cuttings-album, but a circus can hardly exist without the clowns.)

But the seesaw can be pushed so far that it gets stuck, and it is possible to mark the exact moment when it did stick: it was the panic order by the government not to prosecute those British Muslims who publicly called for the murder of a British citizen; I refer, of course, to Salman Rushdie and the *fatwa* pronounced against him. For what is surely the first time in our history, incitement to murder, though repeatedly and unambiguously expressed, was *officially* ignored.

We must not be too literal; the death of Sharifan Bibi

cannot be simply laid at the door of those who spurred on the *fatwa*. But if you listen carefully to some of the words used in the trial for her murder, you may have cause for unease. Take the pleading of the lawyer first:

> It was probably a killing to protect the honour of the family. You may think they had the feelings of their deeply religious father, who was a teacher at a mosque.

Nothing wrong with that, you may say; any defending counsel would put it in such words, to ensure as much sympathy as possible for his clients. No doubt; but those words *were spoken by the prosecution lawyer, not the defence*, and the inexorable laws of physics lay down that anyone who bends backwards far enough will eventually fall over.

But now hear the judge, passing sentence on the two sororicides: 'You must remember you are members of a wider family, the family of the human race.' It's a wonder he didn't express regret that the law gave him no alternative to a life sentence.

It is easy to say that time will eventually dissolve such evil uprightness; already, the members of the younger generation are turning away from such bloodthirsty precepts, if only because they see their indigenous coevals practising a very different style of life: though remember that it takes courage – courage unto death, even – for a young woman of strictly religious Muslim family to insist on a career and a marriage of her own choice, not of her parents. (I still get a naïve pleasure when I come upon children playing, and hear the black ones talking in the same cockney tones as the white.)

Yet we must remember that Islam is a worldwide tree of faith, and beneath some of its branches very ugly things may shelter. Whatever happens over the next few years, few can be happy at what is happening, let alone what may yet happen, in Algeria, where the pot of fanaticism bubbles fiercely on the hob.

Let us not fall into the trap of sentimentality, disguised as admiration. There are many people in Britain who applaud, publicly or covertly, those who cleave to the most rigid fundamentalist Muslim teaching and behaviour. Would that Christians, they say, were as assiduous and serious about their own religion, and no wonder that there are fewer and fewer Christian church-goers, considering the feebleness of what they hear when they go there.

Well, all the Christians need is a few lengths of wood, some piles of twigs, a box of matches and a heretic or two. (Only one or two to start with, that is: if it goes well, we can give a prize for the best translation of *auto-da-fe* – this is a *British* Inquisition, we'll have you know.)

When in Rome . . . do not, please, murder your sister; but if you must, do not feel proud of yourself when you have done so. The world has taken a very long time to get out of barbarism as far as it has, and it will take much longer to complete the process. That longed-for day will only be postponed once more if wickedness is clothed in holiness and bloodlust is mistaken for anointing oil.

Vengeance is mine; I will repay, saith the Lord. Some people have forgotten, and some never knew, that the stress in that sentence is on 'mine' and 'I'.

The Times January 13th, 1992

Dons delight to bark and bite

THE *Times Literary Supplement* is an amazing journal. It is capable of allotting 3,000 words to a review of a book about 11th-century smoke-detectors, written in a remote dialect of Nepalese, printed in an edition of 75 copies and obtainable only in Ulan Bator; invariably, the editor knows the only other man in the world who can deal with it. On the other hand, its high standards, its careful balance and its astonishing range make it indispensable for anyone interested in writing or thought.

It may well hold the record for the smallest number of editors of any such journal – only seven, including the present one, in its 88 years. That continuity must be the clue to its lasting quality. It is difficult to believe that until the mid-Seventies, all of its reviews were unsigned, which gave countless opportunities, gleefully taken, for Professor Hypotenuse to rubbish in safety the life's work of his dear friend and colleague Professor Katzenjammer. H.G. Wells (presumably after getting a bad review) waxed wrathful at 'the anonymous greasers of the *Times Lit Supp*', and I am not revealing hitherto unknown secrets when I say that John Gross, approached to succeed Arthur Crook in 1974, agreed to do so only if the anonymity rule was abolished.

I confess, however, that the page I turn to first is that with the letters on it. I rather think that the space allotted to the paper's correspondents has shrunk in recent years; perhaps I might here make an appeal to the present editor (Jeremy Treglown) not only to restore its former acreage but to increase it substantially. For the one thing that the *TLS* lacks, and as long as I have been reading it always has lacked, is *fun*. Perhaps the analysis of important subjects does not easily lend itself to merriment; your average 7½lb monograph on the dating of Duccio's *Madonna with Three Franciscan Monks* could hardly be a giggle a minute. But that is all the more reason to promote the Letters page, for the fun that is to be had there – quite unintentional, of course – would lighten the spirits even of a reader determined to get through the entire review of the Nepalese smoke-detector study without skipping.

The letters range widely, of course; but the heart of the page, which provides the fun, consists of waspish replies by authors whose books have been reviewed less enthusiastically than the author thinks fitting. But that is only the top layer; there are two more. Some of the very best laughs are generated by authors who are not only cross, but who have written books which are entirely incomprehensible to any reader, however learned, not excluding the other man who knows about the Nepalese smoke-detectors. And the third layer is the introduction into the affronted replies of names cited to bolster the writer's case, but whom nobody at all has ever heard of. Listen to this, in the temper category, from Professor Pangle of Toronto University:

> The discussion of Leo Strauss occasioned by my book *The Rebirth of Classical Political Rationalism: An introduction to the thought of Leo Strauss* [an unwritten rule says that the titles of the disputed books must be longer than the books themselves] is a farrago of unusually brazen misrepresentations. Of the quotations purportedly from Strauss's writings in the review, almost all are of words and phrases or sentences wrenched from context in such a way as to destroy the authentic original meaning, and to substitute in its place a specious and sinister-sounding fabrication.

That's telling 'em then, eh, Pangle? But much juicier

is Professor Finson of the University of North Carolina:

> Eric Sams's review of my book *Robert Schumann and the Study of Orchestral Composition: The genesis of the First Symphony, Op 38*, contains several misleading statements which cannot pass uncorrected. The most unfortunate concerns the production of the libretto for Schumann's *Das Paradies und die Peri*. Wasielewski . . . tells us that the impetus for the project came from Emil Flechsig's translation of a section from Thomas Moore's *Lalla Rookh* . . . Wasielewski also mentions that the composer may have had help from Theodor Oelkers in this transformation.

But here comes M. Michael Issacharoff, taking issue with Keith Gore's review of his *Discourse as Performance*. After praying in aid Benveniste, Genette and Todorov, he gets down to it:

> It is hard to believe that in 1989 a reviewer could still imagine that semiotics is merely a matter of 'reducing one form of discourse to another, to tell us what we already know in the language of the semiotician'. I do not make any claim to being a 'semiotician'. On the other hand, any competent reader would recognise that the thinking in my last five books [another rule is that authors complaining about their *TLS* reviews insist that readers must be intimately familiar with their entire *oeuvre*] has been informed by *concepts* derived from linguistics, semiotics, philosophy of language, literary theory, the theory of reference and speech-act theory.

I could go on for a while yet – I have been collecting these items for some time – but you get the idea by now. One more prize pippin, however, must be tendered; it comes from Professor B.F. Skinner, no less, and demonstrates all three of the elements which we connoisseurs seek on our happy hunting ground: name-sprinkling ('Sperber . . . Levelt . . . Chomsky'), displeasure ('His contribution to an understanding of verbal behaviour was as negligible then as it is now'), and above all incomprehensibility:

> Behaviour is selected by its consequences. Listeners mediate the consequences of verbal behaviour and the ways in which they do so account for the types of verbal behaviour discussed in my book. Cognitive psychologists never speak directly of variation and selection. The process seems to give behaviour an orientation towards the future, and they deal with that as intention, but like purpose in natural selection intention is simply wrong. Behaviour is explained not by the consequences that lie ahead, but by those that have followed in the past.

Many years ago, when I was working on a small magazine, one of its more assiduous correspondents, who thought nothing of sending three letters a week for favour of publication, on subjects as diverse as bee-keeping, the Gold Standard and the innocence (or possibly the guilt) of Richard III, came up with a wheeze which even for him was extravagantly unusual. Why, he asked, doesn't somebody found a magazine *consisting entirely of readers' letters*? I laughed; but I could not get the idea out of my head, and the more I thought about it, the less able I was to see the fallacy, though I was certain that there must be one. For the life of me, though, I still cannot see it. Every newspaper and magazine gets scores or even hundreds of readers' letters a day, of which it can print only a tiny proportion. Add up those writers, and they must come to thousands – tens of thousands, I should think. Interminable arguments would fill the columns, new recruits would rush to write, and of course would have to buy the magazine to see their words immortalised.

The more I think about it, the more I am convinced that my correspondent had an idea as momentous as Newton under the apple tree. It is still not too late, and I have the perfect title: *The Times Literary Supplement Supplement.*

The Times March 22nd, 1990

Supplementary benefit

THE NEW EDITOR of *The Times Literary Supplement*, Ferdinand Mount (Ferdy to all) has been quick to change the layout; its new dress is both handsome and inviting. Ferdy knows, of course, that it is the merchandise, not the wrapping-paper, which sells the goods; it is going to be great fun watching as he carefully, not too quickly, also changes the contents.

I believe that what I call the inertia of newspaper reading is at its most powerful in Britain. To persuade a reader of one newspaper or magazine to change allegiance to another demands an enormous amount of time, money and ingenuity; up and down the land, every breakfast-time, people leap to their feet, fling their newspaper to the floor, stamp on it vigorously, and cry 'I won't have that rag in the house another day.' But next day it is still there.

The corollary, of course, is that when the devotion is felt to be betrayed, the screams of wounded tradition can be heard even above the thudding of the disappointed readers jumping on their papers. When in May 1966, *The Times* ceased to devote the entire front page to small-ads and put news on it, the national suicide rate rose by an average of 16 per cent for the first three months, but this dismal figure (none the less dismal for being made up by me just now) was followed by the result of an opinion poll that asked *Times* readers whether they had come to terms with the new appearance, whereupon 87 per cent of them (provenance of figure the same) declared they had not noticed it.

Ferdy, then, has a considerable task before him. It can be done; Max Hastings, when he was made editor of the

Daily Telegraph, managed, with infinite tact, to bring it at least into the 20th century, though it is true that he had one unique advantage, which was that roughly a third of his regular readers were dead, and indeed buried, or at least embalmed, thus being in no position to complain.

On the eve of the appearance of the new-style *TLS*, there was a feature in the *Guardian* about literary magazines, and naturally views and intentions were canvassed. So, however, were those of Ferdy's chief assistant, Alan Jenkins, and it was something he said that gives me my text for today. Discussing the *TLS*, Mr Jenkins put it this way:

> We have an image problem . . . There's no doubt that it's *perceived* to be a rather stuffy and forbidding publication, and there's no question that in some areas it's *necessarily* forbidding. For example, a book on Byzantine coinage – you can't make it all that interesting to someone who isn't interested in Byzantine coinage; those areas are going to seem of necessity quite unattractive.

That is where I part company with Mr Jenkins's views. He instanced a book on Byzantine coinage, clearly intending his example to provide the most powerful barrier to a wider readership. But from long and searching experience, I believe that no such barrier exists, in the case of Byzantine coinage or in any other topic.

To start at a tangent, I can offer one genuinely enthralling and entirely accessible aspect of Byzantine coinage, which is that the word 'Byzantine' holds the English language record for the number of ways a word can be acceptably pronounced; I believe 'Byzantine' can be spoken in nine ways, every one justifiable. Imagine turning to your neighbour at table and asking: 'What do you do?', to receive the apparently daunting reply: 'I am a Professor of Byzantine Coinage, but I don't expect you to be interested in the subject.' Off you go at once with the pronunciation game, and while the potatoes are coming round you are getting on like a house on fire, particularly if you know something recondite about potatoes.

Now I am going to be serious. I most profoundly believe, and I have been testing my belief all my life, that there is *no* subject which cannot be made interesting, given – this is the great barrier, not the subject itself – that the expert on it knows how to make it meaningful and even exciting to the layman.

Obviously, I demand a great deal; there is many an expert who can do no more by exposition than go on repeating his incomprehensible jargon. I have in my time read more reviews of that kind in the *TLS* than any man should have to do without being paid for his suffering; Ferdy's ultimate aim should be to exclude anything that *only* fellow experts can understand. Nuclear power, fossils, molecular biology, quarks, higher mathematics (my brother-in-law is a higher mathematician), bee-keeping, death, Swedenborg, the internal combustion engine, the Rt Hon. Edward Heath, the *Lusiads*, the theory of chance, the inside of the head of Gary Kasparov, evolution, earthquakes and Mozart: all these things and a great many more have I heard expounded and explained by a man or woman wise and eloquent enough to make me understand their essence, and I am the better and rounder man for it.

Remember that the expert is always keen to explain his subject to the laity, and the reason is obvious: he is tired of explaining it to his fellow experts, who want only to put forward their own version of the subject. That Professor of Byzantine Coinage who said 'I don't expect you to be interested in the subject,' was dying to hear you say, 'Oh, yes, I would love to hear all about it.' That in itself is no guarantee that he can make you understand, but even if he cannot, you are not altogether helpless; ingenious questions can elicit fascinating answers.

I once revealed to my readers that in my library (which I believe is the most eclectic on earth, if not in the entire history of printing), I have, somewhere on my shelves, a book called *A History of False Teeth*. There is no joke or trick; it is exactly what its title said it was, and I read it, enthralled, from beginning to end. Some of my readers responded by asking 'What is the use of knowing the history of false teeth?' If the question is to be answered literally, I have to say that there is no use in it; after all, if I did sit next to the author at dinner, he could not tell me anything I didn't already know. For that matter, I know that camels can't walk backwards, and I recently added to my store of useless zoological information the fact that snakes are deaf, neither of these facts being of any actual or potential use.

But that brings me round the circle to where I started; between you and me, I don't care a bit about Byzantine coinage, and the expert offering to explain it to me would only be explaining himself and his ability at exposition, so that I would leave thinking 'What an interesting man,' rather than 'What an interesting subject.'

And why not, Ferdy? Why not 'What a lucid review,' instead of 'What an important subject'? Come: did not Montaigne himself say '*Quand je me joue à ma chatte, qui sait si elle passe son temps de moi plus que je ne fais d'elle?*' No doubt some of my readers cannot read French; well, what pleasure they are going to have when they are seated next to a professor of that language who can expound its nature in a way they can understand.

Des. res.

W HEN THE FUNCTION of a distinguished building comes
to an end, it is often the very devil to decide what to do
with it. For instance, take the Round House, in London, near
Chalk Farm. (Why is it called Chalk Farm? Even I know that
you can't grow chalk, whether in a farm or a window-box.)
The Round House had a notable history as the place where
locomotives were turned round on the turntable beneath the
conical roof; if I had been about at the time, I would certainly
have applied for the job of pushing the engines round; a more
delightful occupation I cannot imagine. London trams were
much cleverer; they were symmetrical, with a driving cabin
at each end; even the seatbacks, which were hinged, could
change direction with a gentle push.

When the railway no longer needed the Round House, it
became a theatre-in-the-round (well, naturally), and many
a notable performance I have seen there. But its luck ran
out, and it is now derelict and rotting, unlike its handsome
Manchester cousin, the Royal Exchange Theatre, which was
fitted into the vast cathedral where once dealers by the hundred, each wearing a golden sovereign on his watch-chain,
bought and sold bales of the precious thread when cotton
was king.

Battersea Power Station (it was always called 'the power
'ouse' in my youth), is Giles Gilbert Scott's monument,
but it, too, is now abandoned. Battersea was built in two
stages; the first in the early Thirties and the second in the
mid-Fifties, and attracted critical comment from beginning
to end. Scott was making final adjustments for years. But

today, when the controversy is over, you must agree that the skyline of London would have been much the poorer without it.

Most notable buildings acquire legends. Battersea sprouted one that was firmly believed by many; it was said that only three of the chimneys were needed to produce the power, and that the fourth, a dummy, had been added to make it symmetrical.

Then there was the Crystal Palace. Removed from Hyde Park after the Great Exhibition of 1851, it was parked at Sydenham; but what, after all, do you do with a used Crystal Palace? In 1936 it was destroyed by fire; a legend far more lunatic than the Battersea one grew upon the ashes, and in no time was running rapidly round London, to the effect that the Duchess of Windsor had deliberately set it alight in revenge for not being allowed to be queen.

There was also the Windsor Hotel (no relation) in Victoria Street; as I recall, it was a listed building, and uniquely listed, too – it was so stupendously ugly that it was deliberately preserved for years, possibly to frighten naughty children (eat up your spinach or you'll be put in the Windsor Hotel). Mind you, when I contemplate what Victoria Street is like now, I sometimes think it got the wrong end of the bargain.

The Langham Hotel might have suffered a similar fate; before the Hilton group acquired and restored it (very handsomely, I must say), it had deteriorated badly, used for years as a kind of overflow for Broadcasting House just across the road. Its decline was a source of anxiety to me, because it was there I began my career, on a radio programme for the BBC, and I naturally had sentimental feelings for the place. (I wonder if during the rebuilding anybody thought to put up some kind of plaque immortalising me. I would settle for 'The Bernard Levin champagne bar'.)

When the Murdoch Revolution took place there was much discussion of the future of the vacated premises in Gray's Inn Road; helpful as ever, I suggested arson, particularly for the *Times* building, which had been designed and decorated in 'Seifert Venetian', though I doubt if any Doge would recognise it as such. ITN bought the *Sunday Times* building, planning to use it as it was. But they reckoned without the effect of having a few hundred journalists in a confined space for many years; I tell you, we can filthify a palace into a pigsty in no time at all. When the March on Wapping (where *The Times* is now printed) arrived, we went in, through the picket-lines, and stood breathless at the long tables with the gleaming electronic terminals winking greenly, and everything around perfectly clean and shining. It took us 48 hours at most to turn the place into a kind of low-class abattoir. ITN tore down the *ST* entirely, and started again; I don't blame them.

I once toyed with the idea of buying St Pancras station, to shelve my books when I ran out of wall-space and to prevent the house falling down under the weight; BR refused a deal – they said they wanted it for their trains – and so 8,000 of my books are now in store. But I have my eye on St Pancras *Chambers*, which used to be the Midland Hotel and is now full of nothing but ghosts and dust.

All this meandering began when I read, with considerable scepticism, that my old coll, the London School of Economics, plans to buy County Hall and shift the entire LSE empire into it.

County Hall used to house what was latterly called the Greater London Council, but for many years previously was the London County Council – a far more dignified moniker. It was run like the empire of an American 'boss' by Herbert Morrison, one of the most consummate politicians of this century. I recall that in the 1945 general election Morrison, who was supremo of the Labour forces, kept back his *chef d'oeuvre* to the last moment; we went to bed on election eve, and woke up to find every lamp-post in town sporting a sticker which read 'Come on, London, we're voting Labour today!' (And London, and Britain, did.) In the middle of the night Morrison had poured in an army of amateur flyposters.

*

County Hall has been sneered at since it was built, but I have always admired the view from across the river, with the building showing its elegant curve. When the GLC was wound up, it posed a problem; nobody knew what to do with it. There was talk of turning it into a luxury hotel, but the cost of the conversion would have been so enormous that nobody had the nerve (or at least the money) to do so. The building is still empty, which cannot be good for the structure, let alone the interior, but no one had offered a serious idea of what it might become until the LSE decided to have a go. Presumably the coffers are reasonably full, though how to put a price on the place I cannot imagine. Conversion would take years, which brings me back to my youth; when I went up, there was incessant building and renovation going on at the LSE, inspiring Kingsley Martin, long-time editor of the *New Statesman*, to say to the director, 'You reign over an empire on which the concrete never sets.'

As for derelict buildings, which started my hare, I have just learned from an unreliable source that the Hayward Gallery is to be pulled down, together with the Queen Elizabeth Hall. If it is true, may I stake a claim for being allowed to give the first whack with the first pickaxe?

The Times May 27th, 1991

Arcadia on Thames

COME; LET US annoy Sir Godfrey Taylor. He has done me no harm, and indeed I had never knowingly heard of him until an hour ago, but he is thwarting, or at least attempting to thwart, an idea so splendid and imaginative that nothing must be allowed to stand in its way. Sir Godfrey is standing in its way, so we must all annoy him till he desists.

I am a graduate of the London School of Economics, where I sat at the feet of such luminaries as Harold Laski, Morris Ginsberg, Lionel Robbins, Michael Oakeshott, K.B. Smellie and my hero, Karl Popper; from these, I learned practically everything of value that I know.

In 1974, however, I had a nasty shock; I realised that by a few months I was older than the newly installed director of the LSE, Ralph Dahrendorf, and when a man finds that he is older than the head of the institution in which he got his principal education, he is likely to look in the mirror and fumble for razor-blades. (Robert Conquest had a much nastier shock of the same kind; he realised, when J.F. Kennedy won the 1960 election, that the president of the United States was actually younger than he was, though by only a few weeks. I have always believed that Bob, not Lee Harvey Oswald, shot him.)

Imagine, then, the horror with which I realised that when I went up to the LSE as a first-year undergraduate, the present director, Professor John Ashworth, was *eight years old*.

I'll be shooting him, I can tell you, but not before he has

brought to fruition the magnificent idea I mentioned when I started. For he wants to take over County Hall, together with its satellites, the Island Block and the North and South Blocks, and house the LSE in it.

The LSE has been hopelessly cramped since I was a student there. It has expanded to its limit by buying up bits and pieces of surrounding buildings, but it will soon burst, and the work it does suffers from the inadequacy of the premises; the Library of the Social Sciences, the jewel in the college's crown (it has two million works in its stacks, more than any such specialist collection anywhere) will soon need more room, too.

County Hall is empty; when the GLC was abolished, and Ken Livingstone was dethroned (do you remember when he and his gang gave – and for a peppercorn rent – the Festival Hall's entire 5,000 square feet of open space to Brezhnev, to mount a monstrous exhibition of lies and evil?), County Hall lost its *raison d'être*. For a time it was squatted in by a residue of those who, in the Livingstone days, had strolled the corridors, monarchs of all they surveyed, but the law turfed them out, and now there is no one in it, unless the ghost of Herbert Morrison patrols the place at night.

The abolition of the GLC posed problems; it owned County Hall, as had the LCC before it, but if the GLC was dead, to whom could County Hall be left in its will? A new organisation was hastily invented, called the London Residuary Body, and County Hall was put into its hands, along with the South Bank halls. (And do you remember when Livingstone and his cronies instituted tests for political correctness among those wishing to perform in the Festival Hall?)

Which is where Sir Godfrey Taylor comes in. He is chairman of the London Residuary Body, and he is deeply hostile to the idea of bringing the LSE across the river. And that is why we have to annoy him.

He first looked kindly on a project which would have turned County Hall partly into a huge hotel and partly into a block of flats. But it is singularly unfitted for either of these proposed metamorphoses, and in any case the entrepreneurs who proposed the scheme could not come up with the money. Whence young Johnny Ashworth and his vision of the LSE, with students strolling that huge curved corridor, each of them equipped if not with 40 acres and a cow, at least a desk, and even a chair.

I have the detailed scheme – very detailed indeed – for an LSE across the Rubicon, and I must say that I have never seen a proposal for action so meticulously, lucidly and comprehensively drawn up; every time, when reading through it, I said to myself 'Ah, but . . .', I only had to turn the page to find that my objection had been considered and met.

The scheme, then, is sound, and what is more, exciting. But we are far from home yet. The borough within which County Hall falls is Lambeth, so the necessary planning permission will have to be sought from one of the looniest of all the loony municipalities. Here, we have some good news and some bad; the good news is that Lambeth undoubtedly still believes that the LSE is a raging fire of revolution. (I beg you all my readers not to say or do anything that will disillusion them.) The bad news is that Lambeth Council dreams of a Labour government which will restore County Hall and the GLC in the same hour.

The permissions that are sought concern the Riverside Building and the Island Block. The North Block and South Block already have the necessary permissions from the ministry, but these have to be renewed. Very likely, the minister will have to rule in the end. The present environment secretary is Michael Heseltine, and I cannot believe that he would turn down Professor Ashworth, particularly because he must know the truth about the political bent of today's LSE, which we are all pledged to conceal from Lambeth Council.

Oh, can we British not for once thrill to an idea and carry it through? The LSE is one of the most admirable and valuable educational centres this country has; it has,

I believe, a greater proportion than any other of students from other countries, and when they come they find a vast variety of opinions and beliefs and teachings.

It is worth saying that many of the overseas students come from countries where only one political position is allowed, and for the awakening of such young people alone, the LSE deserves to be honoured.

All my life I have mourned the opportunity I missed when I was young; I wanted to go to Cambridge, or failing her, Oxford, and the fates conspired to deprive me of my ambition. I enjoyed the LSE, and I owe it an immense debt of gratitude; my frustrated yearning had nothing to do with the quality of the teaching or the friendships I made. What I longed for – and still do when I go there – was the space and peace of those lawns, the ancient stone of those walls, the well-trodden steps of those staircases, still echoing with great names gone before.

Well, the south bank of the Thames is hardly Cambridge, let alone Arcadia. Nevertheless, the elegant sweep of County Hall, its majestic view over and along the river, its undated handsomeness – these things, with a genuine touch of *rus in urbe*, could provide something like the cloistered calm of the twin great universities, and give every LSE student with enough imagination to understand a glimpse of the gift I missed. Do give in gracefully, Sir Godfrey.

The Times October 3rd, 1991

Civilising mission

SOME TIME AGO, discussing the dramatic changes taking place in the two great poles of our time and place, I used the words '. . . before South Africa can be classified as a wholly civilised nation . . .' A reader, saying that she had been sufficiently intrigued to respond, said – well, let her speak in her own words:

> *My query is – which nation in the world today could earn such a classification? Which led me on to wonder how you would construct a hierarchy of the criteria of being 'civilised'. I thought this might provoke an interesting debate in the columns of* The Times . . .

And so it might, but before it does I would like to have a go myself.

Let us begin with freedom, and even as I use the word I am conscious of the ambiguities that surround it. I have just looked up the famous 'Four Freedoms' speech of Roosevelt; the touching naïvety in it is almost unpleasantly embarrassing:

> . . . In the future days, which we seek to make secure, we look forward to a world founded upon four essential human freedoms.
>
> The first is freedom of speech and expression, everywhere in the world.
>
> The second is freedom of every person to worship God in his own way everywhere in the world.

The third is freedom from want, which, translated into world terms, means economic understandings which will secure to every nation a healthy peacetime life for its inhabitants, everywhere in the world.

The fourth is freedom from fear – which, translated into world terms, means a worldwide reduction of armaments to such a point and in such a thorough fashion that no nation will be in a position to commit an act of physical aggression against any neighbour, anywhere in the world.

That is no vision of a distant millennium. It is a definite basis for a kind of world attainable in our own time and generation.

That speech was made when the second world war had been raging for 16 months; the Blitz was at its height, Hitler's invasion of Russia was six months away, and Pearl Harbor twelve. If Roosevelt's programme was long out of date when he propounded it, it was nothing but a macabre echo four-and-a-half years later, when the A-bomb blew away every illusion, and 80,000 people.

'Everywhere in the world'; it is like a mantra, only less useful. But do not blame Roosevelt; realists, in those days, were very rare, and invariably condemned as cynics. Slowly, reality broke in. If you take out the 'everywhere in the world', and look at what remains, you will find that a fairly small number of western nations have lived up to the second precept for a short time; the rest is silence. No country permits freedom of speech and expression; if you do not believe me, ask Lady Birdwood. No country is without its poor. No country is without fear of aggression or the means of launching it. From time to time, here and there, complete freedom of worship has been allowed; and why? Because it does not touch the tender parts of the state; how many years from now will there be restrictions on some Muslim worship in Britain? My guess is seven.

Very well, these freedoms, if they are the pillars of civilisation, are very weak pillars. In most western countries most people can enjoy them most of the time (good news – Charles Humana is at work on a new edition of his *World Human Rights Guide*, to be published next year and to be consistently looted by me), and such countries would claim to be truly civilised, basing their claim on freedom alone.

But wait. Was Periclean Athens civilised? Of course; perhaps the greatest civilisation in history. Ah, but it rested on a base of slaves, so civilisation cannot be defined by freedom, since the slaves of Athens conspicuously lacked it; there goes the civilisation of civilised Europe, founded as it is on the structure of freedom, however sturdy or wonky. And what about the ancient Kingdom of Tibet, one of the most civilised and wonderful the Earth has seen (which is precisely why the barbarian communists of China had to destroy it); its people had no such upstart notions. And the Incas? And Medici Florence?

We shift our ground. It is culture that denotes civilisation, not freedom. But how do we define culture? Not just artefacts, surely; that is far too narrow a test, and not only because a true civilised culture must – must it not? – exclude evil.

It is easy to see that, isn't it? Look at the 'art' produced under Stalin and Hitler; the only creations that could be called art were those that were banned or hidden. We've proved it, hurrah. But wait again. As far as I know, Japanese art, the most delicate and pure, continued to be created throughout the second world war, while other Japanese were delicately and purely disembowelling prisoners of war. Can a culture be civilised and uncivilised at the same time? This is getting very difficult, but it was supposed to be.

Come back to Athens for a moment. Is it possible to call civilised a society that has such civilised people as – well, you and me, say – knowing that there is a huge majority out there doing nothing but listening to the most simian music and eating potato crisps? Can we, that is, have bi-civilised countries?

And what about nations that are as close as mortals can

get to eradicating poverty and hunger and random violence and dirt and drunkenness, but are boring, such as Sweden? No, that will not do; the Swedes are drunk all the time; so it will have to be Switzerland. Well, the Swiss are not drunk, but if you want me to announce that Switzerland is the most civilised country in the world I shall shrink from the task.

Let us try happiness: in which country is the greatest proportion of its people happy? By this test we would probably come up with somewhere like Botswana. There is nothing wrong with Botswana, apart from the fact that I have no idea where it is, but although I will cheer for this supposedly joyous place, I cannot award it the palm.

Nor France, though a powerful case can be made for her. She knows how to cook, to eat and drink, she excels in the *arts ménagers*, she probably has the best small talk of any contestant, and her country assuredly is beautiful. But her chances of the prize evaporated gradually over the years; she became bad-tempered, the one thing she never was. And how could you give anything but a raspberry to a country that could put up that ludicrous glass pyramid?

I think the answer is Italy, I really do. Much have I travelled in the world of gold, but I do not think I know of a place that demonstrates the qualities of civilisation so strongly. We must discard the shallow image of the charming but hopeless Italian; her recent economic record belies it at once. Yet the Italians, as they have prospered, have not forgotten that the world is a ridiculous place, and that it is better to laugh with the ridicule than try to change it. It is a country that takes its religion seriously but not intolerantly, which has the wisdom her peasants never lost, which has a sharp eye for design, some very good newspapers, a living art as well as an ancient one. True, she has no *haute cuisine*, but her *basse cuisine* is delicious, and she despises her politicians for the right reason: not that they are crooked (though they are), but that they are noisy. She earns a very black mark for letting Venice rot.

And then, look at her past! Look at the stupendous riches of the art that has been created here; look at the love and respect with which she displays her greatest treasure, the opera; look at, indeed, civilisation, and as you look, and wherever you look, you will see how many civilisations have come together to make this boot-shaped place what it is: beautiful, content, good-hearted, sensible, proud of her past, and with every right to be, in a word: civilised.

I told you I wanted to start a hare, and I hope I have. *Après moi le déluge.*

The Times November 21st, 1991

And kiss his dirty shoe

I MAY HAVE missed it – one cannot read everything – but I have not yet seen a statement from Sir Dennis Walters, Lord Mayhew, Mr Michael Adams and Mr Andrew Faulds explaining that the Iraqi invasion is entirely the fault of Israel. It wouldn't be difficult: after all, everyone knows that Saddam Hussein's real name is Solomon Gluckstein, and his profession Israeli agent. His masters in Tel Aviv gave the word, 30,000 Israeli troops were flown into Baghdad disguised as door-to-door carpet salesmen, and lo! Kuwait is yet another part of the Israeli empire, which will stretch when complete from Calcutta to Hatton Garden.

I feel sure that in these tumultuous days the ancient hope, never abandoned, of the Foreign Office – the hope of seeing Israel erased from the map – has been quietly discussed. I am willing to bet (I shall be able to prove it in 30 years' time when the files are opened) that 'position papers' have already been drawn up which advocate a solution based on persuading Saddam to withdraw from Kuwait in return for a free hand (and some discreet help) against the Israelis, while poor Douglas Hurd runs about trying to put salt on the notion's tail.

Ian Mikardo, who had a roughish tongue, was once asked (I think on a radio programme) what were the Foreign Office's real concerns; he replied crisply: 'Homosexuality and anti-Semitism.'

Tut. Mik went too far, and I am exaggerating as usual. But when I see Saudi Arabia, one of the most abominable and lawless states on earth (it rates only 28 out of 100 in

Charles Humana's *World Human Rights Guide*) being touted, not least by Britain, as a pure and enlightened innocent in danger from a tyrant, I do long, in Bill Connor's famous words, for a quiet corner, a handkerchief, an aspidistra and the old heave-ho.

When, and why, did British foreign policy towards the Arab states cease to be one of patronising superiority and become the most creepy subservience? Except for Lebanon and Israel, I cannot think of any country in the Middle East, with however dreadful a government, which wears boots so dirty that our Foreign Office would refuse to lick them, and lick them enthusiastically and often.

I am not so foolish as to suppose that we should ally ourselves only with nations that can boast a system of perfect democracy; simply being in the modern world involves bedfellows who snore, and not a few who are lousy. But what lasting good has the abnegation of our Arabist governments and civil servants ever brought us? Did they rush to support us in the Suez folly? Did the great oil price rise pass us by because we had been nice to the rulers of the oil states? When Iran instigated the attempt to murder a British citizen, did the Arab nations condemn such barbarism? And now, when British citizens were being rounded up for hostages in Iraq, the Foreign Office at first advised them to go dutifully and at once to the place appointed by the Iraqis, carrying one small suitcase. Their predecessors would have advised German Jews in the Thirties to go without fuss to Belsen, and to make sure they brought a pair of striped pyjamas. What has any of our crawling gained for us, unless you enjoy seeing the Arab rulers' princelings, favourites and bastards coming to London for a few weeks' gambling, boozing and whoring?

Turn it round and ask why the Foreign Office has been so implacably hostile to Israel ever since Israel was founded; in the United States it is a criminal offence to take part in the anti-Israel Arab boycott, in Britain the Foreign Office eased its path. Nor can the Foreign Office, at least with a straight face, maintain that its enmity is a response to Israel's behaviour on the West Bank; shameful as Israeli behaviour has been, it does not approach some of the Arab atrocities, as the Kurds and others would testify.

If you want an example of this incomprehensible and profitless attitude on the part of successive British governments, you have only to go back to 1980 to see how deep the need to cringe and simper had already become. Re-reading, as I have been doing, the amazing affair of *Death of a Princess* casts a powerful light on the cowardice, as unnecessary as it was appalling, of British foreign policy.

Death of a Princess, written by Anthony Thomas, an experienced author, and screened by ITV, was based on a real event; in the uncivilised satrapy of Saudi Arabia (it is not a whit better today), a man and a woman taken in adultery were publicly killed. The woman, a princess, was shot; her lover was beheaded. The killings took place in a carpark. Thomas had spent two years investigating the affair; as screened, it was an enquiry presented in dramatic form. In other words, it remained as close as possible to the events of the real killings.

Even before the film was shown, there were demands from Saudi Arabia to cancel the showing, with MPs, mostly the Arabists, joining in. (The ruler at the time was King Khaled, and if *he* had had his head cut off in a carpark it would have done Saudi Arabia nothing but good.) But that was nothing compared to what happened after the programme went out.

Saudi Arabia came close to breaking off diplomatic relations with Britain; the television company which had screened it was denounced as though it had advocated, or indeed organised, the execution of Princess Anne; international ripples became waves when first the Dutch, then the Americans, proposed to show the film on their own television; and the only minister who kept his head was Whitelaw, who made clear that Britain does, on the whole, have free speech, though he did not go on to point out that Saudi Arabia does not.

All this was to be expected; the play was a serious attempt to reconstruct a merciless crime, and the noise would have been harmless nonsense had it not been for what followed. For what followed was not one, nor two, nor three, but *four* apologies by the Foreign Office to Saudi Arabia. And that was not the worst. Among Britain's grovelling there was a stench, not just of a willingness to condone the original crime, nor of a shrug indicating that whatever we might feel about the killing of adulterers in Saudi Arabia it was no business of ours; no, some of the grovelling came close to a fawning admiration of the Saudis' commendable attitude to marital rectitude and the penalty for failing to observe it.

The apologies were accepted; the establishment slandering of Anthony Thomas continued; and Saudi Arabia went on its tyrannical way. That is the nation which now demands that the civilised world defend it against the tyranny of Saddam, so that it can continue unabated the barbarous savagery of its own.

Perhaps we shall have to (see 'bedfellows' above), but I hope we can be spared the bit about gallant, democratic little Saudi Arabia and its colourful customs, especially the free entertainment in its carparks.

The Times August 23rd, 1990

Decline and fall

WE LIKE TO think that we have something of the qualities of the ancient Greeks; when nobody is about we sometimes look in the mirror and feel that a toga would become us quite well, until we remember that the toga was a Roman garment, not Greek, and for the life of us we cannot think what the Greek equivalent was called. Of course, we pride ourselves on knowing a little about The Glory That Was Greece. The Greeks, for instance, invented or developed democracy and geometry, drama and naval warfare, monumental building and the dance, philosophy, poetry, Plato, Pericles and the paean (and pederasty, but we won't go into that). If we know a little more still, we can see clearly how the Greek civilisation has shaped and informed ours, and indeed every true civilisation for some 25 centuries. Another peep in the mirror; add a beard; why, it's Socrates!

But then we come to this passage, about a successful general:

He further increased that reputation by his behaviour on the battlefield after his victory at Corinth in 425. As victor he held the field and could collect and bury his dead. Having done so, he marched off but then learned that two corpses had inadvertently been left unburied. He sent a herald back to the Corinthians asking permission to bury them, thereby abandoning the right to set up a trophy of victory, for victors do not need the permission of the enemy to bury their dead. 'Nevertheless,' Plutarch says, 'he preferred to give up the honour and glory of the victory than to leave two citizens unburied.'

Perhaps ancient Greece, so concerned to bury the last two of the dead on the battlefield, was, after all, not very much like our time, and the Parthenon not very much like the Queen Elizabeth Hall, in either appearance or function. Where shall we go to understand those long-dead people, who have given us so much and been so misunderstood? Assuredly, we will learn nothing of value from, say, Mr Papandreou or Ms Mercouri; for such an enquiry we must go to history, and it so happens that one of the very greatest books ever written takes as its subject this very story. Mind, you will not get from Thucydides an account of the learning, the art, the culture of Greece; except tangentially, he tells us very little about these matters. Nor can we look to him for an amusing anecdote, a pleasant aside, a digression wandering far from the line to which he hews. For those qualities we must go to Herodotus, who tells many a monstrous whopper, but is one of the most lovable of all writers.

There is no getting away from the fact that the glory of Thucydides is an icy glory, and perhaps it has to be, considering its subject. For he says, as Wilfred Owen said:

Above all, this book is not concerned with Poetry.
The subject of it is War, and the Pity of War.
The Poetry is in the pity.

Thucydides no doubt believed in fate; today he would be called a determinist. But when he set out to tell the story of Athens, through the mighty curve of her rise to almost absolute power and her fall to utter destruction, he limited his view of inevitability; for him, what happened was not something willed by the gods from the beginning of time, with no possibility of evading or altering the future. Thucydides says – ignoring pity, retribution, blame, even cause – if A, then B. And, of course, if B, then C. And if C . . .

For centuries, Thucydides' view of the Peloponnesian War has held the field; indeed, in many aspects it must always do so. But before me lies a work, the author of which has undertaken to go through the great narrative again (once and for all, I would say), challenging Thucydides where he is open to challenge, using the material that has come to light since the Thucydidean stamp was set upon the story (much of it, of course, unknown to Thucydides himself), sorting out each detail of the history, looting every scrap of the past to get it right, setting out all the possibilities when he comes to a debatable point, happily introducing other scholars to argue with him in footnotes of prodigious length. The work is in four stout volumes, successively called *The Outbreak of the Peloponnesian War*, *The Archidamian War*, *The Peace of Nicias and the Sicilian Expedition* and *The Fall of the Athenian Empire*. The publication of the books spanned 18 years; the author is Donald Kagan; the publisher is the Cornell University Press. There must be something like 800,000 words in all; and I must warn you now that it is impossible to skip, so monomaniacally complete, so beautifully told, so wisely understood and so Herodotian in its warmth and sympathy is this masterly work. (I must also warn you that if you want to get the books you will probably hang yourself in frustration before they arrive, so hopelessly dilatory is the British outlet for the Cornell UP – though not, of course, as bad as the equivalent for the Toronto UP.)

Were Athens and Sparta doomed to fight until one or the other was destroyed? I do not know; but again and again, in reading Professor Kagan's masterpiece, the reader will be unable to restrain a cry of anguish as Shakespeare's tragic words fit the story:

> . . . and think not, Percy,
> To share with me in glory any more;
> Two stars keep not their motion in one sphere,
> Nor can one England brook a double reign.

The late Edward Crankshaw said of Bismarck that he would in no circumstances have allowed the first world war to take place, but that it was because of his policies that it did. As soon as Pericles' position was unassailable, he decided on a policy of peace, but Sparta could point at the Athenian empire, the very weight of which demonstrated that the two great powers could not live in harmony indefinitely.

So said Thucydides; though Professor Kagan says otherwise. We, who do not have to take sides, can watch from the ringside seat the professor has built for us, and see what *happens*.

What happens happens essentially in his third volume. Among the things the Greeks invented was the word *hybris*, and surely there has never been an instance of it to touch the Sicilian Expedition. However wide Professor Kagan spreads his net of causes and excuses, however much sympathy he urges us to feel, we cannot think but that it was madness. If Bismarck had lived . . . but he did not. If Pericles had lived . . . but he did not. The first words of the professor's Chapter 11 are: 'By the spring of 414 the time had come for the Athenians to attack Syracuse.' To weigh out the exact proportion of truth in that sentence is impossible; history, after all, is always in the past. But the scales cannot even be made ready without taking into account the character and actions of Alcibiades.

If this is a play, he is the villain. The 'triple-turned whore' is painted by Professor Kagan in neutral colours; I have never met an author so fair. But I am not bound by scholarly impartiality: for me, he is one of the great swines of history. His treasons, his scheming, his lying, his boasting, these, surely, must bear a great weight of the tragedy of folly. The professor quotes extensively from Thucydides' record of the speech he made in urging the expedition; across the centuries, we can put a voice to it, a face, a dozen equivalents in modern times. We yearn to stop it, to shout him down, to make the Assembly see that they are going to destruction and the end of Athens. Like men in a dream, we cry out, but there is no sound. The ships sail.

Of course, there were men of sense. Demosthenes (not the orator, but a general of the same name) tried to cut through the madness to the reality; in vain, or at any rate too late. Nicias, the Commander-in-Chief, is irresistibly reminiscent of Haig, and the slaughter to which his bone-headed policies led is even more so.

The fourth and final volume, for those who have followed the mighty river so far, is almost unbearable. After all, we know already what happened, and by now we even have a theory as to *why* it happened. Yet we must drain the cup to the dregs. At Arginusae, the last battle but one, the Athenians were victorious, and Sparta offered peace, as she had done before. But *hybris* spoke, and the die was cast. After the battle of Aegospotami, the catastrophe was complete: history's greatest city had no army, no navy and no hope.

So fell Athens. To be sure, another Athens arose, but the story Thucydides told, and the way Professor Kagan has re-told it, filled it out and, above all, finished it, will linger for ever in the mind and feelings of those who have read his 1,500 pages. No one could finish it without seeing a monstrous parable in the story; a parable of darkness at noon, of eyes which see though blind, of men who believe untruth and reject reality, of avoidable tragedies made certain, of folly enthroned and wisdom scorned. In searching for words with which to praise Professor Kagan as highly as he deserves, I cannot do better than to say that although the great shadow of Thucydides must have been looking over his shoulder throughout, when Professor Kagan wrote The End, the shadow nodded in admiration.

The Times (*Saturday Review*), July 28th, 1990

Neither a borrower, nor a lender be

I HAVE BEEN simultaneously amazed and amused at the recent crop of plagiarism, together with immensely solemn debates on the subject, in the United States. I say the recent crop advisedly, because it is by no means the first time that spirited recycling has come to light in that lovable but somewhat odd country. The most astonishing item in the catalogue was the contribution of Mr Joe Biden, who was seeking the Democratic nomination for president. (If you want to know the difference between American and British politicians, there is an exquisitely hand-carved distinction: American ones 'run' for office, ours 'stand'.)

Presumably, Mr Biden did not trust his own oratory to carry him to victory, and decided to borrow someone else's; so far so good – he had, after all, many great writers, thinkers and speakers to choose from, including Shakespeare, Socrates, Charles James Fox, Confucius, Tolstoy and Levin, not to mention Thomas Jefferson. Talking of Jefferson (today's column, as you may have already guessed, is going to be the discursive kind), do you know the most charming compliment ever paid to that great man? President Kennedy gave a dinner for the surviving American Nobel laureates – in science, medicine, literature and the promotion of peace – and in his speech said words to the effect that this must surely be the greatest concourse of genius in all fields ever brought together under the White House roof – 'Except perhaps,' he added, 'when Thomas Jefferson dined alone.'

Anyway, Mr Biden chose none of these sure-fire exemplars, but instead, in making a speech, waxed eloquent with the words of Neil Kinnock, so help me, who had just enough sense to say he was flattered and then shut up.

That will be hard to beat; but the search goes on. The most recent spate began with an academic, a Mr Maitre, who was the dean of communications, whatever that might be, at Boston University. He was making a commencement address, which might be thought no great labour, nor indeed the kind of speech so likely to go down to history as to need close examination by a Sanhedrin of grammarians; someone, though, spotted a link, and Mr Maitre's shame was revealed: he had borrowed, without permission, parts of a magazine article by a film critic, one Michael Melved.

I have nothing against film critics – very many years ago I nearly became one – and the name of this particular celluloid-scrutineer was hitherto unknown to me. It did, though, strike me as odd – almost as odd as Mr Biden's fatal choice – that poor Mr Maitre, who in turn could have chosen from among Dostoevsky, Molière, Cervantes, Aristotle, St Thomas Aquinas and Levin, should seek inspiration from such a recondite source.

Then it got worse. The *Boston Globe*, reasonably enough – after all, the affair was in its purlieus – recounted the sad story of the fall of Mr Maitre, but gradually the news began to circulate more widely. The Boston correspondent of the *New York Times* therefore deemed it his duty to inform his own paper's readers of the exciting news; unfortunately, he took part of his dispatch verbatim from the original *Boston Globe* report, and was suspended, *sine die*, by his editor.

Then it began to get like flying saucers: a single sighting leads to half a dozen others, and before you know where you are you can't see the moon for the things. Another journalist, this one the Miami correspondent of the *Washington Post*, has been sacked – no half-measures for the nation's capital – for lifting material from the *Miami Herald*. What makes this stage of the plagiarism epidemic even more weird than it was in the first place is the nature of the matter from which came the words the *Herald* purloined: it consisted of *three* articles about mosquitoes.

Now look: I am not interested in mosquitoes, but I recognise that others may not share my indifference. But in the name of Johann Gutenberg how did the *Miami Herald* persuade itself that its readers were so besotted with the creatures that they wanted to read about them three days running? To start with, is there enough known about mosquitoes to fill so monstrous an amount of newsprint? And even if there is, would not the excitement of learning about the little fellows with the characteristic *ping!* wear off rather quickly?

Then it spread to books. A business instructor at Stanford University (I assume that a business instructor at Stanford would have been engaged to instruct the students in the mysteries of business, and a fine example he set them, I must say) lifted whole sections from yet another magazine article, this one about the Ford company, for a book he was writing – or, more exactly, not writing. The book was called *Managing on the Edge – How the Smartest Companies Use Conflict to Stay Ahead*, and I can tell you that however they use it they certainly do not do so to save time on titles.

Sooner or later, I suppose, it had to spread to Japan, but as we all know, when the Japanese copy other countries' inventions they are not content to make replicas and leave it at that, pausing only to undercut the prices of the originals. No; they must improve on the product, and if you can think of a bigger improvement than what follows you ought to be a business instructor at Stanford.

The president of Japan's biggest news agency, the Kyodo News Service, has just resigned over a case of plagiarism. It was not, of course, the Kyodo president who did the plagiarising; he was merely doing the honourable thing of taking the responsibility for the actions of his staff, but the actions in question must have a claim on the title of the greatest act of plagiarism in history. A writer specialising in health wrote a weekly article for the Kyodo News Service on the subject for 51 consecutive weeks, and just as he was sitting down to the 52nd and presumably pouring a celebration drink for completing the year, it transpired that he had stolen the lot from a series that had appeared in a leading Japanese newspaper *17 years previously*.

I suppose I have committed all but one of the many malfeasances that are possible with the use of a pen. Libel, contempt of court, gross inaccuracy, character-assassination, barratry, incitement to violence, *lèse-majesté*, breach of parliamentary privilege, grammatical error (rare, that one), corruption of youth, *scandalum magnatum* – I wouldn't be surprised if there was a forgotten forgery or two, or at least a doctored will; but the one such sin that I have never succumbed to is the one of literary ventriloquism, or passing off the words of others as my own.

The reason has nothing to do with my upright and unblemished character. It is only because I have so much to say on my own account, and have so many opinions, and know so many words in which to give the said opinions, whether invited to do so or not, that the very thought of a need to borrow the words or ideas of others seems to me very comical. Incidentally, did you know that the word plagiarism comes from a Latin word, *plagiarius*, which means a kidnapper, hence a kidnapper of others' words?

I got that straight out of the *OED*. American papers please copy.

The Times August 19th, 1991

Sub specie aeternitatis

A N ANCIENT RUSSIAN proverb says: 'When the cannons are silent, the muses are heard; when the muses are silent, the cannons are heard.' Once in a rare while, though, they make a fearsome counterpoint, and the baying of the hounds of blood mingles with the airs and sweet sounds that give delight and hurt not.

Perhaps there has never been a more profound and terrible experience of the coming together of death and art than what happened, during the second world war, in Terizen. Terizen, more usually known by its German name, Theresienstadt, was one of the Nazi concentration camps, but a special kind. For some time it was a 'Potemkin' camp, used for propaganda, including films, and for that reason conditions in it, though harsh, were much better than in most of the other cities of hell. But the credulous neutrals who saw the camp or the films did not know that as more men and women were sent there, the numbers were kept stable by a regular delivery to Auschwitz.

Most of the inmates were Czechoslovak Jews, and these included a substantial number of musicians. The commandant of the camp, himself a music-lover (artistic folk, the Germans), allowed the doomed musicians to rehearse and perform; one of their highlights was *The Bartered Bride*, another the Verdi Requiem. (There is a story that in the middle of the performance one of the musicians abandoned Verdi's score and began to sound the four notes which began Beethoven's fifth symphony, the phrase which had been adopted as the call-sign of freedom. Alas, it is a myth.) The members of the orchestra all knew that they had no hope of rescue or reprieve, and they did not imagine their heroic dance on the cliff of death would be noted and remembered. Yet the instruments of the condemned orchestra spoke for history, and can still be heard over the cries of evil, be they never so loud.

Here I must cross a very frail bridge. Last Sunday evening, I went to the Royal Festival Hall to hear a concert performance of *The Marriage of Figaro*, conducted by Sir Georg Solti. The chasm between the music in Terizen and my joyous evening in a warm, bright hall, followed by my safe and simple return home, is grotesquely wide, and the bridge is *very* frail. But I had to cross it because, you see, another of the performances by the condemned of Terizen was *Figaro* itself.

And death shall have no dominion. I had left for the Festival Hall with the latest news of the Gulf war in my ears, and I could not but reflect that as the number of bombing raids increased, however precise the aim, human beings, including women and children, would be killed. Some of those would die in agony, their innards ripped from their bodies, their eyeballs melted, their legs smashed; the very crews of the planes which delivered such death might be burnt alive in their aircraft, as the tanks, when the ground offensive begins, will for some become ovens in which they are roasted.

Did those reflections destroy my pleasure at what turned out to be one of the finest of the 70-odd performances of *Figaro* I have ever heard? No; indeed my evening was grounded in a way that made the work even more profound and moving than Mozart invariably and eternally is.

There is war in *Figaro*; Cherubino is called up in Act One, and Figaro tries to make his blood run cold with the prospects, but of course the *farfallone amoroso* is never going to get the smell of gunpowder in his nostrils; directors of the opera who make him truly frightened at the prospect have misunderstood Mozart. The war in *Figaro* takes place not on the battlefield but in the human heart, where the *concerto di tromboni, di bombarde, di cannoni* rages for ever, or at least until the true peace of full understanding is signed by all the High Contracting Parties.

Meanwhile, though we must not be so foolish as to think that if Saddam Hussein could be persuaded to listen to *Figaro* he would come out with his hands up (Hitler was devoted to *The Merry Widow*), we must not fall into the opposite trap and allow ourselves to believe that art can offer no more practical service than consolation. It is not just a romantic fancy of mine to believe that Mozart changed the world, even though I suppose that most of the people in the world have never heard, or heard of, *Figaro*. The scientists tell us that matter is ultimately indestructible, however many times it changes its forms, and it is no great leap to the belief that the same is true of sounds.

Mozart dealt in truth, and nothing in his work, not even *The Magic Flute* or the Jupiter symphony, demonstrates his dealing more clearly and deeply than *Figaro* does. Remember: it is the only one of his operas in which no character is a symbol, but everyone and everything is real and of perfect human scale. Remember also that it is the only one of his operas that starts and finishes in a single day, from sunrise in a homely room to sunset in a stately garden. The souls of the characters have been laid bare, and the reconciliation in which it finishes is not just a happy ending: it is a testimony to a truth more glorious even than the earthly truth of the harmony in which the story and the opera finish.

Shaffer's Salieri instantly recognised that Mozart was a conduit through which God's truth entered the world. And Salieri knew also, and as immediately, that the work which demonstrated most clearly this breathtaking truth ('Whatever else shall pass away, this will not . . .') was this tiny tale of human beings which flowers in that single day into a tree under which all humanity can shelter.

That does not help with Saddam Hussein. But goodness and beauty, particularly goodness and beauty touched by an eternal hand, have a literally miraculous quality: they can spread independently of any human agent. The very fact that an extra item of goodness and beauty has entered the world makes the world better, even if nobody knows that it has entered.

I make so bold as to claim that the men and women of Terizen would have understood what I am saying. They were murdered, hideously. But, after all, they had always known that they were human. Their defiance of death and evil did not mean that they might escape mortality; it was an affirmation which said that music could and does so. The performance of *The Bartered Bride* announced that their blood, even as it was shed, was Czechoslovak and Jewish blood, and they were proud of it; the performance of the Verdi Requiem announced that man must learn to die as well as live; but the performance of *The Marriage of Figaro* announced that although five sparrows are sold for two farthings, not one of them is forgotten before God.

'Men must endure their going hence, even as their coming hither; ripeness is all.' There will be death in the Gulf, and hypocrisy, and a kind of justice; after all, the commandant of Terizen was hanged. But beyond the furthest stars, where love alone rules, all earthly stains, be they of blood or tears, are expunged. *Figaro* abides.

The Times January 24th, 1991

Woodman, woodman, spare that tree

IF YOU WERE seeking the least romantic man in the realm, you would look for him first among the ranks of the spokesmen of Leicestershire county council, and you would be reasonably certain that your search would not be in vain.

What, then, would you think if you read, coming from precisely that source, these words: 'It . . . gives people a visionary feel.' A visionary feel? From Leicestershire county council? Nay, from a *spokesman* for Leicestershire county council? I think you would at least be sufficiently intrigued to learn more about this official and his vision.

But when you discovered what this particular vision encompassed, so great would be your astonishment that you would inevitably think you were being hoaxed. For a recent article in this paper, by Craig Seton, has revealed that there is afoot a serious and apparently feasible proposal to plant in the Midlands an entirely new forest, 150 square miles in area, which would be bigger than Birmingham and Coventry put together and would stretch lengthwise from Uttoxeter to Leicester and widthwise from Lichfield to Burton-on-Trent.

If that does not engage your imagination until your hair stands on end, you must be bald. But it is not a hoax: no one could possibly believe that the Countryside Commission, from which the news emanates, would indulge in such impropriety. Moreover, the environment secretary has given the proposal his imprimatur, and – rather more valuable than his imprimatur – enough money to see that the thing is done.

The Countryside Commission had scoured the land to find an area sufficiently short of trees for the plan, and found five, two of which are sufficiently romantic already, based as they are on, respectively, Sherwood Forest and the Forest of Arden ('Where they fleet the time carelessly, as they did in the golden world'). But the present site, which it seems has fewer trees than most of the rest of the country, carried the day.

And what a day: I can hardly wait for it to dawn, though I shall not see it completed, for the planting alone will take 30 years, and the forest will not come to full maturity for 100. That fact in itself stirs the blood, for to think of a project that will not be finished in one's own lifetime, or indeed in that of two or three generations younger, is a marvellously calming experience. It has that quality primarily because it is based on nature, which cannot be hurried, unlike man-made things; there are many huge projects, such as manned flights to the planets, which will take many decades in the creating, but they will not have the patina that nature, and nature alone, can provide. Why, one day, even that foolish old dream of digging a tunnel between Britain and France will be attempted, though of course it will prove a white elephant and lose all the billions it costs.

No such fate will befall the forest, even though it is a project initiated and cultivated by man. There are man-made dangers, of course; already there is talk of 'assisting tourism' and the idea has even been described as 'a draw to quality investment'. So far from assisting tourism, there should be signs on all the roads leading to any part of the new forest, in all the languages of the earth, to the effect that it is overrun by particularly savage wolves and exceptionally poisonous snakes, and no investment of any kind should be permitted if there is the slightest possibility of it producing a profit. There is also the inevitable chatter about the forest being 'part of the nation's contribution to combating global warming', but that is harmless and can be ignored.

The prospectus says that half of the area will be under

trees, the other half comprising fields, villages and towns. I am uneasy about the towns; suppose they looked like Birmingham or smelt like Burton-on-Trent? Let us insist that there shall be no village with more than, say, 1,000 inhabitants, and for safety's sake none of these should be less than 10 miles from any other. 'Some commercial timber operations' are mentioned; I am not implacably opposed to these – after all, clearing fallen trees and lopping crowded ones are part of forestry conservation – but I insist that the business is scrupulously run and very closely monitored.

All that, though, is nothing but the practical aspect of what is intended. The important part is ours – ours to wonder at, and to imagine ourselves, or our great-grandchildren, wandering through a forest that men had conceived and planted, and that nature, needing no further instructions, had completed. Think of the birds, for a start; they will not need any guidance, let alone thoughts of quality investment, to take up residence. Look up; if you are sharp-eyed enough, you may see a nest, but in any case you will hear them singing, and in any case you will see the light on the leaves and branches, in an infinite variety of combinations, every one a thing of beauty. (I was delighted to learn, years ago, that nature has arranged matters so that on every tree every leaf is assured a measure of sunshine; none is permitted to be hidden from the light altogether. I believe that Corot was the first painter who made use of this amazing truth.)

Rabbits and hares, foxes and squirrels will abound, and if the human beings in the area have enough sense to leave strictly alone the habitat (now inelegantly called the biosphere, or even the eco-system, but who would think to plant a tree, let alone a forest, in an eco-system?) their numbers will stabilise, so that myxomatosis will be needed only for the tourists, should the alarming signposts not deter them.

But there is better still to come. We are assured that the forest will consist of mainly broadleaved trees (that 'mainly' will have to be regularly examined). The wonderful idea of a brand new forest may be thought of as the contribution and penance required of the Forestry Commission, which for decades has been determined to cover every square inch of this country, not excluding Oxford Circus, York Minster and Coniston Water, in their pestilent conifers. If there is no back-sliding, the forest may grant them absolution.

What name shall it have? We must in no circumstances follow the wretched solution devised for the National Theatre, where a preposterous vanity was permitted to name two of the NT's three auditoriums respectively after the long-forgotten mother of an unimpressive Tory cabinet minister, and one of those useful workhorses – among his countless credits was the chairmanship of Battersea dogs' home (well, somebody has to be) – who has not so much been forgotten as little heard of in the first place.

I suppose the search for a name could make a nationwide competition, though the judges would have to be very carefully chosen, lest they decide on Gazza. An appealing solution would be to take the most romantic or charming village name in the area and use that; is there a Weddingportion Culhampton or a Vicar's Beckoning somewhere about? But surely the best solution is before our eyes, at any rate if we have a volume of Shakespeare open before us. Why not just call it Another Part of the Forest?

The Times October 22nd, 1990

Arabian, and other, nights

THE OTHER DAY, I saw a headline on a newspaper article, reading 'A hundred nights at the opera', to which my response was 'Pish, Pooh and Pshaw', and I would have added 'Faugh', if it would not have spoilt the alliteration. For today I shall demonstrate, in a rather spectacular fashion, that I have passed a much more significant milestone.

I passed it in the company of many of my dearest friends, at the Wexford Festival, to which most splendid beanfeast I have annually repaired for almost a quarter of a century, having over that period consumed there a quantity of champagne that would suffice to float a heavy-armed cruiser. (My endeavour is now to live long enough to consume as much more as is required to launch a full-sized battleship.)

Wexford's uncanny genius for exhuming worthwhile operas that have lain dormant for centuries was at work again this year. I cannot remember a better evening there (and not many elsewhere) than Donizetti's *The Burghers of Calais*. They did less well with a feeble thing by Gluck, *La Rencontre imprévue*; the very thought of Gluck trying to be funny chills the blood. For the last night they served up Goetz's version of *The Taming of the Shrew*; it is a splendid score, perfect for the Coliseum.

But to my milestone. When, as a schoolboy, I began to go to the theatre, and later to music, I kept all my programmes. After some years, I could not continue to house them, because I would have needed the Albert Hall as storage; I therefore threw the earlier ones away, and ever since, I have retained the programmes for only a few years back, a reasonable compromise. But from the start, I had numbered them all, in three categories: plays, concerts and operas, each of which had its number sequence, so I could and can tell exactly how many plays, concerts and operas I have notched up, from schoolboy to grave elder. And at Wexford, when the curtain fell upon the Goetz opera, it was that opera which rang for me a great gong, for it marked my *thousandth* night at the opera.

There are many ways of wasting one's time and listening to opera is one of the pleasantest. At its least substantial it can be delightful; at its mightiest it offers insights that can transform a life. In between, we have our memories.

Every operatic generation despises the one below it for not having heard the glories of the past. When the talk turns to opera and I judge I am the senior connoisseur present, I bide my time, and – loftily or off-hand, depending on the company – I murmur that I heard Callas many times, and when that silences them, I add, twisting the knife, that I heard her before and after: I heard her fat, and I heard her thin, and I still do not know whether losing six stone and gaining physical verisimilitude meant also losing something, less tangible, from that magical voice.

Oh, but I heard Stabile as Falstaff, and Vickers as Florestan, and Margherita Grandi as Lady Macbeth in 1947 a thousand years ago, and Flagstad and Windgassen and Schöffler and Ironthroat Svanholm – who, in the same *Ring*, thought nothing of polishing off both Siegfrieds (the weaklings today split them) *and* Siegmund, AND throwing in Loge as well – and more than a dozen of Glyndebourne Mozarts directed by Carl Ebert and conducted by Fritz Busch, who would have no truck with ornaments, not even the tiniest *appoggiatura*, and John Brownlee, who sang *Fin ch'han dal vino* so fast that it was almost impossible to believe any mouth could move so quickly, yet sang it so that every syllable and every stress was perfectly clear and meaningful, and – but I have done quite enough to demonstrate that those younger than I have missed the best of opera, as those who came before me jeered at an opera-lover who never heard Melchior or Lotte Lehmann.

It is a strange, strange form of art, is it not? Music derives its power, surely, from its ineffability: how do you extract meaning from the sounds you hear when you reproduce the marks on the music-paper? Some say you cannot; the feelings music inspires, they claim, are only in *you*, and music, however beautiful or stirring, can never be anything more than sound. I suppose these are the musical equivalent of deconstructionists, a silly lot. True, Michelangeli plays the piano as though he believes it, and there are not half a dozen better pianists living, but we know that when we listen to the last Beethoven quartets we are as close to eternal truth as we shall ever be.

And then some mischievous sprite took it on himself to put words to this phenomenon; not content with words (there was nothing odd about songs, after all), he added actions, nay, great dramas. And opera was born. How did the music then retain its power? And why was it not diluted to nothing, rather than being enhanced? Leave out the slighter composers – Donizetti, Bellini, Weber, Rossini, much of Verdi, Meyerbeer (ahem), and hundreds more which aspire only to entertain, and do it splendidly.

But look at Mozart, Beethoven, Monteverdi, Wagner, Strauss (but only *Die Frau ohne Schatten*), Janáček, I think Mussorgsky, *Falstaff*, and their few other peers: whence came this miracle by which that which cannot be spoken did yet speak?

It is the humanity in opera, however luridly implausible, that does the trick. Crude though so many libretti are, and even more idiotic the plots, the man who invented opera had realised, reaching through the centuries to come, that the marriage of music and human beings lifts both into another realm altogether. Opera is *not* just wonderful sounds made flesh by words. Just as the characters are impossibly brave or wicked or noble, we, as we sit in the darkness, realise, consciously or not, that we have become something higher and more significant, for all that we shall have to shed that aura when the curtain falls and we return to our mundane existence.

Take *The Magic Flute* alone. The plot is a mess and much of the dialogue is feeble and some unintelligible, yet we are transported to heaven not just because of the music, but because the music and words have fused into something greater than both, something indefinable but real.

But such an addiction is dangerous, and not only in the case of Wagner. All great opera makes such demands on its listeners that the thin line between reality and play-acting is erased for the three hours in the darkness, and sometimes we go home still deeply troubled, and wake next morning, and perhaps for many mornings, not quite sure where the line is. Yet no one who has fallen under the spell of this mightiest of the mighty arts will ever ask for the spell to be lifted.

In *Siegfried*, the hero faces one of those legendary tasks: he has to weld the pieces of a shattered sword, and only he can do it. We see the anvil, the fire, the pieces of metal. Naturally, an unbroken sword is hidden near the forge, for the moment when the music announces success. One glorious night, it became clear that the props department had forgotten to put the unbroken sword on the stage, so that the weaponless Siegfried would be obliged *in reality* (and singing all the while) to forge a real sword on an anvil made of plywood with the heat from a fire made of a 100-watt bulb painted red.

How he managed it, I shall tell you when I celebrate my 2,000th night at the opera.

The Times November 14th, 1991

And all who sail in her

SIR ISAAC NEWTON maintained that for every action there is an equal and opposite reaction, and admirers of Sir Isaac will be encouraged to learn that I entirely agree with him. I have watched this systole–diastole pattern for most of my life, in the form of repression–freedom–repression–freedom, and I have never seen the pattern broken. In a sense, it is the most important principle in the world, and if it should ever be falsified, chaos is come again.

Newton's law, applied to liberty and its enemy, means that a denial of freedom will always bring forth an assertion of it. Of course, there may be a considerable time-lag before the pressure for freedom is successful; just as the freedom-lovers increase their demands upon the freedom-haters, these in turn increase the harshness of their rule and the determination to retain it. But as against that, we in freedom's camp know that time is always on our side.

Apart, perhaps, from a few of the more barbaric lands of Africa and the Middle East, the most repressive country in the world at present is China. Through the long years of Mao and his Gang of Four, the Chinese people were powerless to resist, as were the Russian people in the years of Stalin's slaughter – both, incidentally, admired and praised by British fellow-travellers. But the moment the inner pressure dropped, the outer pressure made itself felt; the nascent movement for democracy in China grew rapidly, and its voice could be heard right round the world. For every action . . . well, we know how the first round ended, in Tiananmen Square. What many may not know is that there was a second round.

Before the murderers moved in, the young people who were in the van of the movement built an imitation Statue of Liberty. It was a bit wonky, and bulged in the wrong places, but its heart was sound, and they named it the Goddess of Democracy. The tanks rolled over it, those who sent them having forgotten that all the tanks in the world cannot crush thought, belief or hope. Soon after the blood and corpses were removed, some of the men and women in the democracy movement escaped from China, while others went underground. Between the two groups an idea was born: to charter a ship, moor it near the Chinese mainland, though in international waters, and broadcast the truth into the vast prison-house, to sustain the resisters and give them hope. And the ship was to be named the *Goddess of Democracy*. Most of the dissidents who managed to get out have settled in France, and it was in France that the plans were drawn up; in a surprisingly short time the ship was ready to sail.

And sail she did. Alas, she needed help for this reckless, forlorn endeavour. She got it initially from the French authorities, but they really had no alternative; the last time they had anything to do with an unofficial freedom vessel they blew it up, murdering one of the crew in doing so, and then treated the murderers as heroes. Singapore seems to have behaved well, allowing the *Goddess* to dock without difficulty.

That was not enough; the help of Taiwan was essential, and its rulers, after blowing hot and cold for weeks, decided that to curry favour with Peking was more important than democracy, not that they knew much about *that*. They have impounded the ship's transmitter, and made virtually impossible the final stage of her heroic journey. The *Goddess of Democracy*, it seems, was prayed to in vain.

But of course it was not in vain, for this story is not really about the *Goddess of Democracy*. It is about the rulers of China. As the ship sailed into eastern waters, it was met with harassment from Chinese ships, and – more ominous

– a series of threats; the Chinese refused to rule out violence against the ship, which was unarmed, and which had not ventured, and had no intention of venturing, into Chinese territorial waters. Yet the Chinese rulers behaved as though a vast fleet was approaching, equipped with nuclear rockets and troopships.

The hysteria had begun many weeks ago, when the Chinese said they would not 'tolerate' the presence of the ship off their coasts, following this with formal protests to France. Next, they claimed that Taiwan was in the plot, though there was nothing resembling a plot anywhere in the whole business. There had been no attempt to conceal or disguise the intention of the project's organisers, which was to broadcast to China music, news and statements in favour of democracy. One such statement was to be a pre-recorded message from Chai Ling, one of the leading dissidents, who managed to escape arrest and certain death, and finally found sanctuary in Paris.

Chai Ling – how many divisions has she? The Chinese behaved as though she had hundreds; early on in the project, a spokesman for the Chinese Foreign Office, one Li Jinhua, said: 'The activities of this ship are aimed at subverting the people's government.' Later on, another such spokesman said that the ship was 'an attempt to overthrow the government', and as the dreadnought came nearer to China, the government put up a journalist, Li Yong Ming, from the New China News Agency, whose script might have been written by Mao in one of his more serious spasms: 'The ship is aimed at creating chaos, disorder, subversion and demagoguery. They want by these means to overthrow the people's government of China.'

The question is almost too obvious to ask. What frenzy of fear and guilt gripped the homicidal geriatrics who rule China, if this cockleshell vessel, which flew, so help me, the flag of St Vincent and the Grenadines (pop. 34,000 approx.) frightened them into such gibberish?

*

Possibly they have all gone as mad as Mao, but I doubt it. Perhaps they are worried that there has been no word of sympathy and support from Mr George Foulkes, MP, a Labour spokesman on foreign affairs; he, you may remember, worked himself up to bursting point with indignation when some Americans proposed to broadcast a word or two of truth into Cuba, that land of pure democracy.

I think that the explanation is really very simple. Mao, like Stalin and Hitler, was surrounded by creatures whose sole purpose was to keep reality from getting to the Great Teacher. That is no longer possible; not even a revival of Mr David Hare's *Fanshen* will persuade the Chinese tyrants that they are universally loved, especially by their subjects. They know now that the democracy movement was not killed, but strengthened and extended by their slaughter of the innocents, and they know that every day more of their subjects flock to the banners of freedom.

Those banners must, for the moment, be hidden. The *Goddess*, however, was a visible, audible presence, signalling the truth; that the days of tyranny may be many, but are numbered. That, surely, explains the raving response; and if a pin-prick can provoke such ravings, what will they do when pneumatic drills are at work on the foundations?

For the moment, they are in control. The ship's voyage is over, and the terrible threat it posed has passed; any Chinese citizen saying a good word for it will be in a concentration camp by nightfall. But outside the wire, Newton's truth will remain, as equal and opposite as ever.

The Times May 21st, 1990

Putting it in words

T HERE ARE 15 books on my desk as I write this; I have stood them all up on end, panned out, in a semicircle, and a brave show they make, I must say. But anyone who looked over my shoulder would think that I was in the grip of an extreme form of monomania, for the books are not just all on the same subject; they are all the same book. What is more, I have for many years had the habit of pulling one out of the shelf and reading it right through, then pulling out another and reading *that*, and so on right down the shelf, despite the identical nature of the contents.

In addition, I find myself liking some of them more than others, and on top of that I am always looking out for new publications containing the same matter, which I eagerly snap up. Perhaps I should also have mentioned that I have always been convinced that the whole exercise is a complete waste of time anyway.

There is a simple explanation for this curious behaviour of mine, and I shall shortly give it, although it will lead only to a profound and utterly insoluble mystery, a mystery very similar to the mystery of Shakespeare:

> Others abide our question. Thou art free,
> We ask and ask – Thou smilest and art still,
> Out-topping knowledge . . .

And the Shakespearian analogy goes further than you might think, for the insoluble mystery I mentioned is not what happened on the *Mary Celeste*, or even what song the Sirens sang; it is the mystery of genius, and in this case the genius of a poet whom I believe to be the greatest of all save Shakespeare himself. Those 15 books are all devoted to the wholly impossible and fruitless task of translating the poems of François Villon.

Note that I say 'translate', not 'translate into English'; two of my volumes are translations into German, and two more into Italian, one of these equipped with 316 pages of notes including a *Bibliografica Essenziale* of 303 published items. No one can say that the world has not tried; but why has it failed?

Let us start with the man, remembering that poets are not like the rest of us. To start with, they are untidy, often failing to tuck their shirts into their trousers; they are shockingly unpunctual, and much given to talking to themselves. Some, even more reprehensible than the rest, drink more than is good for them, and others beat their wives (assuming they married them in the first place, which is by no means certain).

Fie! Our man was a burglar, a cutpurse, a jailbird and a murderer; can Ted Hughes say as much? The man whom Villon murdered, incidentally, was a priest; it was said that he started the trouble, but those who did the saying were all friends of Villon; as for the burglary business, one of his more notable coups was to break into the grounds of the Sorbonne and raid the theological faculty, having learnt that they kept their money under the chapel floor. He could never resist a riot, particularly the ones he started, and he was sentenced to death several times, once coming very close indeed to a direct acquaintance with the celebrated M. Henry, the official hangman, the last occasion being for his participation in yet another brawl, this one resulting in the Papal Notary being stabbed.

'*Cucullus non facit monachum*'; for this amazing scoundrel managed to write some 3,000 lines of verse which will live, with all their magic and power, through all the centuries (he has survived more than five already, without any waning of his power to move his readers) and he will remain in demand until human beings cease to be affected by love, wit, rhyme, beauty, passion, glory, melancholy, laughter, malice, friendship, pity, sadness, Paris, hate, mankind, God and acrostics.

All these he understood (we shall come in due course to the one thing he did not understand), and understood so profoundly and surely that my estimation of him as *proxime accessit* to Shakespeare is nothing but the truth.

For the answer to my question – why has every language in the world attempted to translate Villon, and failed? – we must pose another question: why have there been so many attempts? Shakespeare has, of course, been translated into every language, including Swahili, but ten years ago there were at least 14 different Villons in Italian, and the number must be higher by now: even Shakespeare cannot match that. Why does the world go on trying?

Because, of course, it looks so easy. Apart from the six Ballades written in an impenetrable argot (although many ardent Villonistes have claimed to penetrate it), the poems are of a clarity and purity that have no equal in any poetic literature, and that remains true when he is lampooning his enemies or applauding his friends; just as Mozart's transparency leaves a singer with nowhere to hide, so Villon's limpid exactitude leaves a translator without recourse, mournfully realising that the only fitting word is Villon's French one. At which point I put away my 15 volumes of translation.

Take the most familiar of those 3,000 lines: '*Mais où sont les neiges d'antan?*' Listen to some of the attempts (*listen* is the right word).

Lewis Wharton gives us 'But where are they, the snows of yore?', which is dead before the caesura, and buried after it. Anthony Bonner tries 'But where are the snows of bygone years?'; lifeless throughout. H.B. McCaskie (Edward Ardizzone, too, not that it does him any good) proffers 'But where is the snow that fell last year?', which sounds as though it is July and he has just found the Christmas cards in his overcoat. Beram Saklatvala gets a bit closer, although not much, with 'But where are the snows of last year gone?', and anyway he can be improved immediately: 'are' should be 'have'. Peter Dale proposes 'Whither the drift of last year's snow?', but there is no such active motion in the French as his 'whither'. Galway Kinnell abandons scansion altogether with 'But where are the snows of last winter?' Attilio Carminati, with Emma Mazzariol, tries '*Ma ove sono le nevi dell'anno?*', but the stresses of Italian take it too far. Walter Küchler, on the other hand, stresses too heavily, with '*Wo schmolz der Schnee des Winters hin?*' (But Küchler goes on to some tremendous successes, scansion and all, with such parallels as '*Tant crie l'on Noel qu'il vient/So lange schreit man Weihnacht, bis sie da*' (he rhymes perfectly, too).) So we fall back again on Dante Gabriel Rossetti's famous stroke of luck: 'But where are the snows of yesteryear?'

And that is only *one* of the 3,000 lines; better, perhaps, to stop trying to Anglicise him (a wonderfully impossible task!) and look at him in his own context. For there is more in Villon than his crimes; there is even more than his poetry; this brawling scofflaw, always ready with a dagger or a picklock, is also, and most profoundly, a child of God. Again and again, throughout his works and his life, he lays down for a moment his quarrelling, his robbery, his poetic vengeance on his enemies; he even forgets the ladies – bygone and still living – and turns his soul towards Christ.

This is no deathbed conversion, no Gilles de Rais blessing his victims (and burnt alive for his crimes when Villon was nine), no seeking for someone with heavenly contacts to put in a word for him; Villon (which, incidentally, was not his name – it was given to him by his guardian, and must have been one of the few things he did not steal) writes poetry to God as separated lovers write to each other, and no less fervently. Some Villon commentators have argued that he had his tongue in his cheek, a belief based on his habit of

rubbishing his enemies with honeyed words that conceal
their sharp barbs (there are plenty without the honey), but
it is absurd; you cannot miss the note of anguished truth as
he prays, over and over again, for God's mercy, convinced
that it is there even for the most unworthy sinner. When he
prays to the Virgin ('Say to your Son that I am His alone') he
is not begging but promising, and if he breaks the promise
– '*En ceste foy je vueil vivre et mourir*' – he may break it again.
(Don't be afraid of the old French, it can be picked up in half
an hour.)

So certain was he that he would one day be hanged that he
wrote (almost his last lines) *L'Epitaphe Villon*, and subtitled
it *Ballade des pendus*; there are few lines in any language to
touch for pity the words with which he begins:

> *Frères humains qui après nous vivez . . .*

and the words with which he ends:

> *Mais priez Dieu que tous nous vueille absouldre!*

But I promised to tell you what was the one thing he
could never understand, and even as I turn to my promise
I can hear his cry of anguish as he wrestles in vain with the
mystery.

In the *Ballade des menus propos* he catalogues all the little
things (that is what *menus propos* means) of life, thus:

> *. . . Je congnois pourpoint au colet,*
> *Je congnois le moyne a la gonne,*
> *Je congnois le maistre au varlet,*
> *Je congnois au voille la nonne,*
> *Je congnois quant pipeur jargonne,*
> *Je congnois fols nourris de cresmes,*
> *Je congnois le vin a la tonne . . .*

And then and there he falls to his knees, praying God to give him the key of the one great thing, the lock he cannot pick:

> *. . . Je congnois tout, fors que moy mesmes.*

Villon knows everything: the doublet from the collar, the monk from the gown, the master from the servant, the nun from the veil, the swindler from the argot, the fool from the guzzling, the wine from the cask: 'I know it all – except myself.'

No one can open Villon, no matter where, without hearing that iron clang, as of some ancient bell tolling, and no one can fail to hear the pain with which the man who wrote those 3,000 lines heard the bell, and cried out to know, before he died, why he was born.

His entire *oeuvre* was written in less than seven years; after his closest brush with the hangman, he left Paris and the world: where he went no one knows. But he left a body of verse that will live for ever, summed up in the first and last lines of the *Ballad of the Hanged*: 'Brothers, who live when we are gone . . . Oh, pray that God at last will save us all.'

The Times (Saturday Review), November 2nd, 1991

From little acorns . . .

HAVE YOU EVER stopped and thought *why* this country is by far the best to live in? Yes, we are a democracy, the weather, though changeable, has nothing like the extremes of heat and cold that other lands suffer, we murder each other surprisingly rarely, our political rivalries are not serious, we have the Morris men to entertain us, even our banks do not lose *all* our money – but the catalogue of our good fortune could be prolonged for hours.

What we need is a single definition of our good fortune, one which makes us smile as soon as we think about it, and which is guaranteed to make us feel pleased to be alive, and particularly to be alive in Britain.

I have found it. A body called the Committee of Advertising Practice has a remit to frown upon advertisers who make claims in excess of what the facts support.

So far so good. If I am a manufacturer of sausages, and I proclaim in print and on the airwaves that my products are not only the most succulent ever made, but that they stop hair falling out, improve sexual capacity, keep dangerous dogs at bay and poison the rent-collector, I take it that the Committee of Advertising Practice will have a word with me, suggesting that I am coming it a bit too strong.

But where is the line to be drawn between mild boasting, which any manufacturer must be surely allowed, and preposterously baseless exaggeration? Well, the Committee of Advertising Practice have recently adjudicated on a case that must have used up a dozen of their finest pencils on the drawing of line. Golden Wonder Potato Crisps had been advertising themselves by saying that their crisps 'taste better than the other premium brand'. This could have been thought of as a low blow, for 'the other premium brand' is instantly recognisable as Walkers Crisps. But that was not the *casus belli*. The crux was that Golden Wonder had claimed not only that their crisps taste better than those of their rivals (a matter notoriously difficult to adjudicate upon), but that the public, asked for its opinion in this grave matter, had voted with its pocket: Golden Wonder insisted that 60 per cent of a presumably reasonable sample had stated a preference for Golden Wonder over Walkers.

Not so, cried Walkers with something like a sob in their voice; *their* independent research showed with reasonably indisputable certainty that most of the crisp-eating community preferred Walkers to Golden Wonder any day. Pistols for two and coffee for one.

The Committee met; it studied the agenda; Golden Wonder v. Walkers, the crisp-eating public intervening. And it came down on the side of Walkers. The adjudication, like a roll of thunder, was that Golden Wonder's argument was not 'sufficiently rigorous to support the claim'. Ladies and gentlemen, it has been conclusively determined that, however delicious Golden Wonder Crisps may be, they must not advertise themselves as more popular – let alone 60 per cent more popular – than Walkers Crisps.

And here is my evidence that this country is the best to live in, anywhere in the world; I truly do believe that there is no other nation in which, the claims of two rival varieties of potato crisps having clashed, a sober body would meet, consider the evidence, and hand down a verdict.

De minimis non curat lex. But it isn't true. Of course, the Great Potato Crisps Case had to be settled; if two brands of crisps both claim that a majority of the public prefer their product, someone has to make a decision, however haphazardly. At least, that is so in Britain, whence my theme. For surely no country other than this one would concern itself with the rival claims of the rival percentages of a struggle between two brands of potato crisps (which, between you and me, could not by even the greatest expert in the world be distinguished in taste, flavour, crumb residue, colour, number of crisps or ease of opening the packet), and concern themselves so profoundly that a tribunal would have to be set up, before which grave senior figures would deliberate for a fortnight before handing down their decision.

We have heard much lately about the rules which Britain will have to obey when full EC integration has been achieved. No doubt those who have the responsibility of ensuring that general standards must apply in all member countries will take steps to ensure that none has failed to comply. But what will the Commissioner of Uniform Practice say when he comes up against the Great Potato Crisp Battle?

I am not joking; at least, I am, but I am also making an important point. As I say, I do not believe that there is anywhere else in the world a government or government department silly enough to care about two brands of quite indistinguishable potato crisps; but this battle is not about crisps at all. It is about fairness and rules and standards and salt, those qualities on which we rightly pride ourselves, and by which we live and have lived for centuries.

No; crisps are not important. But advertising designed to convince the crisp-eating public of something that cannot be established to the satisfaction of the Committee of Advertising Practice is important. Not *very* important, mind; nothing very terrible would happen if there were a free-for-all in the advertising of potato crisps. But there is, at any rate in this country, an idea that nothing is too small to consider, especially where a matter of honest bargaining is involved.

No doubt I shall be told that I am making heavy weather about a nonsensical body which rebukes the makers of potato crisps for being very slightly extravagant in their advertising. The clue lies not in the crisps, but in the nonsensical body. I am sure the Committee of Advertising Practice has no powers to enforce compliance with its adjudications. *But that is exactly why life here is superior to life anywhere else.*

In some countries, revolutions break out in the wake of a hotly disputed legal judgment. In *our* country, no revolutions break out for any reason whatever, nor do we need any, for we are already seized of the belief that the rules governing the advertising of potato crisps will be applied rightly by the appropriate authority, and so they are.

In other lands, they eat strange things, and have strange rules governing their elections, and entertain strange notions as to what is correct behaviour, and think strange the time and effort expended in a quarrel about crisps. But we do not, and *that* is why this country carries off the palm.

You won't believe it, but there are countries where they put pepper on their crisps. I rest my case.

The Times October 10th, 1991

Three days that shook the world

M Y HERO, H.L. Mencken, was once covering a very boring American presidential convention, so boring that he wandered out of the hall in search of a drink and subsequently fell fast asleep for hours, during which time the crucial question had been settled after a mighty battle among the delegates. He had sent his story back to the *Baltimore Sun* earlier in the day, and only later did he discover that there had been dramatic changes while he was asleep. Pausing only to put his cigar in the other corner of his mouth, he wired the office with the memorable words: 'Insert "not", as the sense requires, throughout'.

Well, the Soviet people got rid of their usurping traitors within the timescale I predicted on Tuesday. I gave them four years to do so and they did it in three days: I can only say that it is very nice to be wrong in the right direction. But if I erred on the side of caution, at least I got the instrument right; on cue and word-perfect, it was the immemorial muzhik who stood firm, looking cross not so much because his freedom was being taken from him but because he had just been woken up by all the noise.

And the muzhik said '*Nyet*'; and behold, it was *Nyet*. And the morning and the evening were, the third day. And Boris Yeltsin saw that it was good, and behold, it was very good. And Mikhail Gorbachev was pretty chuffed too.

Forgive the skittishness, but I *feel* skittish. I have lived all my life in the certainty that a house built upon the rock will stand, and that one built upon the sand will fall, and great will be the fall of it. Do you suppose that I would now allow myself to believe that a pack of thieving scoundrels can turn such tremendous truths upside down in a single day? And not just any day, but *my birthday*?

We who do not have coups may think that they are remote and peculiar things, and we have great difficulty in understanding them. For instance, there is much talk these days about the disillusionment of the Poles and the Czechs and East Germans and members of the other nations who, having lived so long as serfs in the Soviet empire, awoke to find that although they are at last free, life is still hard, queues long, jobs scarce, homes cold, food poor, joy rare. The people of the Soviet Union clearly feel the same disappointment, but for them it is even more painful, because their conditions have become *worse* since the ending of the reign of Soviet terror, and will inevitably become worse yet before the other end of the seesaw starts to swing up.

Here, we are now being told that the seesaw has actually stuck, that the Russian people think that the measure of freedom they now enjoy is worthless, and that they would willingly give it away for a second potato on the ration. That was more or less how the Soviet Union was governed for decades, until the governors truly believed that the hopes of freedom had died out for ever. But it was not only because the second potato never turned up that brave men and women nerved themselves to dissent. Once these had blazed the trail, there was no chance of any of the rest forgetting that even a full belly is not enough. Only those outside the Soviet Union think that the hungry muzhik prefers potatoes to freedom; I would not be at all surprised to find Professor Hobsbawm nodding his head in agreement with such views. (I mean, y'know, Stalin, like, did go a bit too far, I reckon, but you knew where you were with him, eh?)

Turn again to the pictures of the crowds in Moscow surrounding the Parliament building; no, before you do, just savour the words 'Parliament building'. It *is* a *Parliament* building, and there are *members* in it, who were *elected* by the *voters*, who marked their ballot-papers *without fear* in a *secret* ballot, their votes being *correctly* counted and properly allocated in accordance with the *appropriate statutes*.

I promise we shall come to the pictures in a minute, but let me go on for a bit longer with the words. There will be more dangers for those who hold the future of the Soviet Union in their hands; the failure of the coup is by no means a guarantee that there will never be another. In any case, the Soviet Union is not yet fully free; the signal that will mean that its people can hoist the flag of complete democracy is the removal from Red Square of the mock-up of Lenin in his glass tomb.

After all, it was he who destroyed the hopes of freedom for which so many had died, he who fastened the fetters on the wrists of the Soviet people, he who laid out and filled the original Gulag, he who paved the way for the Soviet holocaust. I have never accepted that the mass of the people were deceived; they knew from the first that a darkness more evil than anything in the world's history had descended upon them; it was well for them that they could not know how long would be the wait for the light.

It was a very long time coming, that light, a very long time indeed; when it came, though, it was so powerful that the eyes of strong men watered, and the demand for sunglasses made millionaires of the vendors thereof. And did you suppose that a bunch of pickpockets with hastily assembled titles were going to draw the blinds again without a fight?

Now let us look at the pictures.

The size of the crowd is breathtaking; but so it was, of course, in Tiananmen Square. The usurpers, if they were to give the order to fire, would need to be sure, quite sure, that the order would be obeyed; it was obeyed in Tiananmen Square but not in Dresden; which way were they to look? The villains looked about, anxiously, for a clue, but they should have *listened*. Their fate was decided in one great sound: when the loudspeakers announced that a curfew had been imposed, and the crowds must therefore disperse, a mighty shout went up – a shout not of anger, not of hate, not of suppliance, not of weariness, but of *ironic cheers*. As those splendid rolling cheers gradually died away, both the populace and the usurpers could see that no one had moved. The usurpers, at that point, would have done well to drown themselves, preferably in the Rubicon.

Those ironic cheers will echo in history, and they deserve to. They said that the Soviet people had, in the past few years, gone far towards truth, decency and true self-government, and that they were going to go on until they had reached those goals. But the cheers said more: they said that the Soviet people have the strength, courage and determination to get there, that they know what heritage they have been robbed of, all through the years, that although they have repeatedly been beaten to their knees they have never forgotten how to stand up, that with enough patience and effort of will they can disperse the poverty, ignorance, hunger and brutishness that have been their lot since the terrible curtain fell.

The people who walked in darkness have seen a great light; in three days that shook the world they took their own destiny in their hands and chased from their midst the robbers who would take it from them. Yes, those three days shook the world; but they also shook the tree of hope, and lo! the fruits of courage were showered upon them.

Friends, eat hearty!

The Times August 22nd, 1991

Of making many books

THERE IS A madman running loose about London, called David Campbell; I have no reason to believe that he is violent, but he should certainly be approached with caution. You may know him by the curious glitter in his eyes and a persistent trembling of his hands; if that does not suffice, you will find him attempting to thrust no fewer than 48 books into your arms, all hardbacks, with a promise that, if you should return to the same meeting-place next year, he will heave another 80 at you.

If, by now, the police have arrived and are keeping a close watch on him, you may feel sufficiently emboldened to examine the books. The jackets are a model of uncluttered typography, elegantly and simply laid out; there is an unobtrusive colophon of a rising sun, probably not picked at random.

Gaining confidence – the lunatic is smiling by now, and the policemen, who know about such things, have significantly removed their helmets – you could do worse than take the jacket off the first book in the pile. The only word possible to describe the binding is *sumptuous*; real cloth in a glorious shade of dark green, with the title and author in black and gold on the spine.

Look at it more closely; your eyes do not deceive you – it truly does have real top-bands and tail-bands, in yellow, and, for good measure, a silk marker ribbon in a lighter green. The paper is cream-wove and acid-free, and the book is sewn, not glued.

Throughout the encounter, I should have mentioned,

our loony has been chattering away, although what he is trying to say is almost impossible to understand; after a time, however, he becomes sufficiently coherent to make clear that he is trying to sell the books to you. Well, now, such quality in bookmaking today can only be for collectors' limited editions at a fearsome price – £30, £40, £50?

No, no, he says, the glitter more powerful than ever and the trembling of his hands rapidly spreading throughout his entire body; no, no – the books are priced variously at £7, £8 or £9, with the top price £12.

At this, the policemen understandably put their helmets back on; one of them draws his truncheon and the other can be heard summoning reinforcements on his walkie-talkie. The madman bursts into tears, and swears it is all true.

And it is.

David Campbell has acquired the entire rights to the whole of the Everyman's Library, which died a lingering and shameful death a decade or so ago, and he proposes to start it all over again – 48 volumes this September and 80 more next year, in editions I have described, at the prices specified. He proposes to launch his amazing venture simultaneously in Britain and the United States, with the massive firepower of Random Century at his back in this country, and the dashing cavalry of Knopf across the water, and no one who loves literature and courage will forbear to cheer.

But I go too fast; much, much too fast.

There can hardly be a book-reading family in this country which does not have a selection of Everyman volumes; I have only to swivel slowly round in my chair to see a couple of score on my shelves, their plain, soldierly spines instantly recognisable. And if my eyes were better, I could call them over without stirring: *Tom Jones*, *Tartarin of Tarascon*, *Candide*, *The Brothers Karamazov*, *Don Quixote*, Emerson's *Essays* (the twelfth book in the first 50 original Everyman volumes), Hazlitt's *Spirit of the Age*, Wilde complete, *Rural Rides*, *Utopia*, Mazzini's *The Duty of Man*, *Areopagitica*, *Emile*, Aristotle's *Metaphysics* (for which a great honour was reserved), the *Iliad*, *Everyman* itself, Juvenal's *Satires*, Percy's *Reliques* and the *Everyman Encyclopaedia*.

Everyman's Library is one of the greatest bibliographical achievements in all the history of reading; founded in 1906, it sold 60 million hardback copies – 15,000 a week for three-quarters of a century – in a range that marked a target that had never been hit before and, I think, has never done so after. (Well, perhaps Allen Lane with Penguin.) The two men who created the monument were J.M. Dent and Ernest Rhys, and their intention was to put out, in a series of standard formats, the whole world's classic literature.

Roll that round your mind for a moment; the *whole* world's classic literature. Editors and translators were summoned up by regiments, printers and binders were shipped wholesale, the sky was blotted out with distributors and booksellers, and the world threatened to fall through a hole in the universe with the weight of readers.

However, that did not happen quickly, and many times it looked as though it would never happen at all; Dent's financing was precarious (he had sworn he would never borrow), and the first years were painful and difficult. Yet he never let himself forget the mighty oath he had sworn: to create 'the most complete library for the common man the world had ever seen'.

'The common man'; that was to be Dent's customer. When the publisher got down to work, only a quarter of a century had passed since elementary education had been made compulsory in Britain, and general secondary education was only four years old. The nation was barely literate; Dent gambled on the thirst for learning and reading the law had unleashed, as Dickens, a generation earlier, had found a huge well of self-improvement. His trust was not misplaced; the precarious years were forgotten as the volumes – a shilling each – were torn from the shelves.

'A good book is the precious lifeblood of a master-spirit, embalmed and treasured upon purpose to a life beyond life.'

So said Milton, and his words were adopted by Dent and Rhys for the immense project. But they still needed a name for it. This is how Rhys cried: 'Eureka!'

> Good titles, like good lyrics [Rhys was a poet as well as a playwright, novelist, essayist and editor] drop from heaven. The finding of one, attractive and explicit, was the puzzle. We discussed a score of likely names for the series, but not one quite convincing. Then, when we had begun to despair of the search, one day on my way through Garrick Street to the publisher's office in Bedford Street, the lines of the old play: 'Everyman, I will go with thee and be thy guide, In thy most need to be by thy side' came into my head. Here, unexpectedly, was the waiting word, *Everyman's Library*.

The next problem was what should be the first title in the series: it was solved instantly, for what could it be but Boswell's *Life of Johnson*? The second was less obvious: Lockhart's *Napoleon*. Altogether, in the first 50 volumes, there were Bacon's *Essays*, the *Fairy Tales* of Hans Andersen, Lamb's *Tales from Shakespeare* (ugh, actually), *Ivanhoe*, the *Meditations* of Marcus Aurelius and the six novels of Jane Austen.

It took 50 years for the thousandth Everyman to appear and neither Dent nor Rhys lived to see it. The choice for so grand, so splendid an achievement was not as easy as for the first, but there was no pandering to general popularity, and the honour went to Aristotle's *Metaphysics*.

Finis coronat opus; or so it seemed, not many years ago, when we heard the news that the whole mighty edifice was to be abandoned. No more reprints, no more acquisitions, no more weeding the garden for those plants that had failed to show staying power (all through the years, the wholesome practice of culling and replanting had continued). Everyman volumes would now have to be sought in second-hand bookshops, and there followed a sorry sight: publishers selling the Everyman rights on like a game of pass the parcel.

I don't know where the rights had got to when our wonderful madman took the stage, nor does it much matter. Campbell has not simply rescued the Everyman's Library, nor even revived it; he has recreated it. Every beautiful volume will be accompanied by a substantial newly written introduction, as well as a bibliography and a chronological table of events matched to the author's life and work. Already, Campbell has added new Everyman volumes to the canon; his first 50 include for the first time Lawrence's *Sons and Lovers*, Ford Madox Ford's *The Good Soldier*, Lampedusa's *The Leopard*, Scott Fitzgerald's *The Great Gatsby*, Joyce's *Portrait of the Artist* and Pasternak's *Doctor Zhivago*. (Assuredly, Dent and Rhys would applaud, knowing that such an enterprise can never stand still.)

Campbell points out that many paperbacks are as expensive as, or even more than, some of his fine-edition masterpieces; Proust in paperback, for instance, is £11 *per volume*. But although such comparisons are significant, and the quality of Campbell's editions outstanding, what is most important by far is the fact that the Everyman's Library, that great monument to learning, pleasure, solace, understanding, wisdom, thought and genius, will continue on its eternal voyage, a voyage which can never end in dropping the anchor, for its cargo may never come to rest. Instead, it must sail for-ever from port to port, bringing the good news, the great news, the incomparable news, the news that it is still true, and always will be, that In the Beginning was the Word.

The Times (*Saturday Review*), September 21st, 1991

When scorpions ruled the earth

M R STANLEY WOOD, a palaeontologist by trade, has discovered a fossilised scorpion's head, which he claims is 340 million years old. Well, it could be 680 million for all I care. But he added that the head was two-foot wide, from which he deduced that the whole thing would have been 10-foot long.

I have to say, with the very greatest emphasis, that I do not wish to know that. I am one of those unfortunate people who suffer from a phobia; my particular terror is of all varieties of creepy-crawly, though the disorder is at its most intense when the eight-legged kind comes scuttling towards me. And when I learn that in the Carboniferous era, scorpions more than three yards long abounded, I tend to get into bed and pull all the bedclothes over my head, though not before pushing the chest of drawers against the door and making sure that the cyanide pill is at hand.

Moreover, this is not the first time Mr Wood, may he be found as a fossil 340 million years hence, has caused me to climb half-way up the chimney and stay there. He is greatly given to the practice of finding horrors from bygone ages and describing them in a manner well calculated to turn my sleep to screaming nightmare. He seems to find most of his beasties at East Kirkton, in Scotland, and so far, in addition to the 10-foot stinging Thing, he has produced giant milli-pedes (as any insectophobe will tell you, the more legs the greater the horror), harvestman spiders (whatever they may be, and I fear the worst) and *millions* of the scorpions.

Then it gets worse. It seems that the received belief about

the Carboniferous period has hitherto been that it was ruled by the giant amphibians, who spent their time snoozing from morning to night in the Carboniferous warmth. But no, says Wood; the giant scorpions would have done them in in no time: 'Amphibians', he insists, 'couldn't afford to lie about sunning themselves with these carnivores scurrying around.' I suppose not; just listen to Wood as he warms to his work:

They would capture their prey and drag it under cover. Then they injected their digestive juices into their prey, and waited until it had become a soup. Then they sucked it up.

Well, it takes all sorts . . . There really is a man who thinks nothing of finding the traces of 10-foot scorpions, together with millipedes that would stretch from *here* to right over *there*, and boasting about his finds – boasting, I may say, to such good purpose that his fellow palaeontologists have taken to calling him 'Stan' and agreeing with him that at East Kirkton at least, the scorpions once ruled the Earth. There is some argument about whether his friends were aquatic giant scorpions or terrestrial giant scorpions, but I refuse to take sides; the horrible things might have been *flying* giant scorpions for all the comfort it would bring me.

Do you remember a film called *Them*? The things of the title were a family of giant ants, at least as big as Stan's scorpions, and the female of the species, towards the end of the film, was gravid with millions upon millions of itty-bitty ants, all of which, when they were born, were going to grow up as giant ones, which in a few ant generations would have overrun the entire earth. (I suppose the giant scorpions might have been induced to deal with them, but I wouldn't have bet on it.) Just in time, the hero shot the monster, and the ant larvae perished in their mother's womb.

It will not surprise you to learn that I did not go to see that film; all I know of it was from reading the reviews, and that was quite bad enough. (I did look at the pictures outside the cinema where it was showing, but I did not do so twice.) I took comfort, though, from a faraway memory, so far away, indeed, that it came from my schooldays. The giant ants in the film had, of course, the same shape and proportions as real ones. But I remembered, or I thought I did, that if the length and breadth of a solid object are multiplied by χ, its mass is thereby multiplied by χ squared. (Or is it cubed?) The giant ants, therefore, could not have existed. Score one for peace of mind.

That, though, was fiction; according to Stan, Stan, the scorpion man, his 10-foot stingers were as real as – well, as his giant millipedes. (The scorpions were, so to speak, made to measure, so the reassurance from the mathematical formula did not apply to them.) And remember that I have not even started to discuss the harvestman spider, largely because I fear that if I did so, I would find Stan insisting that the thing was five yards across – when there would be nothing for it but a spoonful of honey to help the cyanide pill go down.

The Thing doesn't have to be a prehistoric one. Staying in the country, always a dangerous custom for the arachnophobe, not long ago, I found One of Them in my bathroom; it was about the size of a fully-grown octopus, and I flew down the stairs gibbering, in the hope of finding someone still about – other than Stan, of course – to take an interest in my plight. Fortunately, my hostess had not gone to bed, and the brave girl picked it up with a tissue and sent it on its way. (The real phobic, like me, screams as loudly at seeing some normal person dealing with the enemy as he would if he met it alone.)

I suppose we can argue that we are still top creature; we are here, after all, and where are the giant scorpions, the mile-long millipedes, even the basking amphibians which the scorpions turned into soup and then so horridly slurped up? Order after order of almost incredible creatures once ruled the earth, and went their way, none knows whither (well, apart from the ones that fetched up at East Kirkton). But why are we so sure that the same fate is not lurking somewhere to account for us? After all, the number of theories purporting to explain why and how the dinosaurs died out are as numerous as the stars above us.

The truth of the matter is that the universe, whoever is in charge of it, moves in a mysterious way its wonders to perform. But I do feel that it need not have paused in its performance to create 10-foot scorpions and similarly proportioned millipedes, to say nothing of the giant harvestman spider, or for that matter the common or garden one, *Tegenaria domestica*.

I forgot to say that Stan's other discoveries have included the remotest ancestors of frogs. I have no fear of frogs; indeed I rather like the little fellows. But I recognise that one man's smile is another man's cold sweat, and I send greetings and sympathy to all the batrachophobics who are reading this. Mind you, frogs eat spiders. But who will serve up Stan as soup for his scorpions?

The Times February 22nd, 1990

The heart has its reasons

IT HAS LONG been obvious to me that if we were to seek a single safe and inexpensive panacea for the improvement of the entire population's well-being, it would be the immediate closing down of the Health Education Authority.

This body, which is in danger of terminal indigestion from the quantity of our money it has swallowed, must by now have frightened to death so many people that it is no wonder that the population is falling. Well, would you want to live, much less bring children into the world, if you were daily assured by the HEA that your only chance of survival, and that a slight one, was to change immediately to an exclusive diet of pasteurised muesli washed down with turnip-juice?

The HEA and its food-wowsering allies (that reminds me – Mr Geoffrey Cannon has been commendably silent for some time, Bacchus be praised) have lately had a nasty experience. In Helsinki, a huge survey – the subjects were studied over a period of 15 years – was set up with 1,200 men all of whom had lifestyles that would have stretched the members of the HEA unconscious on the carpet if they had got to hear of the matter.

These death-inviters smoked, they drank, they were overweight, they had high blood pressure, they positively oozed cholesterol. When collected, they were divided into two equal groups. One half were monitored in the greatest detail throughout the 15-year study, and were put on strict diets and regimens, the very things the HEA would approve of, or rather insist upon. The other half of the Finnish guinea-pigs were left to their ruinous ways, being given no warnings or threats; they were simply thought of as the control group, and left blissfully alone.

Five years passed, during which half of the 1,200 had continued to tread the primrose path to the everlasting bonfire, while the other half had – well, let me quote directly from the *Sunday Times*:

> Researchers were surprised to discover that within five years the death rate was twice as high among those told repeatedly to cut down on calories, saturated fats, cholesterol, alcohol and sugar. The group was also told to eat more polyunsaturated fats (mainly soft margarine), fish, chicken, veal and vegetables, and to cut down on smoking and exercise more.
>
> After 15 years, the 'healthier' low-cholesterol sample continued to die more rapidly, 67 deaths in all, 34 of them due to heart disease. The control group, whose risk of heart attacks was theoretically higher, had only 14 cardiac deaths and 32 deaths from other causes.

None of this surprises me in the least. For as long as I can remember, I have started my breakfast with a steaming jug of cholesterol; my lunch consists of three or four saturated-fat sandwiches, and my usual dinner is a substantial plate of calories (with melted butter). As for drink (this bit's true) it is a poor day – a wretched one, even – when no champagne, pleasantly cool, slides over my tonsils. Of course, I am not such a fool as to take exercise, and my only worry in these matters is that I don't smoke – not because I think it unhealthy, but because I dislike the taste. (I propose, instead, a course of nicotine injections.)

Yes, yes, Levin must have his fun. But he must also have his seriousness, and this is it, coming up.

There is a hint, and a truly terrible one, buried in the summary of the data accompanying the news of cholesterol's beneficial properties. I quote again:

Several big trials of cholesterol-lowering treatments have failed to bring a reduction in deaths, with some showing a peculiar increase in numbers dying from non-cardiac causes such as suicide, accidents and violence; *such increases were also reported in the Helsinki trial.*

My italics; and well they might be. Do you not see the point even now, you pests? Do you not understand the cumulative effect of your bullying, your scares, your self-righteousness, your belief that you may, or indeed must, shove your noses into the dietary and other habits of perfect strangers? Has not a single one of you ever heard of Marie Lloyd? When the man who invented jogging dropped dead while doing it, was there *nothing* in your minds other than sympathy for his family?

Your silence is eloquent; were you compelled to answer all those questions you would say 'No' to every one. Very well; I must teach my grandmother to suck eggs.

In matters of health (body or mind), in matters of comfort, of familiarity, of habit, of companionship (even if the companion is a cat), of regularity, of satisfaction, of surroundings, of everything and anything which goes on indefinitely in its usual way if left alone, while we are quite contented that it *should* go on indefinitely in its usual way if left alone – of all these things and all things like them, we hold these truths to be self-evident, that *nothing that is experienced as hateful can be doing the experiencer any good.*

Of *course* the 'reformed' Helsinki subjects died sooner than did the slobs. But that had nothing to do with the diet and the rest of the measures that were supposed to make the poor devils live for ever; the clinching clue was the apparently inexplicable finding that in the ranks of the born-again fitness-freaks there was a tendency for them to go off their heads and end their lives in violence. The pattern of their lives had been disturbed, whence these significant blips on the actuaries' charts.

*

Habit is one of the most powerful forces in mankind, and there is no culture that dispenses with it, or tries to, without experiencing seriously negative consequences. I come back to my discovery, some years ago, about jogging; I was in Los Angeles, where the joggers are numerous as the grains of sand on the seashore. As each one went by, I could see – I was on the edge of the jogging-path, not more than a foot or two away from them – that every one of them had a face contorted in anger and disgust. No, it was *not* the grimace that accompanies great effort; it was self-hatred. Believe me; when I realised the meaning of those faces, I should also have realised that I could have saved a lot of Finnish doctors 15 years of selfless labour, merely by gathering them round me, standing them doubles of whatever sensible people like to drink in Finland, and explaining.

Leave well alone. The food-wowsers will tell you that a bad diet is bad for you, and so it is. But they define bad as disregarding the rules they have themselves drawn up. The *real* bad diet is one which makes the eater of it first disquieted, then unhappy, then angry. You do not have to be a doctor to know that disquiet, unhappiness and anger are not good for the heart. Measure *those* indicators, gentlemen, not the intake of cholesterol and polyunsaturated fat, and base your conclusions on what they tell you. Meanwhile, if you seek a place where they now know that a little of what you fancy does you good, try Helsinki.

The Times January 6th, 1992

Merrily on high

ON JUNE 12th, 1458, Magdalen College, Oxford, was founded. On the same day in 1819, Charles Kingsley was born, and on June 12th, 1842, Dr Arnold of Rugby died. In 1759, June 12th saw the death of William Collins, and when *this notable day* came round in 1897 Anthony Eden was born (born to trouble as the sparks fly upwards, as it turned out). Then again, Harriet Martineau (runner-up to Mme de Stael for the title of the Ultimate Bluestocking) was born on June 12th, 1802. There was yet another birth on that day, and it is one that will stop every reader for a moment: it was June 12th, 1929, and the new baby girl was Anne Frank. Finally, the first railway in Japan was opened on this auspicious day in 1872, and the Rotherhithe Tunnel, likewise, in 1908.

An interesting and varied date, then, is June 12th. But all the June 12th milestones I have listed, and all the June 12ths that have no notable event to celebrate, *and all the June 12ths yet to come – yes, all of them to the end of time –* are nothing to June 12th 1991, which will be with us in some three weeks.

I am not joking; indeed, when I contemplate what is going to happen on June 12th next, I have to fight off the tears, for all that I was the first to prophesy it, amid incredulity and unkind laughter.

On that day, the people of Leningrad will vote in a referendum. The referendum will not, except perhaps metaphorically, decide who governs their municipality, let alone their country; indeed, in all ways but one – but the one is tremendous beyond imagining – it will leave Leningrad exactly as she was before. For the referendum is to decide whether they shall cease to call their brave and noble city by its evil, usurping, shameful name, and re-christen it by the name to which it answered through 211 years of history: St Petersburg.

On 16th June, 1703 (Old Style, and quite right too), the Tsar laid the foundation stone of a mighty fortress, dedicated to Saints Peter and Paul. From then on, the city that rose (with astonishing speed) was called St Petersburg, and St Petersburg it remained until 1914, when it took the pitiful name of Petrograd, only to be thrust even deeper into the mire when, on the death of Lenin in 1924, it sank to the level of being called by his name, and Leningrad it has been ever since.

But no longer, for surely the citizens will not cling to the rotting lie instead of embracing the reincarnated truth. When the members of the city council were asked to vote on the question 'Do you want our city to regain its former name of St Petersburg?' there were eight abstentions, 18 Noes, and 229 Ayes, and I cannot think that the citizens will be any less eager to embrace the symbol of their now rapidly approaching freedom.

That freedom has been hard won. It was in Leningrad, in 1934, 17 years after the chains of communism had bound all Russia, that the Great Terror began, when Stalin had his faithful henchman Kirov murdered; it was the signal for the unleashing of a slaughter that eventually took the lives of roughly (no one will ever know for sure) 15 millions of human beings. An almost greater shudder still accompanies, or should, the story of Leningrad's heroic stand in the second world war, when the Leningraders' resistance to the Nazi assault led to a mighty siege; it was called The 900 Days, which was the length of it. The reward of the Leningrad heroes was death; Stalin's paranoia culminated in his having the leaders of the resistance killed. (Incidentally, the article on Leningrad in the new *Encyclopaedia Britannica* has not a word to say on these terrible and tragic events, and reads like the work of a rather dim 17-year-old whose understanding of the Soviet system has been gained entirely from reading an Intourist brochure.)

A different kind of resistance came later; Leningrad bred many of the toughest *refuseniks* – those whose only wish was to leave the Soviet Union, with nothing but what they were wearing, and were refused. But Leningrad has always had braver and more defiant people than Moscow; one recollection of my only visit to the Soviet Union is of the distinct difference between the two that I spotted; Muscovites commonly walked with their eyes cast down, Leningraders with level gaze.

Well, for what Leningrad has suffered and endured, no recompense would be sufficient; for what she has hoped, deliverance is near. And what a deliverance!

The Soviet Union endured for some three-quarters of a century. It was supposed to free all people from bondage and imposed a slavery more terrible and complete than any seen until then; it was heralded as the bringer of equality, and created a ladder of hierarchies steeper than those of the most cruel of ancient emperors; it was defined as a system that would make all mankind one, and turned a mighty nation into 270 million informers, spies and *agents provocateurs*; it was proclaimed as the provider of bounty that would make its citizens uniquely prosperous and comfortable, and scores of millions of families still know no better home than a corner of a crowded room, and scores of millions have grown to maturity without ever setting eyes on meat; it was followed as the light of the world, and turned into the blackest and longest night in the universe. And now, at last, the foul thing is dying, and with it the lie on which it stood.

Well, now, I know of no era or culture which, having the technology to make bells, did not do so. They are, indeed, one of the oldest symbols of mankind's feelings; bells, almost since time began, have accompanied solemn ceremonies and governed scenes of rejoicing, marked notable days and laid down the hearers' duty, warned of attack and signalled victory, roused the sleeping, harried the lazy, informed the unaware and, above all, called the faithful to prayer.

If I find it difficult to believe that the people of Leningrad will vote to retain its justly hated name,* I find it unthinkable that they will rechristen their city without the accompaniment of bells. But Leningraders are spirited folk, and if they are going to call upon the bell-ringers to note so splendid an event, they are not going to do it by halves; when the news of the ballot is promulgated, we may be treated to the greatest campanological din in history, with every bell saying the same joyous thing: 'And this gospel of the kingdom shall be preached in all the world for a witness unto all nations.'

Then there will be only one more action for the people of Leningrad to take, accompanied and supported by millions all over the crumbling nation. It is to demand that the ridiculous wax figure in the Red Square mausoleum, which not even the simplest *moujik* now believes is the body of the man whose wickedness enslaved a whole nation, whose successor murdered innocent millions and whose name defiled a great city, should be shovelled into – it is the enslavers' own slogan! – the dustbin of history. And when *that* is achieved, the sound of the bells will deafen the world, and St Petersburg will once again bear a name its citizens can be proud of.

The Times April 20th, 1991

*They did not.

A little local difficulty

WATCH. A MAN, in a restaurant, is about to light a cigarette. He bends his hand claw-like, palm inwards; he tilts his other arm till it falls, then he rests on it the elbow of the arm with the hand which holds the lighter. He inclines his neck and closes his lips over the cigarette, which is the way he pulls it out of the packet. The cigarette is now between his lips; he inclines a little more, and pushes up the spare elbow, so that mouth and lighter meet. Using his thumb alone to spark the flame, he brings cigarette and ignition together; he does it by using the last possible inclination of his neck and head. He keeps the flame alight as he takes the first puff, then the claw-like hand drops the lighter on to the table, followed by the cigarette packet. He inhales.

And that is only lighting a cigarette; what do you think he has to do to wrap up a parcel?

We are speaking of Quentin Crewe, author, wit, traveller extraordinary, gastronome and wine-bibber, vividly blue-blooded member of several aristocracies, record debtor, eternal optimist, delightfully malicious, easily moved to laughter, uxorious and philoprogenitive yet astoundingly successful as a persistent fornicator, impossible – literally impossible – to quarrel with, a man with an immense number and infinite variety of friends, and a man who by every test, prognosis, appearance, examination, precedent, behaviour, diet and actuarial computation should have been dead long ago, indeed should never have survived infancy.

For he was born with an appalling handicap: the wasting disease called muscular dystrophy, by the implacable progress of which the sufferer loses more and more of his physical capacities – whence my description of the way he has to light a cigarette. (He refuses to reveal how he goes to the lavatory, much less how he lives up to my description of him as a champion wencher.)

We are all familiar with the tantalising game of wondering how we would behave in extreme conditions: under torture, in battle, imprisoned, gone blind. We are also familiar with authenticated examples of the way human beings can rise to the occasion: the pale, henpecked conscript who wins the VC, the colourless bank clerk who tackles the armed robbers. And the man who is born with muscular dystrophy.

I am convinced that had I been in Quentin's place, I would have let go and died, probably in my early twenties. How has he not only survived, but triumphed?

That question, at least, can be answered. His book *Well, I Forget the Rest* (the title is a line from Browning) is published today by Hutchinson, and I assure you that although you will be amazed and fascinated by it, you will also be enraged. The amazement comes from the things he has done – things that only a very few, and those with all their bodies intact, would have dared do. The fascination is provided partly by the felicity of his writing and partly by the quality and character of the man. But the rage that will send you stamping about the room comes from the almost unbelievable insouciance; it is so unshadowed, so gay, so genuine and so impudent that the reader is hard put to it not to wish him irreversible psoriasis as well.

Quentin's malady moved slowly; he was cruelly mocked by his coevals as a child, but when I first knew him he could walk, though clumsily. As more and more mobility was taken from him, he was plainly determined to cram into his life every experience, good and bad, that he encountered, from sitting at the feet of Lady Violet Bonham Carter ('. . . familiar with every nuance of political thought since Gladstone, on whose knee she had sat, sceptically counting the number of times he chewed each mouthful and finding it woefully fewer than the thirty-two that every nanny told every upper-class child to emulate') to staying with Willy Mostyn-Owen's mother ('a dotty pyramid of a woman who drank copious amounts of sherry and embarrassed her children').

Gradually, it becomes clear that he would have been a gormandiser of life even if his body had been like other people's; I do not think I have ever read an autobiography in which so much happens on every page. Most of the things that happen are very funny, at least as he tells them, for Quentin has never wavered in his conviction that life is a tremendous joke; he sees everything through comic spectacles, including death – no, *especially* death.

Some of the things he has done for a living are positively weird; he spent years reading to Percy Lubbock in Italy, for instance, and I often wonder how the dialogue went back in London: 'And what do you do?' 'Well, actually, I read to Percy Lubbock.' 'Er, how frightfully interesting.'

As his body slowed, he made sure that the earth, his private carousel, would spin faster. Jobs in journalism came and went, marriages (three so far, with five children so far) also came and went; still he enjoyed life, indeed enjoyed it ever more intensely: there is a wonderful scene of carpet-biting, in the style of Hitler, by Jocelyn Stevens, and an account of the stupendous generosity of Joseph Berkmann, who would give dinner to a dozen or so friends (I was one of them) and serve with the meal a dozen or more great vintages of, say, Latour or Mouton-Rothschild; there were so many glasses that we each had a table to ourselves.

But every time the music stopped, Quentin's Bane was seen to have advanced a little further. Somewhat irked (only somewhat, you understand), he decided that life was getting too tame. Beachcomber (J.B. Morton) recorded the exploits of Evans the Hearse, the first man to push a pea to the top of Mount Snowdon with his nose. But Beachcomber was joking; it was no joke when Quentin announced that he was going to traverse the Empty Quarter of Saudi Arabia;

only three Europeans had ever done so, and assuredly none of the three had done it in a wheelchair.

There came a moment when he could no longer walk even with two sticks, yet the smile never faded, and the absurdity of the universe was kept prominently in mind, even when he watched three executions. The horrors of the desert journey would have killed many an ox or elephant (one night he rolled on to a scorpion and couldn't roll off), but perhaps muscular dystrophy doesn't kill you; at all events, it doesn't kill *him*, for he completed the trek and promptly bustled off to South Africa, there to bait the upholders of apartheid into a double fury, the second half being their realisation that it wouldn't look good if they beat up a bleddy cripple. (Perhaps I should have mentioned that he didn't go straight there: '. . . I made a journey of it, travelling up the Nile, visiting Sudan, Ethiopia, Kenya, Malawi and what was still Rhodesia . . . In Ethiopia, I telephoned the Emperor's granddaughter Mary . . .') After that, he went right across the Sahara.

Did I not tell you that you would be enraged? He lives in France now, probably planning a trip over the Alps in the new motorised wheelchair devised by his friends Anthony Snowdon and Jeremy Fry. Then, no doubt, the Pyrenees, perhaps the Tuscarora Deep in a special bathosphere which will take a wheelchair, the Himalayas . . . the Moon . . . When will he weep, like Alexander, because there are no more worlds to conquer?

It makes no difference; for it is the inward journey he has made that demonstrates his mastery over his fate. I know very many people who know Quentin; I have never heard any of them speak of him with pity. Indeed, I have never heard any of them discuss his disability. Except, perhaps, to wonder how he still attracts the ladies, and what exactly he does when he has attracted them.

The Times September 12th, 1991

Countercheck quarrelsome

WHEN MALCOLM MUGGERIDGE died, there were, most fittingly, substantial appreciations and reminiscences throughout the media. One brief note, easy to miss, struck me speechless – a condition in which I am very rarely to be found. It recorded the astonishing and dismal news that one of Muggeridge's friends, the well-known novelist Anthony Powell, had, in the mid-Sixties, fallen out with Muggeridge to such an extent that he had not spoken to his former buddy for 17 years.

The world being what it is, I do not suppose that that is a record. But it must be something of a record among civilised, mature, successful men of the world. The question immediately arises as to what St Mugg (it was I who coined the canonisation, and I was delighted when it caught on – as was he) had done to Mr Powell to invite non-speaks from 1964 to 1981. Did he make a pass at Mr Powell's mother-in-law? Did he cheat Powell of a legacy by forging a will? Did he poison Powell's cat, throw stones at Powell's children, squeeze Powell's toothpaste from half-way up the tube?

None of these things. He wrote a fiercely adverse review of one of Powell's novels. And after that, all Powell's communications with his friend the critical reviewer were shut down entirely, not for the ensuing weekend, as one might think reasonable, but for 900 weekends. And what makes the business even more bizarre is that Mr Powell now says that he took the review to be a coded message from Muggeridge, saying that *he* did not want any more association. A line from

Twelfth Night springs unbidden to mind: 'Why, there's for thee, and thee, and thee – are all the people mad?'

Well, are they? Remember where they were when the trouble started: Powell was not a distant acquaintance of Muggeridge's, or someone he disliked already, or a neighbour with whom he was always quarrelling. He was a close friend. Yet the friendship was shelved for 17 years after the friend in question had given him a lousy review.

I must say, though it will be dismissed as mere anecdotal evidence, that if I ceased to speak (for 17 years) to every friend who rubbished one or more of my books by way of review, there would be a hell of a lot of Tipp-Ex in my address-book. Why, my very first book was knocked about most bruisingly by Anthony Howard, though not only was he a friend, but a friend I had recently done not one but two signal services in the way of friendship. Well, did I turn on my heel when I next ran into him? Did I send him a curt message to the effect that I never wished to hear from him again? Did I lie in wait till I could do him a harm?

Of course not; I wouldn't be such a damned fool, and not only because if I had stopped talking to him I would have missed, over the years, a great deal of political gossip of the most delightfully scandalous kind, oodles of which he always has on offer.

Turn it round. Not long ago, Ludovic Kennedy wrote a short book, one of the Counter*Blasts* publications, advocating the legalisation of euthanasia. When I had finished stamping the entire series into the ground in one column, I turned my fire on Ludo's contribution in another, and I must admit that I went quite far. Ludo replied to me on the correspondence page, defending his argument against my assault. And did he, in his letter, say or imply that he would never again break bread with me? Of course not, for he, too, wouldn't be such a fool. Instead, he referred to me in his letter as 'My old friend Bernard Levin', and plainly meant it.

Ludo isn't a saint, any more than I am; what distinguishes

us from those who bear Waughlike grudges for years on end is a sense of proportion. If I may broaden the area of hurt a little, I can instance an occasion at Lady Pamela Berry's luncheon-table when I enraged Paul Johnson to such an extent that – I was sitting beside him – he turned his chair round to give me his back, and ignored me to the end of the lunch. Paul, as it happens, has a fiery temper, but when I next met him it was obvious that he had altogether forgotten his anger half an hour after he got home.

And yet it seems that even a man of Anthony Powell's quality and success could not bring himself, for 17 years, to speak to Malcolm Muggeridge (incidentally a man to whom the very idea of breaking off a friendship because of a hostile review would have seemed the funniest thing imaginable) after he, Muggeridge, had thought less highly of his, Powell's, book than Powell had.

'Let not the sun go down on thy wrath.' Good advice, so often unheeded. I can no longer remember what was the cause of the breach between Dickens and Thackeray, but I can recall the splendid scene at the Travellers' Club, when Thackeray flung his arms round Dickens and cried: 'For God's sake, let's be friends – life isn't long enough to bear grudges!'

Nor is it, particularly when the grudge is based on something as trivial as a bad review. I used to be a theatre critic, a trade in which it is impossible to avoid making enemies, unless one takes literally the Hollywood adage: 'If you ain't praising them, they ain't listening.' On the other hand, a critic should be wary of making friends among those whose work he is called upon to judge, because the theatre's skin is almost unbelievably thin, and friendships can crumble much faster than they can be built up.

Mind you, there are sensible people even in Shaftesbury Avenue. My regard for the work of Tom Stoppard could not be higher; I regard him as one of the greatest theatrical artists alive. One play of his, however, I thought very poor;

I steeled myself and said so, whereupon I got a wonderfully Stoppardian letter in which he said that he had pondered much over his play in the light of my review, but that in the end he felt unable to agree with my estimate of it.

I did lose a friendship once, in the strangest way. I wrote a column about an exhibition of paintings; the artist was, and is, one of the most successful in the land, and is very highly regarded. Rejecting the general view, I made clear that I thought his very great technical accomplishment only pointed up the sterility and poverty of his imagination. A few days later I received a letter from an old friend of mine, who was (something I did not know) a passionate admirer of this artist's work; the letter was so savage that it truly shocked me. The shock passed; but the writer had said she wanted nothing more to do with me, solely because of my article. Of course, I should have argued with her, trying to point out the absurdity of breaking off a friendship because I liked the work of a certain artist less than she did. To my regret, I just shrugged and let it go. If she reads these words, I would like her to know that my affection and admiration for her have never been diminished, and that, as Thackeray knew, life is too short to bear grudges.

The Times December 6th, 1990

You say tomato

L ET US BEGIN with Archimedes. We all know the story ('Eureka! Eureka') of his leap from the bath as the law of displacement was demonstrated before his delighted eyes; those who know a little more about him can say how he died.

He was intent on tracing a theorem in the sand, so intent that he did not see the Roman soldier stooping over him, nor hear the soldier's barked command to identify himself, whereupon the soldier killed him. (We can pause here to mourn the further discoveries he might have made, but only if we keep in mind one of the most powerful truths of history, demonstrated perfectly in this case, that death is more powerful than murder: the name of Archimedes will be known for ever, but the name of his killer was forgotten even before the sage was buried.)

It was a good way to die, was it not? For his death came from the power of his concentration on his geometry, and that concentration came in turn from his belief that the truths of mathematics, which are eternal, are more important than war and peace, which are ephemeral.

That is dangerous doctrine, of course, particularly at this moment. True, we have progressed; I do not think that however long the Gulf war drags on we shall see well-dressed ladies with well-bred voices handing out white feathers to men in mufti presumed to be of military age. Yet there is, or should be, a place for those who want to say 'Leave me alone'.

When the Nazis staged their abortive Austrian *putsch* in 1934, some of Karl Kraus's friends, convinced that Hitler was about to take over the country, went to his home to tell him he must get out. 'Don't bother me,' said Kraus, insisting that the particular comma-problem he was working on (he was a fanatical linguistic purist) took priority.

'But Hitler is here,' they said, 'what do commas matter now?' 'Fools!' he cried, 'if you had cared enough about commas, Hitler would *not* be here!'

If there is no part of you that wanted to cheer at Kraus's magnificent reply, you should oblige your imagination to take more exercise. There is a much smaller, but no less haunting, illustration of the power of living *sub specie aeternitatis*, in Tolkien's *Lord of the Rings*; at the siege of Gondor, when Gandalf on Shadowfax remains alone to defy the enemy, a cock crows, and Tolkien holds up the action to make the point that the cock knows and cares nothing of the battle, even though it is the last battle, the battle for the world. (The cock's crow is answered by the horn-calls of the men of Rohan, coming at last to save the city.)

Robert Ardrey, best known for his pioneering ecological studies such as *The Territorial Imperative*, was earlier a playwright and film script-writer. *Thunder Rock* was an ingenious patriotic parable designed to give strength to the coming struggle (the play was first staged in 1939); it is set in a lighthouse where a man, disgusted with the world and its troubles, has gone to live as a hermit, ignoring everything outside his fortress. It doesn't work, but for a striking reason: the ghosts of shipwrecked men and women break into his life, and in the end he rejoins living humanity.

Perhaps Diogenes portrays the breed of *fainéant* best; when Alexander, having heard of the wise man who rejected society, went to call on him, the conqueror of the world asked Diogenes humbly, 'How can I help you?'; the curmudgeon's reply was, 'Well, to begin with, you can stand out of my light'.

Which, of course, brings me to tomatoes. I have recently seen a huge advertisement (a quarter of a page) for the said delicacy. (I was once dragooned, over the telephone, into settling an argument going on at a friend's house: is a tomato a fruit or a vegetable, and whichever it is how can we prove it? Hardly pausing for breath, Solomon Levin said it was a vegetable, and the test was that you put salt on it; were it a fruit, you would put custard on it.) The ad was couched in a wonderfully old-fashioned style, as witness:

> The mouthwatering flavour of this astonishing Tomato is a *revelation* – until you've enjoyed it for yourself, you simply cannot possibly imagine how absolutely delicious a Tomato can be! . . . Just imagine the taste-thrills you'll enjoy as you prepare the fresh-off-the-plant super-salads and sauces . . . just picture the mouthwatering snacks you'll glory to, as you sink your teeth into the ruby-red, rich, delicious flesh of these astounding Tomatoes right off the bush!

There is more of this, about fifteen times as much, but that will give you the flavour. But although I do not propose to buy a dozen Tomato plants and sink my teeth into etc., I do glory – the word is not too strong – in a country at war that is willing to stop what it is doing and contemplate an advertisement for tomato plants couched in terms as luscious as the goods are guaranteed to be. Perhaps, of course, I should be commending the advertiser; after all, I presume that the tomato-plant seeds did not come from Iraq, and I would have no objection if they had, for tomatoes are notoriously unwarlike.

During the second world war, Sir Hugh Roberton, founder and conductor of the Glasgow Orpheus Choir, was a complete and unwavering pacifist. Some clown in Parliament demanded that this underminer of the nation's will should be silenced, whereupon Churchill growled, 'I don't see why being a pacifist should make a man sing flat', and no more was heard from the super-patriot.

It all comes back to Wodehouse (an unlikely companion

for Karl Kraus). In the middle of one of Bingo Little's matrimonial crises, Jeeves is attending to Bertie, who is so distracted by his friend's problem that when Jeeves murmurs, 'The tie a little tighter, Sir, one aims at the perfect butterfly effect', Bertie so far forgets himself as to cry out, 'Oh, Jeeves, what do ties matter at a time like this!', whereupon Jeeves, shocked, says, 'There is no time, Sir, when ties do not matter.'

I am on the side of Jeeves. I know that men and women and children have died in the Gulf war already, and many more will die before the contest is over. I am not such a feelingless brute as to think that a shrug is sufficient for an epitaph on them. But there must be a corner where ridiculous prose extols tomatoes without diminishing the struggle, let alone those who die in it, and another echo from the second world war points up that moral. There was rationing, of course, for every kind of foodstuff, and even clothes; pregnant women had priority for milk. Though jokes were made, it was no joke, but there was one, and only one, part of the system where stern necessity relaxed. Though they had no serious nutritional value, children's sweets were not forgotten; there was a page in the ration-book for them, and by handing over the appropriate coupon together with the price, a precious packet of bulls-eyes or a bar of fruit-and-nut could be had.

Whoever thought of that escape-hatch (probably Churchill again) had taken the measure of the people, and measured rightly. So let it be with the tomato fanatic; let no one say there is no place in this grim time for him and his miracle vegetables. They also serve.

The Times January 28th, 1991

Time, gentlemen, please

CONSIDERING THE NUMBER of times I have said that if I were minded to make away with myself I would certainly do it on New Year's Eve, I think my readers would be well advised to turn this page for a moment, to see if my obituary is on the next verso. No? Then I shall continue.

'Another year! – another deadly blow,' said Wordsworth, adding, 'And we are left, or shall be left, alone'. Too many of my friends and acquaintances, heedless of my exhortations, have taken to dying, choosing 1990 to do it in; there was one horrendous visitation which obliged me to deliver two memorial addresses in a week.

I am not normally a gloomy fellow; I flatter myself that I can still set the table on a roar. But the end of a year is inevitably a measuring; someone rang me up a few weeks ago to ask if I would be interviewed under the heading 'My health and I' (that's nothing where lunacy is concerned – another interview was requested for, so help me, a series called 'My image and I'), and after I had declined, which was immediately, and giggled a bit, which was soon after, it occurred to me that 1990 had included not only fallen arches (well, one fallen arch) but about 240 yards of computer print-out on the couch of a most diligent cardiologist searching for the visible traces of an irregular heart-beat which he had happened upon auscultationally. (Don't be alarmed; I have had an irregular heart-beat since I was born, and it has not troubled me. He was only seeking the evidence and providing reassurance.)

There are other aspects of mortality. I used to have an exceptional memory; indeed it was so exceptional that it was truly freakish. But there was a trap in it, which I never spotted; because I could retrieve at will and with the greatest exactitude matter many years or even decades old, I kept no files, no cuttings, no sources, nothing. So perfect was my recall that for years I did not even keep an address-book, knowing that the details required were ready to be produced from the appropriate synapse. Now, the familiar stigmata of fading memory can be seen in an inability to remember people's names, for instance, or a doubt as to whether I have already sent that letter; this, as I say, is a familiar experience as the years advance, but for me the pain is greater than for most, because I have to measure the natural level of failing memory against the unnatural level of my former success.

I had better face the truth; I am never going to read Motley's *The Rise of the Dutch Republic*. It has been sitting on my shelves since I was a schoolboy, and if you add up the words in all the promises I have made to take it down one day and read it, you would probably find that they come to more than there are words in the accusing volume. (The trouble is that it sits – I have no idea why – next to the Rawlinson version of Herodotus, and every time I think I will break my duck at last, my fingers stray to my old friend.)

The point of all this is not just that I am never going to read Motley; it is that I have finally admitted as much, and you wouldn't believe the relief I felt when the guilt lifted. I got over my Proust-guilt long ago, I am happy to say, and powerful reinforcement for my conclusion that the first 70 pages of *Swann's Way* are all that is necessary was provided very recently in the *TLS*, where I found a review of the *eighteenth* volume of Proust's letters. This covered 1918, and assuming that the epistolary torrent comes at the rate of one splash a year, there must be three more to come, since Proust died in 1921 (even he, I take it, cannot write letters posthumously); it gives me a warm feeling to know with the utmost certainty that, having decided not to read the *Recherche* itself, I am certainly not, *a fortiori*, going to read the letters.

*

I suppose I am clearing the decks; Motley is a very good symbol of the necessity of knowing what we cannot do. Once, we thought we could do anything, and you would be amazed at the length of time it took me to understand that that is a fallacy; I am by no means the worst – some go on to the end of their lives never knowing that they have wasted reality in the chase of a dream. Yet even I cannot gainsay that 'coming to terms' is one of the most depressing phrases ever coined. I never could run a mile in four minutes, so it does not distress me that I can't now; but I could once recite without faltering the whole of *Lepanto*, and it distresses me beyond measure to find that I can no longer do so.

But it is worse even than that. The other day, a most cheering announcement was made: it seems that Birmingham is going to be pulled down. Unfortunately, it is going to be put up again, but that cannot be helped. The point, where I was concerned, was that the key date of the rebuilding is to be 1995. I repeat: I am not given to gloom, let alone general pessimism, but the thought came into my head unbidden, and bid it leave as I might, it stayed there, thumbing its nose at me. Would I see the end of Birmingham's reincarnation? (I have no wish to do so, of course, because whatever they put in its place will be at least as hideous as what is to be demolished, but I wouldn't want to miss it for *that* reason.)

And how about this? In a couple of weeks' time I shall celebrate (if that is the word, and the way I feel at the moment it certainly is not) the 20th anniversary of the first column I wrote for *The Times*. William Rees-Mogg, who had not long since become the editor, invited me to join the paper, and I did so at the beginning of 1971 (also the year my first book was published). The *Times* office was then still at Printing House Square, and space was by no means easy to come by (it is a damned sight more difficult at Wapping, I can tell you – or even if I can't, my colleagues can and will), and I parked myself in his outer office and got down to work. He had initially asked me to write one column a week, but a year or so later he asked me to do two, and later on raised it, so help me, to three. (That nearly killed me – so nearly, indeed, that I eventually took an immense sabbatical, well over a year long, and came back determined never again to write more than once a week; you see how my promise was kept.)

I have been fortunate beyond most journalists in my relations with *Times* editors; the present one is the fifth I have worked with, and never a cross word. Wailings and moanings, yes; Rees-Mogg's screams of horror, as he contemplated yet another couple of thousand words of the most extravagant libel, could be heard on the other side of the Thames.

Mind you, I was in at the birth of one of the most magnificent phrases an editor ever finished a leader with. He came out of his room one day, put a galley-proof on my desk, and said, 'Can I really print that?' I looked at it, and replied, 'If you *don't* print it, I will never speak to you again.' It was, of course, the famous peroration: 'Anyway, George Brown drunk is a better man than Harold Wilson sober.'

Twenty years a columnist! I am sure that I do not hold the record, but I would be interested to know who does. Of course, there have been journalistic careers lasting 50 years or more, but the very existence of the modern columnist is very recent as newspapers go; certainly I was the first of these on *The Times*. To think that I have been giving my opinion – which is the rough and ready definition of the breed – year in and year out for two decades, chills my blood, which has anyway cooled quite enough for my liking with the passing of time. I hope – well, I *suppose* – that unless I go completely gaga I shall never run out of opinions to express; I have never yet sat down to write a column without having at least three suitable subjects in mind, and that's a comfort, I can tell you.

Yes, but what about the rest of it? To put it bluntly: have I time to discover why I was born before I die? Silly question: the knowledge can come, complete and rounded, in the twinkling of an eye (an assurance first given to the Corinthians), and I am no more barred from the discovery

than anyone else. Nevertheless, I have to admit that I have
not managed to answer the question yet, and however many
years I have before me they are certainly not as many as
there are behind. There is an obvious danger in leaving it
too late, but there is a still more intriguing question in this
exploration: why do I *have* to know why I was born?

Because, of course, I am unable to believe that it was
an accident; and if it wasn't one, it must have a meaning,
from which follows the truth that with sufficient diligence
and determination a meaning can always be understood.
Villon, whom I read more and more now, summed up
the desperation of the unanswered question:

> Prince, je congnois tout en somme,
> Je congnois coulourez et blesmes,
> Je congnois Mort qui tout consomme,
> Je congnois tout, fors que moy mesmes.

No, I cannot translate it; it is untranslatable, and always
will be. Shut up and read him in the original until you
understand.

'Until you understand'; must we be in some other-world
corner with a dunce's cap on, until our darkness is lightened?
No, it cannot be like that; nothing is given, but everything
is there to seek. Nor am I convinced that when the ultimate
question is put to me, and I reply, 'Well, I was a frightfully
good columnist for at least twenty years', it will be judged
sufficient. True, this is the first day of Mozart's year, and
if we listen carefully until New Year's Eve 1991 we can get
some tips; but even they will be only tips on how to seek
the answer, not the answer itself.

'Be still, then, and know that I am God.' But what about
poor devils like me, who suffer so badly from St Vitus's
dance that we cannot be still? Perhaps, after all, I did take
the rat-poison as the clocks chimed midnight; have another
peek at the obits, would you? But stay: Surely such dreadful
and momentous news would be on the first page. Turn back!

Index

Abbott, Lewis 23
action, and reaction 193
actors, political opinions 138
Adams, Michael 168
adultery punished 142–3, 170–1
advertising, excessive claims 203–6
Aegospotami, battle 176
Africa: aid to 57, 58–9; colonial 58, 59;
    democracy 56, 57, 58; free xvi, 57–8;
    human rights 58
AIDS, increase in 2
Alcibiades 175
Aldus Manutius 19
Alembic Press 20
Alexander the Great 237
Algeria 144
All Things Considered (Levin) ix
Allan Quartermain (Haggard) 128
Altered Standpoint, Fallacy of the 104, 107
American Civil War 141
Americans, geographical ignorance
    91–4
Anderson, Lindsay 134
Anglican church, and mercy 110
Annie Get Your Gun (musical) 134
anthropology, modern 128
appoggiaturas, forbidden 42
arachnophobia 216, 218
Archidamian War, The (Kagan) 174
Archimedes 236
Ardizzone, Edward 199
Ardrey, Robert 237
Arginusae, battle 176
Arnold, Thomas 224
art: food as 89; and religion 76
Artaud, Antonin 54
artistic judgment 84–5
Arts Council grants 42
Ashendene Press 20
Ashworth, John 159, 161
Atex word-processor ix, 19
Athens: Periclean 165; and Sparta 174–6
Atkins, Sue 69, 70, 72
Atlantic Extension, Law of xiii
atom-bomb, Soviet acquisition 32
Attlee, Clement 100

Australia sheep cull 1
Austro-Hungarian Empire 141

Balickas, Vincas 114–15
Ballo in Maschera, Un (Verdi) 76
Baltic States, Soviet Union and 112–15
Baltimore Sun 207
Barber, Anthony x
Barker, Felix 133
Bartered Bride, The (Smetana) 181, 184
Basle, Stücki restaurant 86–90
batrachophobia 219
bats, legal protection xii–xiii
Battersea Power Station, London
    155–6
Beachcomber (J.B. Morton) 230
beauty: and goodness, transforming
    touch 183–4; hatred of 126
Bedford, wartime 5
Beethoven, Ludwig van 54, 103, 181, 191
Belgian Congo (later Zaire) 57, 59
Bell, George, Bishop of Chichester 6
Bellini, Vincenzo 191
Bennett, Arnold 47
Berenson, Bernhard 24
Berkmann, Joseph 230
Bernard Shaw (Holroyd) xv, 60–4
Bibi, Sharifan 142, 143–4
Biden, Joe 176–7
Birdwood, Lady Jane 164
Birmingham 187; rebuilding 242
Bismarck, Prince Otto von 175
Blunt, Anthony 30
Boakes, Commander Bill 45–6
Bomber Command (Hastings) 10
Bonham Carter, Lady Violet 229
Bonner, Anthony 199
books, vitality 99
Boston Globe 178
Boston University 178
Botswana 58; and civilisation 166
boxing, by women xvii, 69–72
Boyle, Andrew 31
Bradbury, Ray 39
Bradford, immigrants in 143
Brezhnev, Leonid 160

245

Brien, Alan 136
Briggs, Douglas 105
Britain: as the best 203, 204, 205–6;
  colonies 58; and EC regulations 205;
  free speech 164, 170; and Israel 168,
  169–70; race relations 143; and Saudi
  Arabia xvi–xvii, 168–9, 170–1;
  security services 31; urban violence
  xi–xii
British Rail 7, 9
British Transplantation Society 105
Britten, Benjamin 29
Brook, Peter 52
Brown, George 8, 243
Browning, Robert 25
Brownlee, John 190
Brownlow, Kevin 52–3
Bruno, Frank 28, 71
buildings, derelict 155–8
*Bulletin of the British Museum (Natural
  History)* 23
Burchfield, Robert 38
Burgess, Guy 30
Burghers of Calais, The (Donizetti) 189
Burke, William 107
Burton-on-Trent 187
Busch, Fritz 42, 190
'Byzantine', pronunciation of 152

Callaghan, James xi
Callas, Maria 190
Callil, Carmen 62
Calvinism 110
Cambodia 2, 3, 141
Campbell, David 211, 212, 215
Cannes Film Festival 52
Cannon, Geoffrey 220
capital punishment debate 116–19
Caprice Restaurant, London 134
Carboniferous scorpions 216–17, 218
Carey, John 62
Carminati, Attilio 200
Carter, John 18
Carter-Ruck, Peter 84
Carthage, Rome and 121, 123
catch-phrases, political xi
Catholic church, and mercy 110
Caxton, William 19
Chai Ling 195
Chalk Farm, London 155
chaos, IRA and 10
Chatto & Windus, publishers 61, 62, 66
chess, battles 138–9
Chimaera Press 20
China, repression in 193–6
cholesterol and mortality 220–3
Christians, fervent 145
Christie, George 40, 41
Christie, John 41
Christie, Mary 40, 41

Churchill, W.S. 238, 239
civilians: indiscriminate killing 6; and
  soldiers 11
'civilisation', definition 163–7; and four
  freedoms 163–5
classics for the common man 212–15
Climate of Treason, The (Boyle) 31
coalminers, women as 69–71
Cold War 33
Coliseum Theatre, London 134
Collins, William 224
Colmar, Issenheim Altar 126
colonialism 58, 59
Committee for Advertising Practice
  203, 204, 205
compensation claims 11–12
Connor, Bill 169
Conquest, Robert 159
Conservative party and capital
  punishment 117
Cornell University Press 174
Corner, Adam 8
Corot, Jean Baptiste Camille 187
counselling 11
Countryside Commission 185–6
County Hall, London 157–8, 160–1
Covent Garden, *see* Royal Opera House
Crankshaw, Percy 175
Crewe, Quentin xviii–xix, 228–31
Crook, Arthur 146
cryonics 106–7
Crystal Palace, London 156
Cuba 196
culture, and civilisation 165

Dahmer, Jeffrey 120
Dahrendorf, Ralph 159
Daily Express 132
Daily Mail 129, 132
Daily Telegraph 1, 132, 152
Dale, Peter 200
Davies, Hunter 62
Davis, Carl 54
Dawson, Charles 23, 25
Death of a Princess (TV documentary)
  170, 171
death, resentment of 106–7
democracy, African 56, 57, 58
Demosthenes 176
Dent, J.M. 213, 214, 215
destruction: mindless 124–5, 126–7;
  property development as 125, 127
Diaries (Mencken) 83–4
Dickens, Charles 234
diet and health 220–3
Diogenes 237
Disraeli, Benjamin 47
Doe, Samuel K. 56
Donizetti, Gaetano 189, 191
donors of organs, definition 105

Douglas-Home, Sir Alec xi
Doyle, Sir Arthur Conan 23
dress, at Glyndebourne 41−2
Dropmore Press 20
drugs, value of 108
Dürer, Albrecht 101

East Kirkton (W. Lothian) 216, 217, 218
Ebert, Carl 190
EC, *see* European Community
Eden, Anthony xi, 224
elections and laughter 46−7
'elitism' use of 38−40, 42−3
Encyclopaedia Britannica 225
*Enquiry Into the Nature of Certain
    Nineteenth Century Pamphlets, An*
    (Carter & Pollard) 18
Enthusiasms (Levin) xv
ephemera, political x−xi
Erasmus, Desiderius 19
Estonia 112−15
Europe, American knowledge of 92−4
European Community (EC),
    regulations 205
evening dress, at Glyndebourne 41−2
Everyman's Library 212−15
Evil Eye 61, 64
evil, tempered by good 110
expertise, explanation of 152−3

Falklands war 7
Fall of the Athenian Empire, The (Kagan) 174
Fallacy of the Altered Standpoint 104, 107
Fanshen (Hare) 196
Farr, Tommy 71
Faulds, Andrew 168
fear, freedom from 164
film critics 178
Fine Press Book Fair 20
Finson, Professor 148
First Nights, theatrical 133−4, 135
Five Seasons Press 20
Flagstad, Kirsten 190
food, as art 89
Foreign Office xvi−xvii, 168, 169, 171
forest, plans for 185−8
Forestry Commission 188
Forster, E.M. 103
Forsyth, Frederick 61
Foulkes, George 196
Four Freedoms 163−4
Fox, Charles James 47
France: Catholic church in 73, 75, 76;
    and Chinese resistance 194, 195;
    'civilised' 166; food as art 89
Frank, Anne 224
Franklin, Benjamin 97
fraternity, duties of 4
Fredman, Myer 75
free speech 163, 164, 170

freedom: 'civilised' 163−5; encroachment
    on xiii; and repression 193
Freedoms, Four 163−4
French Revolution 141
Froben, Johannes 19
Fry, Jeremy 231
Fuchs, Klaus 32
Fyfe, Sir David Maxwell 29

Gallery First-Nighters Club 135
Gance Abel xv, 52, 53, 54
Garamond, Claude 19
Gault-Millau guide 86
Gay News 26
General Will 102
geography, ignorance of 91−4
Germany: Allied bombing 5−6; Green
    party 36; post-war 141
Ginsberg, Morris 159
Girardet, Frédy 86
GLC, *see* Greater London Council
Gluck, Christophe Willibald 189
Glyndebourne xv, 40−3, 190
God, hatred of 126
Goddess of Democracy (Chinese radio
    station) 194−6
Goetz, Herman 189
Golden Cockerel Press 20
Golden Wonder Potato Crisps 203−4
goodness: and beauty, transforming
    touch 183−4; possibility of 110
Gorbachev, Mikhail 113, 115, 139, 140,
    141, 207
Gore, Keith 148
Grandi, Margherita 190
Gray, Dolores 134
Greater London Council (GLC) 157,
    160, 161
Greece, Ancient 165, 172−6
Green Party 36−7
Greene, Graham 1−2
Gregynog Press 20
Grillparzer, Franz 84
Gross, John 146
grudges, bearing 232−5
Guardian, The 135, 152
Guide to Communist Jargon (Carew Hunt) 38
Gulf war (1991) 5, 11, 236, 239; in
    perspective 5, 7, 9, 92, 95, 182, 184;
    restraint in 8; USA and 92, 94, 95
Gutenberg, Johann 17, 21

habit, power of 223
Haggard, H. Rider 128
Haig, Douglas, Lord 176
Hamish Hamilton, publishers 129
Hamlet (Shakespeare) 16
Hanborough Parrot Press 20
Hancock, John 97
Handel, George Frederick 74

Hannibal 121–3
Hannibal's Footsteps (Levin) 121
happiness, and 'civilisation' 166
Hare, David 196
Hare, William 107
Harris, Arthur 'Bomber' 6
Harvey, Len 71
Hastings, Max 10, 151–2
Hasupuweteri people 128–9, 130, 131
Haydn, Franz Joseph 54
Hayloft Press 20
Hayward Gallery, London 158
Health Education Authority 220
health, lifestyle and 220–3
Heath, Edward xi
Heaven and Hell (Swedenborg) 25
Hedgehog Press 20
Helsinki health survey 220–1, 222, 223
Henderson, Archibald 62
'Henry, M.', official hangman 198
Herbert, A.P. 83
Herodotus 173
Hereford Cathedral 75
Hermit Press 20
Heseltine, Anne 49
Heseltine, Michael 48–50, 51, 161
Hindley, Myra 109–11
Hitler, Adolf 7, 165, 196, 236–7; evil
    xii, xvii, 102; and homosexuals 29;
    and music 183; and Poland 112
Hobsbawm, E.J. 208
Hogarth Press 20
Hollis, Sir Roger 31
Holroyd, Michael xv, 60–4
'Home Front' 11
Home Office 111
homosexuals 26–7, 28; 'outing' 27–9
Hong Kong xv, 77
Hope-Wallace, Philip 135–6
hospitality, supreme 77–81
hotel, favourite 77–81
House of Commons, insanity in 44–5
Howard, Anthony 233
Hughes, Ted 198
Humana, Charles 165, 168
humanity, qualities of 108–11
Hurd, Douglas 51, 168
Hussein, Saddam 2–3, 7, 171, 183; as
    Israeli agent 168
Hüttenbrenner, Anselm 84
hybris 175, 176

In These Times (Levin) ix
Independent Television News (ITN) 157
index, cumulated, need for 61
India Lunacy Act xviii, 44, 47; Prime
    Ministerial sanity xviii, 44, 47
injury, compensation for 12
Into the Heart (Good) 129
IRA, *see* Irish Republican Army

Iraq: British hostages 11, 169; citizens of
    7; genocide 2
Irish Republican Army (IRA) 8, 10
Islam 144
Israel, Britain and 168, 169–70
Issacharoff, Michael 148
Issenheim Altar, Colmar 126
Italy: and 'civilisation' 167; and music 75
ITN, *see* Independent Television News
ivory towers xx

Jackson, Michael 128, 129, 131
Janacek, Leos 191
Japan: art 165; plagiarism in 179–80;
    railway system 224
Jefferson, Thomas 97, 177
Jenkins, Alan 152
Jesus Christ: biography of 65–8; on
    music 76
Jews as violinists 76
jogging, and self-hatred 223
Johnson, Paul 26, 234
journalists, plagiarism 178–9
Joyce, James 83
Juvenal 121

Kagan, Donald 174–6
Kant, Immanuel 25
Karpov, Anatoly 138, 139, 141
Kasparov, Gary 138–9, 140, 141
Kaunda, Kenneth 56
Keats, John 25
Keith, Sir Arthur 24, 25
Kelmscott Press 20
Kennedy, J.F. 159, 177
Kennedy, Ludovic 233
keyboards 19
Khaled, King of Saudi Arabia 170
Khmer Rouge 2
King Solomon's Mines (Haggard) 128
Kingsley, Charles 224
Kinnell, Galway 200
Kinnock, Neil 178
Knopf, publishers 212
Korean War 7
Kraus, Karl 236–7, 239
Küchler, Walter 200
Kurds, persecution xvii, 2–4, 170
Kuwait 168
Kyodo News Service, plagiarism
    179–80

Labour party, and capital punishment
    116–17
Lambeth, London Borough 161
Lane, Allen 213
Lang, C.S. 'Doc' 74
Langham Hotel, London 156
Larkin, Philip 82–3, 84–5
Laski, Harold 159

Latvia 112—15
laughter, elections and 46—7
Law of Atlantic Extension xiii
Lehar, Franz 183
Lehmann, Lotte 191
Leicestershire county council
    afforestation policy 185
Lenin, V.I. 112, 209, 225, 227
Leningrad: change of name 224—7; 900
    days' siege 225
Leopold II, King of Belgium 59
Li Jinhua 195
Li Yong Ming 195
Libanus Press 20
life, meaning of 243—4
lifestyle and health 220—3
Lincoln Cathedral xix
Lindemann, Frederick Alexander 30, 33
Linotype 19
Listener, The 39
literary criticism 146—7, 152, 153, 154;
    and grudge-bearing 232—5;
    rejoinders to 147—9
literary ventriloquism 180
Lithuania 112—15
litter: and Glyndebourne 41; in New
    York 34—6, 37
Livingstone, Ken 160
Livy 121
Lloyd, Marie 222
Lloyd Webber, Andrew 134
London County Council (LCC) 157, 160
London Residuary Body 160
London School of Economics (LSE)
    100, 157, 158, 159—62
Longest Journey, The (Forster) 103
Longford, Frank Pakenham, Lord xviii,
    108—11
Look Back in Anger (Osborne) 133
Lord of the Rings (Tolkien) 237
Los Angeles, joggers 223
lost tribes 128—9; and modern America
    129—30
Louis, Joe 71
LSE, *see* London School of Economics
Lubbock, Percy 230
Luftwaffe 6

McCaskie, H.B. 199
McGonagall, William 85
Maclean, Donald 30
Macmillan, Harold xi, 51
Madonna 128, 129
Magdalen College, Oxford 224
Magic Flute, The (Mozart) 192
Magnificat (Stanford) 74
Magritte, René 60
Mahler, Gustav 95
Maitre, Mr (communications dean) 178
Major, John xi

Managing on the Edge . . . 179
Mandarin Hotel, Hong Kong xv,
    77—81
Manningham-Buller, Sir Reginald x
Mao Tse-tung 193, 195, 196
Marriage of Figaro, The (Mozart) 182—3, 184
Martin, Kingsley 158
Martineau, Harriet 224
Mary Celeste 22, 198
Maxwell, Robert xiv—xv
Maxwell Fyfe, *see* Fyfe
May, Alan Nunn 32
Mayhew, Christopher, Lord 168
Mazzariol, Emma 200
Measure for Measure (Shakespeare)
    15—16
Melchior, Lauritz 191
Melved, Michael 178
Members of Parliament (MPs): insanity
    44—5; means of support 46; and
    publicity 46
memory, fading 240—1, 242
Mencken, H.L. 83—4, 207
Mendelssohn, Felix 84
Mengistu Haile Mariam, Lt-Col 56, 57
mercy, and the churches 110
Merry Widow (Lehar) 183
Messiah (Handel) 74
Meyerbeer, Giacomo 191
Miami Herald plagiarism 178
Michelangeli, Arturo Benedetti 191
Michelangelo, Buonarotti 126
Midlands forest, planning 185—8
Mikardo, Ian 168
Milan, Rondanini Pieta 126
Milton, John 99, 214
miners, female 69—71
Mines Act (1842) 69
Misleading Cases (Herbert) 83
Mobutu, Col Joseph-Desiré xvi, 56—7,
    58, 59
Moi, D.T. arap 56
Monster Raving Loony party 45
Montaigne, Michel Eyquem de 154
Monteverdi, Claudio 191
Moral Dilemmas 1—2
morale, wartime 6—7, 8, 9—10
Morgan, Charles 133
Morison, Stanley 18
Morrison, Herbert 157, 160
mosquitoes 179
Mossad 3
Mostyn-Owen, Willy 230
Mount, Ferdinand 'Ferdy' 151, 153, 154
Mozart, W.A. 54, 190, 244; humanity
    191—2; *Marriage of Figaro, The*
    182—3, 184; transparency 199; and
    truth 183
Muggeridge, Malcolm 232—3, 234
music: in church 73—6; and immortality

music (Cont.)
  184; power of 191
Muslims, in Britain 142–5; *fatwa* 143–4
Mussolini, Benito 57
Mussorgsky, Modest 191
Mystery Cleared Up 22

Nanny State xiv
Napoleon (film) 52–5
National Theatre 188
National Union of Journalists 116
Nazis' Austrian *putsch* (1934) 236–7
New China News Agency 195
New Left Review 38
New Statesman 39
New Theatre (later Albery) 135
New York: garbage police 34–6, 37;
  murders in 34, 35–6; theatre critics 132
New York Times, The plagiarism 178
Newdigate Press 20
newspaper-reading, inertia of 151
Newton, Sir Isaac 193, 196
Nicias 176
nihilism 125, 127
Nonesuch Press 20
Now Read On (Levin) ix
Nunc Dimittis (Parry) 74
Nyerere, Julius 58

Oakeshott, Michael 159
OED, *see Oxford English Dictionary*
Oklahoma! (musical) 134
Old Testament 76
Oleander Press 20
Open Society and its Enemies, The
  (Popper) 101–2
opera: as addiction 192; and evening
  dress 41–2; humanity in 191–2;
  language of 42; and original
  instruments 42
opera-going 189, 190–2
organ donor cards 104–5
organ-banks, living 105–6, 107
Osborne, John 133
Ottoman Empire 141
Outbreak of the Peloponnesian War, The
  (Kagan) 174
'outing', homosexual 27–9
Owen, David 46
Owen, Robert 173
Oxford English Dictionary (OED) 39

Pacific 1860 (musical) 134
Paddington station bomb 10
Pangle, Professor 147
Parry, Sir Hubert 74
Patch, Blanche 62
patients, as organ-banks 105–6, 107
Peace of Nicias and the Sicilian Expedition
  (Kagan) 174

Pears, Peter 29
Pearson, Hesketh 62
Peloponnesian War 174–6
Penguin Books 213
perfection, struggle for 126
Pericles 172, 175
Petite Messe Solennelle (Rossini) 75
Philadelphia Orchestra 94, 95–8
Philby, Kim 30
pigs' kidneys as human transplants 104, 106
Piltdown Forgery, The (Weiner) 23
Piltdown Man 22–4, 25
Pinero, Arthur 62
plagiarism: American 177–9; Japanese
  179–80
Plantin, Christophe 19
Pliny 59
Plutarch 172–3
poetry in translation 199–200
Pol Pot 2, 141
Poland 112
Political Correctness xiii, xx
political office, pursuit of xviii, 48–51
politicians, insanity 44–7
politics, ephemerality x–xi
Pollard, Graham 18
Polybius 122
Pontecorvo, Bruno 32
Popper, Karl 101–3, 159
potato crisps, merits of 203–6
poverty, freedom from 164
Powell, Anthony 232–3, 234
Powell, Enoch 143
prime-ministerial office xviii, 48–51
prime-ministerial sanity xviii, 44, 47
printing 16–21; uglification 19
private presses 20
prizefighters, female 69–72
property development, destructive 125, 127
prostitutes, advertising 13–16
prostitution, attitudes towards 14–16
Proust, Marcel 241

Quakers 76
quarrels xviii, xix, 147–9, 232–5
Queen Elizabeth Hall, London 158
Qwerty keyboard 19

Raczynski, Edward, Count 112
Rais, Gilles de 200
Rampant Lions Press 20
Random Century, publishers 212
Rattle, Simon 42
readers' letters 149–50
redundant buildings 155–8
Rees-Mogg, William 242–3
Reith, John 30
religion: and arts 76; music in 73–6
Rencontre imprévue, La (Gluck) 189
repression, freedom and 193

Requiem (Verdi) 76, 181, 184
Rhys, Ernest 213, 214, 215
Richardson, Eddie 108–9, 110, 111
Ring cycle (Wagner) 190
Rise of the Dutch Republic (Motley) 241, 242
Robbins, Lionel 159
Roberton, Sir Hugh 238
Roberts, Glenys 69, 70
Rome, and Carthage 121, 123
Roosevelt, F.D. 163–4
Rosenberg, Julius 32
Rosseteti, Dante Gabriel 200
Rossini, Gioacchino 75, 191
Rotherhithe Tunnel 224
Rothschild, Victor 30, 33
Round House, London 155
Rousseau, Jean-Jacques 102
Royal Air Force 6
Royal Exchange Theatre, Manchester 155
Royal Festival Hall, London 160, 182
Royal Opera House, Covent Garden 134
Rushdie, Salman 143
Russian Federation 39
Russian Parliament 208–9, 209–10

St Pancras Chambers, London 157
St Pancras Station, London 157
St Petersburg 225
Saklatvala, Beram 200
Salieri, Antonio 183
Sams, Eric 148
Sanders of the River (Wallace) 128
Saudi Arabia xvi–xvii; adultery
    punished 170–1; Britain and 168–9,
    170–1
Schöffler, Paul 190
Schubert, Ferdinand 84
Schubert, Franz 84, 85
Scipio Africanus 123
scorpions, Carboniferous 216–17, 218
Scott, C.P. 19
Scott, Giles Gilbert 155
Screaming Lord Sutch 45
Second World War (1939–45) 5–7, 8,
    10–11, 12, 239
self-hatred 126, 127
selfishness xix
Senegal 58
Seton, Craig 185
Shaffer, Peter 183
Shaftesbury, Anthony Ashley Cooper,
    Lord 69
Shakespeare, William 15–16, 39, 42–3,
    188, 197, 199
Shatalin, Professor 140
Shaw, Bernard xv, 60–4, 74
Sicilian Expedition 175
Siddiqui, Dr 143
Siegfried (Wagner) 192
Silence of the Lambs, The (film) 120

Simon King Press 20
Singapore, and Chinese resistance 194
Skinner, B.F. 148–9
Smellie, K.B. 159
Smetana, Bedrich 181, 184
Snowden, Anthony, Lord 231
Sollas, William 23
Solti, Sir Georg 182
Solution of the Piltdown Problem, The 23
Solution, Unprovable 22
sororicides and the law 142, 143–4
South Africa 2
South Bank Halls, London 160
Southworth, June 129
Soviet Union 226; admiration for 100;
    and the atom bomb 32; and Baltic
    States 112–15; Democratic Party 139;
    disintegration xiii–xiv, xix, 2, 57,
    139, 207; famine 140, 141; potato
    harvest 139
Sparta, Athens and 174–6
Speaking Up (Levin) ix, xi
Spencer, Frank 23–4
squatters 124
Stabile, Mariano 190
Stalin, Joseph 32–3, 63, 140, 165, 193,
    196, 208; and Baltic States 113; evil
    xii, xvii, 102, 113, 225; as hero 100
Stanford, Sir Charles Villiers 74
Stanford University 179
starvation, and waste 1
Stevens, Jocelyn 230
Stokes, Richard 10
Stokowski, Leopold 95
Stoppard, Tom 234–5
Strauss, Richard 191
stress, compensation for 11–12
Stücki, Hans 87
Stücki restaurant, Basle 86–90
Suez crisis 7
Sunday Times, The 132, 221
Svanholm, Set 190
Swann's Way (Proust) 241
Sweden, and 'civilisation' 166
Swedenborg, Emanuel 25
Switzerland, and 'civilisation' 166
sympathy, misdirected 4

Tabard Press 20
Taiwan and Chinese resistance 194, 195
Taking Sides (Levin) ix
Taming of the Shrew, The (Goetz) 189
Taylor, Sir Godfrey 159, 160–1, 162
Teilhard de Chardin, Pierre 23
telephone-boxes, prostitutes' ads in
    12–13, 16
Tennyson, Alfred, Lord 126
Terizen (Theresienstadt), concentration
    camp 96, 181–2, 184
testamentary dispute 82–5